1979

TRAGIC REALISM AND MODERN SOCIETY

TRAGIC REALISM AND MODERN SOCIETY

*Studies in the Sociology
of the Modern Novel*

JOHN ORR

University of Pittsburgh Press

First published in Great Britain 1977 by
THE MACMILLAN PRESS LTD

Published in the U.S.A. 1978 by the
UNIVERSITY OF PITTSBURGH PRESS,
Pittsburgh, Pa. 15260

Library of Congress Cataloging in Publication Data

Orr, John, 1943 –
    Tragic realism and modern society.

    Includes index.
    1. European fiction—19th century—History and criti-
cism. 2. European fiction—20th century—History and
criticism. 3. Literature and society—Europe. I. Title.
PN3491.07   1977   809.3'83   77 – 12897
ISBN 0 – 8229 – 1129 – 9

Printed in Great Britain by
J. W. ARROWSMITH LTD
Bristol and London

Nastasya Filippovna looked bewildered at the prince.
'A prince? Is he a prince? Fancy that, and I took
him for a footman just now and sent him in to
announce me! Ha! Ha! Ha!
                    DOSTOEVSKY
                    The Idiot

Contents

Introduction

A few introductory remarks are needed to explain the shape and pattern of the following study. It is intended as an original contribution to the sociology of the novel. But its intent is also polemical. It contains criticism of the anti-realist conventions which have recently dominated the sociology of literature. Consequently, the book can be read in two ways. Chapters one and four, on the theory of tragic realism, can be read as a prolegomenon to the individual studies of the novel in the second part of the book. Or Part I can be taken as part of a general debate about literary realism. My reasons for including the anti-realist material in the second and third chapters were twofold. Firstly, I wanted to show that many anti-realist arguments are not as far removed from the mimetic tradition as their proponents think. Secondly it seems to me that the period I am dealing with, that of the modern novel from 1848 to 1948, is one for which anti-realist arguments have least to offer and for which, in fact, they never produce a feasible account at all.

The division of the book into two parts, theory and practical criticism, also needs explanation. It is an attempt to explode the current hypocrisy of the sociology of literature. Originally conceived as a response to a vacuum in literary theory, the literary–sociological approach is itself in danger of becoming vacuous. As an approach which stresses the importance of the literary text, it has been singularly defective in studying them. Part II is a detailed study of specific texts, a feature of literary criticism which no one can avoid without losing all credibility. Without losing sight of a general theory of tragic realism, I have tried to substantiate it mainly from the novels under discussion, and not from novels which I have had to omit.

I think this is justifiable because of the vast range of tragic realism in modern fiction. In order to give the detailed attention to individual texts necessary for my purposes, I have been selective in a particular way. I have chosen to concentrate my attention on what I have called, perhaps arbitrarily, the political novel, though it seems to me that the political dimension in tragic realism is greater than in other forms of modern fiction. In practical terms, this means that elements discussed in the novels under consideration may be absent from other texts I have omitted, and vice versa. This notwithstanding, I have tried to outline the general features of tragic realism. In a sequel to the present study, I hope to discuss its place in modern drama, a topic which again I have omitted from consideration here.

I also ought to mention a term which plays a large part in the second half of the book without prior introduction. This is the idea of passion. It is discussed at length in the chapter on Tolstoy and Dostoevsky and recurs consistently thereafter. I have consciously tried to place passion in the classical rather than the romantic tradition. It is a feature, of course, of both tragic and realist fiction, but I have argued that it becomes most significant in literature where the two intersect. In this respect, passion is the antithesis of the romantic agony. But all told, I am less concerned with passion as a form of personal sensibility than as a form of relationship which, in turn, entails a relationship to a wider society. In the political novel of tragic realism, that relationship tends to have its widest significance.

Finally I wish to express the hope that despite the conscious limitations I have set upon this study, the immense importance of this way of writing for the development of world-literature will come across to the reader. For while this book is concerned with a particular kind of criticism, it is more concerned with the destiny of the novel itself.

J. O.

Part I

1 Lukács, Williams, Auerbach: Tragedy and Mimesis

If one wished to be cruel, one might argue that, by and large, realism is a twentieth-century concept applied to a nineteenth-century phenomenon. [1] In actual fact, its terms of reference are very wide indeed. It is an artistic phenomenon typical of the modern capitalist and industrial age as a whole. Even then, it appears historically time-bound compared with our idea of tragedy. For tragedy goes back to ancient Greece, to the origins of European culture itself. The real seems culturally conditioned, the tragic timeless. Yet the intersection of realism and tragedy has been one of the great events of literature since the middle of the nineteenth century. To sense the importance of this, one has to dispense with the commonsense idea of real. In everyday language, it is used to imply a constraint upon the imagination, the very opposite of visionary thinking. Clichés such as 'Let's be realistic', or 'He's not living in the real world' are of little use in discourse about art. For realism is about a particular form of artistic imagination. The link between tragedy and realism is vital. It involves the synthesis of a relatively modern and a profoundly classical sensibility. Nowhere are its effects more profoundly revealed than in the relationship between the novel and modern society.

The three major literary critics to discuss this relationship have been Georg Lukács, Raymond Williams and Erich Auerbach. Lukács and Auerbach have always been explicit about their representationalist aesthetics. Auerbach actually titled his most famous study *Mimesis*—imitation. For both, literary realism is the pinnacle of modern artistic achievement. Though not as explicit, Williams is almost as equally committed to the virtues of realist fiction, and significantly analyses them in the very English novels which the two German critics inexcusably overlook. But beyond that, all three have a sense of the intertwining of tragedy and realism in modern fiction. Their criticism produces different explanations of a common theme—the inseparability of the decline of tragedy from the decline of realism. To separate their emphases, one could say that Lukács is concerned mostly with realism, Williams with tragedy, and Auerbach with tragic realism. From each of these angles each has made a vital critical contribution, a starting point from which to look at the relationship of tragic realism and modern society. All three share a version of the historical eclipse of realism. But one can only understand the decline of tragic realism by looking at the historical fact of its persistence, and in the political novel we have one of the major forms that persistence has taken. Our present study is therefore intended to illuminate an important relationship between literature and recent history, and one thing should immediately become clear. No sociology of the novel can exist without a historical consciousness. For, like its readership, every literary text has a historical location. Aesthetic sensibility is inseparable from the experience of life over time. What is read finds its aesthetic validity in what has been lived. The novel, specifically, has an enduring relationship to history and society. It exposes the academic separation of the arts and the social sciences as a pedagogic myth. There is no literary critic who can understand the novel by turning his back on society, and no social scientist who can understand modern society by turning his back on the novel.

The term 'tragic realism' belongs to Auerbach. It is essential to understand why Lukács never uses it, for this failure is a limitation not only on his sociology of the novel but also his general aesthetics. The main answer can be found in the separation within Lukács's intellectual career created by his conversion to Marxism. In his pre-Marxian *Theory of the Novel* he is concerned with the relationship of the literary hero to an alien world. In his later Marxist writings, his main concern is how the totality of the literary text reflects the social reality of a given historical epoch. This presented a problem for Lukács which he never finally resolved. To the extent that his awareness of the sociological significance of literature increased, he began to sacrifice his concern with its tragic elements. In *Theory of the Novel*, as in *Soul and Form* where he concentrates on the theatre, Lukács displays many of the cultural characteristics of the German intelligentsia during the Second Reich—a spiritual inwardness, introverted melancholy and mystic irrationalism he was later to condemn so dogmatically. At the same time, one can see in his concepts of 'the problematic hero' and 'the tragic vision' the seeds of a dialectical theory of literature later made sociological but simultaneously betrayed by a rather sophisticated historicism.

Even in the early work the tragic is largely absent from the situation of the problematic hero. Lukács postulates three possible types of relationship between the soul of the hero and the external world. These he refers to as literary forms. The first, as in *Don Quixote*, is where the hero's vision is too narrow for the complexity of the world. The opposite form, prevalent in the nineteenth century novel, is when the soul is larger and wider than the destiny life has to offer it. 'Here', he states, 'the tendency is towards passivity, a tendency to avoid outside conflicts and struggles rather than to engage in them, a tendency to deal inside the soul with everything that concerns the soul.' This heroic inwardness actually subverts traditional literary forms. It leads to 'the disappearance of epic symbolisation, the disintegration of form in a nebulous and unstructured sequence of moods and reflections about moods, the replacement of a sensuously meaningful story by psychological analysis'.[2] A more serious consequence follows. The external world 'must be entirely devoid of meaning'. The extreme example of this type of hero is Oblomov. One that Lukács was not to know about was already beginning to form in the imagination of Thomas Mann – Hans Castorp, the introverted problematic hero of *The Magic Mountain*.

The point at which the problematic hero becomes tragic is crucial in the study of the modern novel. But in his third literary form, Lukács found a middle way between these two extremes which avoids tragic collision. In Goethe's *Wilhelm Meister*, he saw a compromise between the soul and the external world being effected through the self-constraint of the hero. This led to the 'reconciliation of the problematic hero, guided by the loved experience of the ideal, with concrete social reality'.[3] We can see a degenerate version of this preference for the *Bildungsroman* in Lukács's later acceptance of socialist realism, and a degenerate version of the passive problematic hero in his concept of modernism. What is clear from the outset, though, is his preference for affirmative rather than tragic fiction. It was his complete pessimism about its prospects which played a part in his conversion to Marxism. Amidst the collapse of the old European order after 1914, he felt that affirmative reconciliation was not possible within the bourgeois world. Bourgeois culture was gradually dying. This pessimism is retained in his Marxist attitude to the literature of mature capitalist societies. With rare exceptions, such as that of Thomas Mann, it is judged to be in a process of deterioration. But it is no longer a deterioration of literary form alone. Rather, it is a degeneration in the portrayal of social reality which Lukács attributes to the abandonment of the quest for artistic totality.

It is with the quest for totality that the problem of realism is inextricably linked. According to Lukács both art and science, including Marxism, strive for 'the whole man in the totality of his social world'. Though they accomplish this by different means, the struggle of both is against the social division of labour, against class divisions, and against alienation. In his Marxist writings, Lukács distinguishes the intensive totality of drama from the extensive totality of the novel. His view of the novel is liberated from the previous rather narrow problematic of the hero into a concern with its total vision of society. He gives us a classic definition of its representational functions:

The novel's manner of portrayal is *closer* to life, or rather to the normal appearance of life than that of the drama. . . . By representing a limited section of reality, it aims to evoke the totality of the process of social development. . . . The novel has the task of evoking the full span of life,

the complexity and intricacy of its developments, the incom-
mensurability of its detail. Hence the problem of the 'totality of objects'
as the representational aim of the large epic . . . should be understood
in a very broad sense, i.e. this whole includes not simply the dead objects
through which man's social life manifests itself, but also the various
habits, customs, usages etc. characteristic of a society and the direction it
is taking. Society is the principal subject of the novel, that is, man's social
life in its ceaseless interaction with surrounding nature, which forms the
basis of social activity, and with the different social institutions of
customs which mediate the relations between individuals in social
life.[4]

But this immaculate textbook formula is also misleading. It contains no
reference to the problem of characterisation. Nor does it reveal Lukács's
notorious historicist reservations about Western European literature after
1848. In truth, both are debilitating and eliminate, at times, the dialectical
elements in his literary-sociological thought.

What it does make clear, however, is Lukács's preference for viewing
realist literature as epic, rather than tragic. More important than the fate
of the characters is the historical and sociological dimension of the text.
Totality in the novel is identified with the epic, rather than the tragic
vision. In his study of Russian realism Lukács interprets both Tolstoy and
Sholokhov as predominantly epic writers, writers who portray agrarian life
in all its totality at different historical stages. In comparison with this the
tragic fate of Anna Karenin and Gregor Melekhov is secondary, and in the
case of the Cossack hero, is not even recognised as tragic at all:[5]
Interestingly enough, when history itself becomes tragic in Lukács's eyes,
with the intensification of class-struggle in modern times, literature ceases
to be truly realistic. Lukács's study of western literature after 1848 is in
terms of the failure by most great novelists of the period, such as Flaubert
and Zola, Proust and Kafka, to be truly representational at all. While
critical realism and historical tragedy are largely incompatible, the period
of bourgeois ascendancy permits what Lukács curiously calls 'the tragedy
of birth'.

Here his idea of tragedy in the novel loses any consistency it might have
had. Balzac, the archetypal critical realist in Lukács's criticism, is realist by
virtue of living too soon to witness the tragic class-struggles of advanced
capitalism. At the same time his works reflect the tragic struggle of man
against capitalist degradation, a struggle which is lost by 1848. Hence
Balzac is a tragic writer even though many of his heroes are not tragic at all,
but actual beneficiaries of the new capitalistic order. After all Balzac
himself entitled his vast work *La Comédie Humaine*. The inconsistency in
Lukács's attitude seriously impairs his distinction between realism and
naturalism, above all in his derogatory attitude towards Flaubert and
Zola. It also transforms the following comparison between Balzac and

Flaubert into a ritual ideological formula almost entirely devoid of meaning:

> Balzac depicted the original accumulation of capital in the ideological sphere, while his successors, even Flaubert, the greatest of them, already accepted as an accomplished fact that all human values were included in the commodity structure of capitalism. In Balzac we see the tumultuous tragedy of birth; his successors give us the lifeless fact of consummation and lyrically or ironically mourn the dead. Balzac depicts the last great struggle against the capitalist degradation of man while his successors already paint an already degraded world.[6]

This passage actually tells us more about Lukács than it does about Balzac or Flaubert. He uses Flaubert to exemplify his secret fear that historical tragedy (i.e. the class struggle after 1848) prevents tragic fiction. On the other hand, he uses the example of Balzac to disguise affirmative reconciliation—for that is what Balzac really means to him—with a tragic mask. Reading his studies on European realism, one senses that he re-enacts in his criticism the literary myth of his own historical conversion to Marxism. There is an early period of bourgeois security, prior to 1914, when he could safely preoccupy himself with the tragic vision. But later there is a clearer recognition of the universal nature of the class-struggle. This destroys the late-romantic inner space of tragedy. In Balzac there is an artistic refraction of the early Lukács—the luxury of being tragic. In Flaubert there is the 'realisation' of the later Lukács, that a mature capitalism, confronted by class struggle, permits no such luxuries at all.

Lukács's studies of literature after 1848 contain a studied evasion of tragic realism. In this cause, the role of the problematic hero is itself diminished and played down, replaced as it is by the Soviet critical orthodoxy of the 'type'. The evasion of the tragic continues right up until *Doctor Faustus*. Here he acknowledges Mann's tragic realism but in a distorted manner. *Doctor Faustus* is less the concrete tragedy of Adrian Leverkuehn than the abstract tragedy of modern art, namely its 'vulnerability' to barbarism and fascism.

While the distinction between realism and naturalism runs right through the sociology of literature providing even those who try and stand it on its head with their basic terms of reference, the nature of both genres remains problematic. Naturalism is a catch-all term for a diversity of trends in modern literature from the documentary novel to the novel of private experience. Lukács discovers its essence in polemical writings by novelists rather than in literary texts, where it is falsely attributed to ideological attitude rather than literary accomplishment. Continuing this tendency in his post-Stalinist work, he changes the term to modernism, and promptly lays all the blame for its shortcomings at the feet of existentialism.[7] While the links between existentialist philosophy and modern fiction are genuine, it is false to see literature purely and simply as the crystallisation of a philosophical world-view. Lukács's sociology of the novel is idealist and materialist at the same time. Binding fiction to history, it also binds it to philosophy. When no clearly defined ideological position is stated by the writer, he still insists on interpreting literary talent in terms of cognitive attitude. Thus the virtue of Thomas Mann amidst the crises of late-capitalism is his attitude of 'mature resignation'. But this is little more than a projection by Lukács of his own view of life had he remained in the western camp. It hardly squares with the physical suffering and the artistic struggle which Mann describes during the period when he wrote *Doctor Faustus*,[8] and it unconsciously betrays the arrogance of the tendentious critic who identifies his own response on reading the novel with the original state of mind the author possessed when writing it.

A more serious defect is Lukács's tendency to see the differences within realist literature as basically political. The only distinction of genre he makes is between 'critical' and 'socialist' realism. In the former, the problematic relationship of hero to alien world is transformed into the critical attitude of literature to life, the opposition of the writer to the society his work portrays. On the other hand 'the typical situation of socialist realism is to educate men for socialism'. While the dialectic element of critical realism is substantially restricted, in socialist realism it is in danger of disappearing altogether. In his theory of literary evolution, the transition to socialist realism is like a bad parody of the transition to a classless socialist society, which it is intended to parallel. For, like the bourgeois state, critical realism is meant to wither away. Not only has history been a constant source of embarrassment to Lukács's theory, his literary criticism has also been inconsistent. To all intents and purposes, he treats Solzhenitsyn as a critical realist without having the courage to say so openly. But despite his ambivalence, one thing is still clear. In socialist realism, the tragic has no real place.

Another grave defect in Lukács's theory concerns the relationship of realism and revolution. Socialist realism is post-revolutionary. But what of that period when man is stranded between the stable world of early capitalism and the halcyon days of socialism yet to come? Here we can only draw a literary blank. The real and the tragic both seem to vanish, one to be restored under a new form, the other to disappear for ever. But the relationship between tragedy and revolution is an important one, despite the fact that Lukács shirks it. Among other critics, Raymond Williams has attempted to answer the question which Lukács never even posed. For Williams, tragedy is a response to social disorder. While such disorder can appear in many forms, the tragic writer responds to disturbance without necessarily knowing, in any rational sense, either its causes or its possible solution. This historical reality runs counter to our conventional notions of tragedy and revolution:

The idea of tragedy, in its ordinary form, excludes especially that tragic experience which is social, and the idea of revolution, again in its ordinary form, excludes especially that social experience which is tragic.[9]

But in fact revolutionary doctrines which advocate human liberation do have a tragic dimension:

> This (Marxian) idea of 'the total redemption of humanity' has the ultimate cast of revolution and order, but in the real world its perspective is inescapably tragic. It is born in pity and terror: in the perception of a radical disorder in which the humanity of some men is denied and by that fact the idea of humanity is itself denied. It is born in the actual suffering of real men thus exposed, and in all the consequences of this suffering: degeneration, brutalisation, fear, hatred, envy. . . .
>
> And if it is thus tragic in its origins—in the existence of a disorder that cannot but move and involve—it is equally tragic in its action, in that it is not against Gods or inanimate things that its impulse struggles, nor against mere institutions and social forms, but against other men. This throughout has been the area of silence, in the development of the idea.[10]

The tragic aspect of violent revolution to which Williams refers ties in with his idea of the 'long revolution' against human alienation. For the long revolution initially produces new kinds of alienation. The connection between liberation and its unintended effect is tragic. The same insight can be found in Trotsky's *Literature and Revolution*. But as a revolutionary political leader, Trotsky never really made it explicit. What it suggests for literature is a unique role in confronting revolution. While political ideology portrays the revolutionary event as epic, fiction emphasises its tragic dimension. The contrast can clearly be seen by juxtaposing Trotsky's own *History of the Russian Revolution* with *The Silent Don*. One proclaims the victories which have been gained; the other the terrible losses which have been incurred.

Williams, like many other critics, accounts for the rise of Elizabethan tragedy in terms of the disordered transition from a feudal to a bourgeois society. But what is more significant is his explanation of the subsequent failure of tragedy. The new ordering principle of capitalist England militated against it, not only socially but also culturally. Puritanism was inimical to the tragic vision. In fact Williams practically reverses Lukács's explanation of the effect early bourgeois society had on literature. Tragedy lacks a social context. The transformation from feudal rank to bourgeois class society, destroys the social context within which highness of rank could be equated with greatness of passion. Before the industrial revolution was a period of 'bourgeois tragedy' in which realism had yet to be grasped and the social context of tragic passion had already evaporated. The difficulty with his account of the renaissance of tragedy in realist forms is that Williams concentrates almost entirely on drama. Missing from his account of modern tragedy is a detailed attempt to explain its growth in the novel. His attempt to establish types of modern tragedy suffers in the process. Of particular interest is the inadequacy of a twofold distinction he makes, on the one hand between bourgeois and liberal tragedy, and on the other between social and personal tragedy. The former involves a process of historical transition, the latter a growing separation between two incompatible modes of writing. Briefly, a few points can be made about them. The former distinction is partly justified in terms of the development of modern drama, but the term liberal is misleading. Williams means by it a society in which actual social practices are incompatible with general values. But while this is a feature of a liberal capitalist society, it is not an appropriate designation for its tragic literature. For, as we shall see, in the novel of tragic realism, the tragic hero is almost never liberal in the economic or political sense of term. On the separation of personal and social tragedy in twentieth-century fiction, another point can be made. Tragic realism is of necessity social in meaning, and Williams' idea of personal tragedy is either a misjudgment, as in the case of O'Neill, or, in the case of Lawrence, an instance where the tragic has already vanished. The idea of personal tragedy in fiction is largely meaningless.

Williams is important for two main reasons. He shows the absence of tragedy from bourgeois pre-liberal societies and gives a historical explanation of it. He also emphasises the vital connection between tragedy and revolution. Where perhaps he falls down is in underestimating the conservative vision of the tragic writer, and its importance in the development of the tragic novel. Like Lukács, he often gives too much credence to the attitude of the writer towards his own work. His interpretation of *Women in Love* as 'personal tragedy' follows much too literally Lawrence's own polemical rejection of modern tragedy as 'transgression against the social code'. It is one thing to concede that Lawrence was consciously moving away from social tragedy but another to suggest that he in fact found an alternative sense of the tragic. As we shall see, there is no way in which the tragic cannot be a reflection upon the social, despite the polemical attitude of the writer to his creative work. The death of Gerald is not tragic because his death lacks any sense of human loss, does not deprive of us of any of the human qualities to which we aspire. And Birkin's failure to realise his vision of passion is no more tragic because he survives into the qualified happiness of marriage.[11]

In Auerbach's *Mimesis* there are two crucial elements lacking in Williams' account of modern tragedy. Firstly, there is a more fully developed explanation of the conservative resistance of the writer to his age, and secondly, a historical account of the transformation from tragic drama to tragic realism in the modern novel. Auerbach is not fully explicit about the conservatism of the tragic writer. But we can extrapolate from his view suggestions which tend in this direction. This is particularly so with regard to Shakespeare. As everyone realises, Shakespeare's tragic heroes would not have been possible without the development of the Renaissance humanism which stressed the importance of man as an individual being. To that extent his heroes are a literary reflection of the changing culture of a new age. Yet, as Auerbach reminds us, tragic drama was still aristocratic in its convention. Tragic nobility is identical with nobility of rank. The high style of Elizabethan tragedy contrasted with the low style of medieval comedy, where the lower-classes came to prominence only through their comic stature. The clash between Renaissance culture and literary convention was exceptionally fertile in Shakespeare, and for good historical reasons. Hamlet and Lear appear on the stage of the English theatre at the same time as the bourgeois appears on the stage of English history. But it would be a mistake to think of the hero of Elizabethan tragedy as a mirror of the material aspirations of an emergent bourgeoisie. Psychologically akin to the bourgeois in some ways, the tragic hero is still noble of rank and his fate signifies, both actually and prophetically, the threatened historical position of the aristocracy.

Moreover Auerbach goes on to stress the anti-popular nature of Shakespeare's writing:

> . . . The tragic in Shakespeare is not completely realistic. He does not take ordinary reality tragically or seriously. When common people or soldiers or other representatives of the middle or lower classes appear, it is always in the low style, in one of the many variations of the comic which he commands. . . . Shakespeare's world-spirit is in no way a popular spirit—a point which distinguishes him from the admirers and interpretors in the *Sturm und Drang* period and the romantic period. The dynamic throbbing of elemental forces which we feel in his work has nothing to do with the depths of the popular soul with which men of a later age connected it.[12]

Tragedy is confined to nobility of rank. But the quality of the noble is diffuse, timeless and finally universal in its impact. Tragic nobility is something which cannot be repeated in bourgeois drama, as Auerbach makes clear in his study of Schiller's middle-class tragedies. And later, after the French revolution, the universal status of citizenship was a formal, abstract designation without reference to the quality of life. As a material attribute and a spiritual quality, the noble has no substitute in bourgeois life. It is not surprising, therefore, that in Victorian England Shakespeare was to outlast his successors. The stiff, mannered, anti-poetics of the Victorian Shakespeare may have reflected the *embourgeoisement* of tragic nobility, but there was simply no bourgeois drama to put in its place. Not only does Shakespeare's popularity over the centuries point to the universal nature of the noble but also to the absence of anything equivalent in the bourgeois theatre. This remained the case in European drama until the advent of Ibsen.

Prior to that, however, a revolutionary breakthrough into modern realism had occurred in the novel. The novel was the first literary form to treat seriously the nature of non-aristocratic life. As it has often been pointed out, its rise is contemporaneous with the rise of bourgeois society. Elements of realist fiction asserted themselves quite strongly in the picaresque novel of Fielding and Defoe, but only in the moral seriousness of the nineteenth-century novel do we find the essential basis of realism. An important distinction remains between serious and tragic fiction. The novel of tragic realism is an exceptional literary occurrence in modern bourgeois society. In the novels of Tolstoy and Dostoevsky, it finds its greatest expression outside bourgeois society altogether. The lesson of Austen, Dickens, Balzac and Eliot is that serious realism does not of itself generate tragedy. It depicts society and social relationships in specific settings. But tragic realism goes one step further by portraying the irreparable loss of the human qualities either actual or possible in the lives of its characters. Yet it operates, unlike Shakespearean or Racinian tragedy, with a guiding idea of history and society. Its greater proximity, in content, to contemporary social life, is at once a liberation and a constraint. There are no limitations of style upon its portrayal of reality. But tragic drama has a different sort of freedom which eludes the novel. It can portray the history of its own society as antique myth. It is not bound in the same way to time and place and so the world it evokes can constantly be recreated in the image of the world which witnesses it. While the reader of the novel can identify with its hero's fate in the same way as an audience can identify with the fate of the actor standing on the stage in front of them, the characters of a novel are bound to a specific society and a distinctive web of social relationships. The novelist cannot create tragedy out of myth but must find it within reality itself. More or less contemporary with the world it reveals, tragic realism expresses without any form of social exclusion the conflicts and contradictions of that same world.

Auerbach illustrates the difference between the serious and the tragic through his comparison of Stendhal and Balzac. The tragic elements in Stendhal's fiction are explained partly in terms of the persistence of an aristocratic sensibility in a predominantly bourgeois society:

> Stendhal is an aristocratic son of the *ancien régime grande bourgeoisie*, he will and can be no nineteenth-century bourgeois. He says so time and time again. . . . Such traits make him appear a man born too late who tries in vain to realise the form of life of a past period: other elements of his character, the merciless objectivity of his realistic power, his courageous assertion of his personality against the rising *juste milieu* and

much more, show him as the forerunner of certain intellectual modes and forms of life, but he always feels and experiences the reality of his period as a resistance. That very thing makes his realism so energetic and so closely connected with his own existence: the realism of this *cheval ombrageux* is a product of his fight for self-assertion. And this explains the fact that the stylistic level of his great realistic novels is much closer to the old great and heroic concept of tragedy than it is to the later realists—Julien Sorel is much more of a 'hero' than the characters of Balzac, to say nothing of Flaubert.[13]

This experience of 'the reality of his period as a resistance' is the key to tragic realism. By initially opposing the change of his period the tragic writer puts his finger on its very pulse. Stendhal's, and later Dostoevsky's, passion for aristocracy is significant by virtue of the fact that it can never be realised. For the very nature of literary realism pulls them in the opposite direction, the revelation of aspects of life previously considered beneath the dignity of serious fiction. By comparison with Stendhal Auerbach finds the resistance of Balzac to be much weaker. He is a natural offspring of the French Revolution, bequeathing us a truthful portrait of the middle and lower Parisian bourgeoisie. On the other hand, his depiction of high society is melodramatic, false and unintentionally comic. His penchant for exaggeration reflects his failure either to be truly tragic or serious in contrast to Stendhal:

> In Stendhal the freedom of the great heart, the freedom of passion still has more of the aristocratic loftiness and of the playing with life which are more characteristic of the *ancien régime* than the nineteenth-century bourgeoisie.
>
> Balzac plunges his heroes far more deeply into a time-conditioned dependency; he thereby loses the standards and limits of what had been earlier felt as tragic, and yet does not possess the objective seriousness towards modern reality which later developed. He bombastically takes every entanglement as tragic, every urge as a great passion; he is always ready to declare every person in misfortune a hero or a saint; if it is a woman he compares her to an angel or the Madonna; every energetic scoundrel and above all every figure who is at all Sinister, he converts into a demon: and he calls poor old Goriot *ce Christ de la paternité*.[14]

Melodrama of this sort degenerates at the hands of lesser writers into sentimentality, and Auerbach clearly sees in Flaubert 'the objective seriousness' which Balzac lacks. This, along with his belief that modern society facilitates the entry of the lower classes into literature, entails a rejection of the distinction between realism and naturalism. There is no generic distinction here at all. At the same time he sees in Flaubert's objective seriousness an immense problem of characterisation—the loss of the point of view and, with it, the loss of sympathy of the reader for the hero. While true of *Sentimental Education*, it is not true of *Madame Bovary* in spite of what Flaubert himself wanted. Auerbach claimed that Flaubert's attempt at impartiality had eliminated the tragic element from his greatest novel. No tragic heroine can suffer, as Emma Bovary does, from 'unconcrete despair'. The diffuse *ennui* of provincial bourgeois life does not provide the basis for tragic catharsis. But here Auerbach, for once, is wrong. What Flaubert provides is the social context of Emma's malaise. It is portrayed as a lived predicament amidst provincial middle-class men who are either cynical, uncomprehending or stupid, and as such is a thoroughly realistic one. Environment is not distorted, or eliminated, as it is in the contemporary novel of private experience to provide a false context for emotional alienation.

Auerbach's failure to recognise the tragic realism of *Madame Bovary* illustrates his quandary in dealing with the twentieth century. Writing during the last war, in Turkish exile, there is a sense of remoteness in his writing. His failure to understand Joyce, his ambivalence towards Virginia Woolf clearly show this. For despite his recognition of the development of much modern fiction away from tragic realism, and indeed from realism itself, he also failed to recognise the durability of the genre he had delineated. In his own study, it seems to end with Zola's *Germinal*, and Auerbach is hesitant about its fate thereafter. But tragic realism does proceed beyond *Germinal*, and the second part of this work is intended to pass beyond the blank wall which Auerbach seemed to have encountered. The consistent thread of tragic realism is the alienation of its heroes from bourgeois society. But socially and politically speaking, there are varieties of alienation which do not conform to a single pattern. Despite this diversity, a pattern of development can be traced from the quasi-aristocratic hero of Stendhal to the non-aristocratic heroes of later fiction. They all stand outside the main currents of bourgeois life within novels which are nonetheless produced for a predominantly bourgeois readership within liberal capitalist societies. The relationship of the novel to the bourgeoisie provides us with a fundamental paradox. The greater the entry of the enlightened middle-classes into the modern novel, the greater the chances for serious fiction, but the lesser the chances for tragic realism. In the nineteenth century, England is the homeland of serious fiction, but the tragic qualities of the English novel are rare. Only in *Wuthering Heights* and occasionally in Hardy is tragic realism attained. In the case of both writers it is strongly rooted in a regional culture. In Hardy's case this culture often becomes a fixation, so that local custom and dialect appear esoteric and constrict the tragic stature of his heroes. To portray alienation in the novel has been one of the most formidable literary tasks of the modern age. And we shall see that in many cases the failure to do so by talented writers is an instance of the breakdown of tragic realism.

Finally we must pose a question so far avoided—what is the essence of the tragic? The death of the tragic hero is insufficient. For in tragic realism, the hero can sometimes continue to live. The tragic lies in the irreparable loss occasioned by the experience the hero has undergone. The loss lies initially not in the character or hero, but in the events themselves. As Williams has remarked, 'We think of tragedy as what happens to the hero, but the ordinary tragic action is what happens through the hero'.[15] The tragic is embedded in the web of social relationships of which the hero is the focal point. The tragic lies in the destruction of a certain set of relationships, but in a double sense. It obliterates past actions and prevents future ones, destroying both what is actual and what is possible. The link between the two, the past and the future, the actual and the possible, is sustained fictionally through characterisation. It is to the qualities of the character that we look for the possibilities of action which the tragic denies. Auerbach has called this quality of writing 'figural realism', and in chapter four there is a fuller account of the importance of figural realism in the political novel.

Meanwhile, having shown the historical evolution of tragic realism, I wish to discuss the anti-realist aesthetics premissed upon the more recent eclipse of all realist fiction. For it seems to be that such discussions owe more to the realist paradigm than their critics care to admit. Indeed the following two chapters are more than an intellectual digression. If the dependence of the anti-realists on a realist paradigm can be demonstrated—and in some cases they have merely inverted its terms of reference—then the whole puzzling question of modern fiction remains wide open. The long process of decay which the critical theorists, formalists and structuralists have attributed to realist fiction itself becomes a suspect argument. And seen in this light, tragic realism may once again be recognised as the dominant genre of modern literature.

2 Repudiations of Realism I: Critical Theory

With respect to literature, the most striking feature of critical theory is that it has no theory—only significant fragments. Theodor Adorno and Walter Benjamin, its two most eminent critics, both resisted that totalising mode of theorising which is characteristic of Lukács and Auerbach. What they have bequeathed us are a series of essays on often unrelated themes. Adorno, possessing a Nietzschean resistance to philosophical standardisation, based his literary criticism on the principle of a detotalising totality.[1] This principle is part of his wider conception of theory as negative critique of existing culture and society. In Benjamin's work, this negative critique takes the form of a cryptic meditation on public life, which is viewed as an ever-recurrent threat to the freedom of the individual spirit. In Herbert Marcuse, one of the more programmatic thinkers of the Frankfurt School, there is an attempt to use the scattered insights of his colleagues to produce a theory of the relationship between art and modern society. But at best it is carried out inconsistently, without the understanding of modern literature which they possessed.

Nonetheless, Marcuse's totalising formula of 'one-dimensional society' is significant in posing problems for literary realism. For he sees in all advanced industrial societies the effective destruction of those libertarian aspirations originating in the French Revolution. *One-Dimensional Man* brings up to date the culture-pessimism of German sociology. Literature is seen to be deprived of the critical function it possessed in the West before the rise of fascism. Culturally tolerated, it has nonetheless lost all capacity to oppose existing culture and existing institutions. Unlike Auerbach, Marcuse does not link the critical function of literature to the development of realism. Rather the 'two-dimensional' features of literature are based upon a refusal of reality, that is of an official reality of established institutions. It is this negative refusal of reality, so crucial to two-dimensional culture, which Marcuse extracts from the writings of Adorno and Benjamin.

Walter Benjamin, a marginal contributor to the Frankfurt School, more conservative and less Hegelian than its leading members, nonetheless provided the basis of its literary theory. Benjamin's personal preference for the story, or tale, strongly influenced his analysis of the novel. The former he saw as pre-bourgeois, the latter as the main literary form of bourgeois society. At the same time he saw a negative link between the tale and the avant-garde experiments of his own time. Both the traditional and the experimental were beyond the domain of bourgeois life. During the thirties he came to see an important link between the two in the theatre of Bertolt Brecht. With its epic form and popular appeal, Brecht's work had a playfulness Benjamin saw as reminiscent of the freedom of the tale. Both were unhindered by mimetic constraint. All told, Benjamin's attitude towards modern technology was ambivalent. He saw its culture threatening the tale and the novel with total extinction. On the other hand his fascination with mechanical reproduction expiated this deep-rooted fear. After his exile from Germany, it found expression in his commitment to new modes of artistic production in film, newspaper and theatre.[2] After this point, significantly, Benjamin began to lose interest in the novel.

In his earlier work, where he compares the novel and the tale, Benjamin is strongly influenced by the young Lukács. He sees the tale as a communal experience whose content can be taken from any aspect of life and be told by anyone. The individual is equally narrator or listener, and the context of his literary experience is collective. By contrast, the novel arises from the solitude of the individual in bourgeois society. Not only its content, but also its form, expresses this solitude. It is written in isolation and read in isolation, the basic mode of artistic communication in bourgeois society. By contrast with the simplicity of the tale, its mimetic qualities give 'evidence of the profound perplexity of living'. For the fictional hero, the real author and the solitary reader, alienation remains the essential experience. Like Lukács, Benjamin sees the novel as 'the form of transcendental homelessness'. This homelessness is overcome only by the novel's ending. For unlike the timeless myth of the tale, its narrative is temporal, and for the novel's hero 'the meaning of life is revealed only in his death'. The hero's death is the reader's solitary catharsis. Benjamin sees in the novel a tragic vision based upon the relationship between the fate of the novel's hero and the response of the solitary reader to it:

> The novel is significant, therefore, not because it presents someone else's fate to us, perhaps didactically, but because the stranger's fate, by virtue of the flame which consumes it, yields us the warmth which we never draw from our own fate. What draws the reader to the novel is the hope of warming his shivering life with the death he reads about.[3]

Perhaps Benjamin's idea of the tragic finitude of the novel is too forlorn and despairing. But it is significant in a number of ways. The alienation of the problematic hero is reformulated as a tragic vision of the world, which centres around an unresolved quest for 'the meaning of life'. To this quest, the representational functions of the novel appear to be subordinate. Yet the two are not necessarily incompatible. Unfortunately Benjamin, did not pursue his own insight and, left hanging in the air, the 'meaning of life' strikes one as the cliché which it has since become. The reason for the identification of reader with hero is never sociologically grounded. Benjamin never suggests what historical or sociological aspects of the hero's fate attracts the reader to him, and their unity of being is founded on little more than mutual solitude.

Significantly, and perhaps perversely, Benjamin's interest in the modern novel increases to the extent that he sees it resurrecting the qualities of the traditional tale. The novelists he writes about never substantiate his embryonic theory of the novel. In Proust he sees human hope being sustained through the remembrance of a past world which the alien present cannot destroy. In Kafka he sees a world at once ancient and modern, of Chinese ancestor cults and atomic physics, where an accurate vision of modern science is conveyed to Kafka by mystical tradition. In his longing for the past and his fascination with the future, Benjamin produces the formula for a conservative literary revolution—elimination of the solitary individual associated with the novel and the bourgeois world. In the following passage on Kafka there already exists the critical vision which later reappears as 'historical reality' in Marcuse's *One-Dimensional Man*—a unity of mystic tradition and impending global annihilation:

> An appeal has to be made to the forces of this (mystical) tradition if an individual (by the name of Franz Kafka) was to be confronted with that reality of ours which realises itself theoretically for example, in modern physics and practically in the technology of modern warfare. What I mean to say is that this reality can no longer be experienced by an *Individual*, and that Kafka's world, frequently of such playfulness, and interlaced with angels, is the exact complement of his era which is preparing to do away with the inhabitants of this planet on a considerable scale. The experience which belongs to Kafka, the private individual, will not probably become accessible to the masses until such a time as they are being done away with.[4]

The passage is remarkable for the way in which Benjamin reveals Kafka's vision of planetary extinction. Yet, at the same time, he appears to be mesmerised by it. It is almost as if he thought it inevitable, as if he accepted Kafka's theological vision of the bureaucratic organisation of destiny, as if he longed for the primordial oblivion of a prehistoric world where there are no human beings but merely the spirit-forms worshipped by the Chinese ancestor cults. In superseding the bourgeois novel, Kafka had taken the novel form to the point of extinction, and in Benjamin's eyes that extinction was identical with the extinction of humanity itself. In the critique of Kafka, there is a rejection of humanism, which seems to coincide with a rejection of the novel itself.

What did Benjamin put in its place? He looked for an art in which no spirtitual inwardness was possible, in which artistic forms relied upon technique for their effectiveness. The cult of technique, the expulsion of inwardness, of all subjectivity, was a typical German reaction to the age of technology.[5] Benjamin replaces his precious lament for the novel and the tale with a rather crude cult of metaphysical materialism. By claiming that artistic possibilities must be explained by the artistic technique itself, Benjamin mystifies the artistic means of production rather than explaining it. It leads him into false analogies and comparisons. He claims that film is a superior art form to painting because of its superior equipment. He suggests the relationship of painter to cameraman can be seen as that of magician to surgeon. He openly extols the 'scientific' qualities of the latter over the illusionist qualities of the former. The image of the cameraman as an artist by virtue of his precise powers of scientific dissection of reality is strange enough in itself. But Benjamin's acclaim for 'the thoroughgoing permeation of reality with technical equipment' reveals a culturally schizophrenic attitude towards modern art. Despairing of the loss of cultural tradition he sided with those modern experimental techniques most effective in eliminating it.

Benjamin saw the main institutional threat to the tale and the novel arising out of the increase of information in modern society. In Adorno's notes on literature this is a main focus of concern. He regarded the production of information as a major threat to the position of the modern novel. Just as the painter had been deprived of his traditional subject-matter by photography, so the novelist had been undermined by journalism, the culture industry, and at times the cinema. In choice of subject-matter, the novelist is compelled to concentrate upon themes which have not been made worthless by information. For all modern societies forms of non-artistic communication have a general, and even an intellectual, seal of approval. The intelligentsia itself complies with the growing standardisation of knowledge. The psychological imagination of Dostoevsky, for example, which makes man's being intelligible through fiction, is replaced by a scientific psychology which legitimates the purely empirical investigation of human nature. Everything factitious in science and information forces the novel to surrender its realist qualities. 'If the novel wishes to remain true to its realist foundation and say how things really are,' Adorno states, 'it has to repudiate a realism which, by producing a façade, only helps to foster a trade in deception.'[6]

Adorno's concern here is most certainly one which Lukács and Auerbach neglected—the relationship of fiction to other forms of culture and knowledge. But his attitude towards literary realism is significantly ambiguous. On the one hand, he seems to suggest that the novel must substantially change its representational qualities; on the other hand, he appears to claim it must give them up altogether. A demand for a change in the portrayal of the real merges into a demand for the refusal of the real. Alongside the claim that realism is immanent in the literary text is the assumption that science and information make the mimetic function increasingly pointless. In refusing the reality of an increasingly informational culture, Adorno looks to literature for a rebellion against 'the lies of representational art' at the same time. He finds it in the early development of twentieth-century literature, the novel of the twenties where the major writer gained a degree of inner emancipation from the constraints of the administered world. The twenties novel is superior to the realism which preceded it, precisely because the relationship between writer and society is mediated by aesthetic imagination.

Unlike Lukács, Adorno sees Flaubert as the last great representative of the classic bourgeois age. For he, through his objective craftsmanship, had perfected the realist illusion, raising the curtain for his audience and inviting them to participate in the events before them as if they were really there. The subjectivity of the realist author lies simply in the manner of presenting the illusion and, in Flaubert, also in the purity of language. Later novelists, Proust, Gide, Musil and Thomas Mann, reveal a reflexivity impossible in the traditional novel. By a variety of techniques, such as internal reflection, remembrance or irony, the author distances himself from his narration in such a way as to allow for the provisional suspension of the objective world. Adorno saw in Proust a writer who provided a counter-fiction to the cult of the fact which realism had done so little to oppose. Each claim of remembering how things actually were generates in Proust's fiction a counter-claim of how they might have happened differently. Capturing the chimerical quality of remembrance with microscopic precision, Proust's very sensitivity strengthens aesthetic sensibility. The inner space of the interior monologue enables the narrator to establish an inner space unavailable to him in an alien world. The free moment of the stream of consciousness is the artistic refusal of objective reality. This reveals the fundamental ingredient of great art—aesthetic distance. The modern literary movement culminates in Proust in a series of variations in aesthetic distance akin to moving camera positions in a film. The writer safeguards his art by the distance he creates in writing from the world his writing portrays.

After fascism, with the growth of the Cold War, Adorno became gloomy about the prospects of aesthetic distance. The extreme work of Kafka represented its final elimination and the destruction of all subjectivity. Instead of a return to realism there is the use of shock, the horror of *Metamorphosis*. The contemplative security of the reader is destroyed by shock-effects. But this is not an act of literary sensationalism. It is an authentic response to a world where the contemplative attitude has become an object of derision. Shock and dissonance are the only artistic weapons left in a world which faces the threat of nuclear catastrophe with complete equanimity. As a response to the urgency of the contemporary predicament, shock and dissonance are the supreme negative acts. Adorno sees in the compositions of Arnold Schoenberg the supreme musical expression of negative dissonance, the result of a revolution in form similar to Kafka's transformation of modern literature. The solitary catharsis of the bourgeois novel with its quest for the meaning of life is no longer possible. Those who read Kafka or listen to Schoenberg can expect only permanent discomfort and perturbation.

Adorno's schema of modern literature contains three stages. The first is that of classic realism culminating in Flaubert. The second is that of aesthetic distance developed as a counter-response to Zola's cult of the documentary fact. The third is the literature of shock inaugurated by Kafka and developed by Samuel Beckett. It is the final stage which provides the fiction of Marcuse's One-Dimensional Society, whose historical parameters are the economic collapse of 1929, and the rise of fascism in Europe and of Stalinism in the Soviet Union. Marcuse in fact attempts to reduce Adorno's three stages to a dichotomy between two-dimensional culture and one-dimensional society. In the former pre-fascist period art is seen to be in opposition to bourgeois society. Latterly it becomes absorbed into the dominant culture of a totalitarian industrial world. Here the negating power of art is itself neutralised. Like Adorno, Marcuse is sensitive to the development of new forms of culture which challenge the influence of serious art. In their famous wartime essay on the American mass culture industry,[7] Adorno and Horkheimer had argued that late-capitalism's relationship to culture would henceforth be determined by the profitability of mass culture, and not by the legitimating potential of serious art. The audience for classic literature is not eliminated but its cultural significance is henceforth negligible. Because of the dominance of mass-culture, it can no longer play a significant role in people's lives. For Marcuse, this was evidence of the 'repressive tolerance' of the liberal order in the cultural sphere. The classics could be mass-produced and consumed meaninglessly. In such a way their negative oppositional function was destroyed.

Marcuse's vision of two-dimensional culture is significantly different from Adorno's 'aesthetic distance'. He sees classic art from a Freudian perspective as a form of creative sublimation. Whereas Adorno saw the artistic negation of the objective world in terms of cognitive reflexivity, Marcuse regards it as a psychic mechanism occasioned by the deferring of sexual gratification. Two-dimensional culture means both traditional realism and reflexive modernism—Proust and Thomas Mann as well as Goethe and Tolstoy. Marcuse reinterprets Benjamin's nostalgia for a lost world as sublimated romance, and sees it exemplified in the songs and poems of Brecht. Dominated by Freudianism, Marcuse's theory of culture lacks any criterion of literary evolution. It certainly comes to grief in a very ethnocentric dismissal of the treatment of sexuality in modern American literature. Having praised the sublimated art of the European classics, Marcuse goes on to write:

Desublimated sexuality is rampant in O'Neill's alcoholics and

Faulkner's savages, in the Streetcar named Desire and on the Hot Tin Roof, in Lolita, in all the stories of Hollywood and New York orgies, and the adventures of suburban housewives.[8]

Revealing the literary snobbery of the Frankfurt School, this passage also shows Marcuse to be as remote from modern American literature as Adorno was from jazz music. Marcuse's identification of desublimated and revealed sexuality is not merely an attack on pornography. It is anti-realist in its assumption that any literary treatment of sexuality denigrates the artistic process. Thus Marcuse is unable to distinguish an important facet of literary evolution in O'Neill, Faulkner and Williams from its vulgarisation by the mass culture industry.

Marcuse's interpretation of avant-garde literature is also inconsistent. At times he sees the shock-effect and its opposite, Brecht's alienation-effect, as posing a subversive threat to the existing order. At other times he seems to suggest they are easily capable of absorption. During the Vietnam war, Marcuse regarded the New Left cultural revolution in America as evidence of a renaissance of the avant-garde culture of the twenties, such as surrealism and expressionism. Towards the end of the war, disillusioned with his followers, he attacked efforts to dissolve the separation of art and life, seeing in them attempts to destroy the negating power of 'the great refusal'.[9] But his view of the prospects for sublimated art is equally pessimistic. The cultural processes of a mass consumer culture with their emphasis on instant gratification are desublimating, and thus destructive of the imaginative processes on which art depends.

Both Adorno and Marcuse turn their back on realism but in different ways, Adorno through reflexivity, Marcuse through sublimation. For both, artistic achievement is subordinate to the requisite aesthetic attitude towards the world. Literature is the means by which the writer severs himself from a world he finds intolerable. He must do so, ideally, through whatever means is historically appropriate, not through what his writing objectively reveals. Realism is inappropriate, the critical theorists argue, because the established order has expropriated the real. Fiction is not therefore an autonomous quest but a calculated counter-response to whatever institutionalised forms threaten its existence. In order to be authentic, its representational function has to be discarded. Literature is to be acclaimed not for the truths it reveals to us about society, but for the refusal of its creators to be compromised. The two things are not necessarily related.

The paradox of critical theory is that while possessing an important sociological insight into the decline of literary realism at the expense of other forms of modern culture, it does not wish to compensate for the loss it laments. Adorno's active fatalism, embodied in his notorious slogan 'No poetry after Auschwitz', inadvertently condones a cultural paralysis of will. In trying to legitamely protect the integrity of the artist in an age which denies it to him, the critical theorists make him a much too precious figure, almost as if artistic inwardness alone guaranteed creative achievement. Adorno's demand for inner cognition, Marcuse's championing of sublimation, while both important to the psychology of the writer, have together become vulgarised attitudes. Nowadays interest in the personal lives of great writers has reached the level of a clichéd prurience. Those who read and write the sexual biographies of famous writers mimic critical theory without knowing it. It is a cultural commonplace to regard every great writer as having a secret inner life and a Freudian commonplace to regard that life as based upon the manifestation or restraint of his sexual instincts. By frantically reading his fiction in order to find clues to his life, the prurient critic or reader not only destroys the whole point of fiction, but treads the same road as the critical theorists in the opposite direction. Critical theory sees in the secrecy and asceticism of literature its distance from life, while the prurient reader sees in it a deviation from life and looks for the lover or fetish which 'made' that deviation possible. While information about writers is a means to understanding their work, their work should never be used purely and simply as a means to understanding their life. In fact the mass media culture which Adorno condemns has probably done much to stimulate this fruitless attitude. But the counter-argument of critical theory, obsessed by inwardness and sublimation, has probably done little to stop it.

Like Lukács, the critical theorists often confuse the attitude of the writer with his literary text. They differ significantly because their concern is with aesthetic attitude, not ideological attitude. Hence Adorno's contempt for all demands that literature should be politically progressive and little more besides. The significant advance they make is to assess aesthetic attitude in a historical and sociological context, the complete opposite of *l'art pour l'art*. On the other hand, aesthetic distance in the modern novel has also meant distance from reality, since in Adorno's eyes reality has already been expropriated by the reified enemy he calls 'the administered world'. Distance from reality remains even after aesthetic distance has been eliminated.

The negative refusal of critical theory actually legitimates the retreat from society we see in the heroes of Miller and Burroughs, Salinger and Bellow, and even Gunther Grass's *The Tin Drum*. With the public world ever diminished by inroads of information and documentary, it is only here, warily, that artistic integrity is preserved, in what Paul Goodman has called 'the private experience of modern society'. Here the problematic hero is reduced to a confessional autobiography of the solitary ego, as the only alternative to that other literature of the *nouveau roman* where the ego has been totally eliminated. Neither tragedy nor realism can exist, either in society or its fiction. Rather tragedy can only refer to the relationship between the writer and the repressive open society which undermines his art through desublimation or information. The prospects for the novel are pessimistic if we take the analysis of the critical theorists to its logical conclusion. Routed by the false public discourse of a highly rationalised world, it becomes the surrogate pleasure of a defeated intelligentsia still feeling the guilt of its own subjectivity. At best, such guilt can be transformed into refusal; at worst, it is totally eliminated. Like so much modern criticism, critical theory has left its own image in the mirror of modern fiction. Thankfully it has not recognised the fact, for if it did, it would not altogether like what it sees.

3 Repudiations of Realism II: Formalism and Genetic Structuralism

It might seem that any movement concerned with establishing a pure literary science would be at the furthest remove from the sociological study of literature and society. However, the Russian Formalists have produced methods of criticism which cannot be ignored.[1] Developing out of the *Opojaz* movement of 1914, they were in revolt against two opposing trends of literary thought—the positivists who veered towards a posture of sociological determinism and the idealists who saw literature in terms of religious or mystical symbolism. In addition, no greater contrast can be found than between the formalists and the Russian radical critics of the 1860s who tried, through the yardstick of social utility, to subordinate literature to life. The formalists stressed the *Literaturnost*, or literariness, of all fictional texts, and the scientific autonomy of literary criticism. At its worst, this emphasis degenerates into an introverted analysis of literary techniques. At best, however, it illustrates the literary text as the dominant element in literary-sociological criticism. On nearly all occasions, however, the formalists officially repudiated literary realism. We therefore have to ask the question: How was this repudiation justified, and does it mean a total incompatibility between the formal method and the concept of mimesis?

In trying to answer this question, it should be stressed that the formalists were more interested in the folk-tale and the development of modern poetry than in the novel. Their contemporary connections were with the new schools of Russian poetry, Futurism and Acmeism, which had broken away from the pre-war Symbolist movement of the so-called 'Silver Age'. One of their major preoccupations was the relationship of sound, rhythm and meaning in the new verse forms. Yet many formalists, including Jacobsen, Shlovsky, Eichenbaum and Tomashevsky, tried to come to terms with the problem of realism in the modern novel, or as they themselves called it, 'the realist illusion'. Because of the varied, eclectic nature of the movement, some are closer to realism than others. The most analytical repudiation of realism is by Jacobsen, the most polemical by

Shlovsky. Again Tynjanov's theory of literary evolution is inimical to a realist position. On the other hand, Eichenbaum's idea of literary environment and Tomashevsky's neo-Aristotlian thematics are important for representational analysis.

Many of their objections to realism in art are either specific to features of Russian art criticism or part of a wider objection to all forms of positivism. But Jacobsen concentrates on the logic of the concept itself, pointing out both its inconsistent usage and intrinsic relativism. He claims that realism is usually endowed with two distinct and often contradictory meanings. It can refer either to whether the artist perceives his work as true to life or whether his audience does. To these two meanings, a third is often added—the perception of realism as specifically a nineteenth-century artistic movement. Jacobsen easily picks holes in the relativity of such criteria. What is perceived as real on this basis within a specific work or genre will change from age to age. Conservative critics base their criterion of realism on a past epoch, radical critics on the current one:

> The words of yesterday's narrative grow stale: now the item is described by features that were yesterday held to be the least descriptive, the least worth representing, features which were scarcely noticed. 'He is fond of dwelling on unessential details' is the classic judgment passed on the innovators by conservative critics of every era. . . . (But) to the followers of the new movement, a description of unessential details seems more real than the petrified tradition of their predecessors.[2]

The historical relativity of changing judgments is unacceptable to Jacobsen. For 'maximum verisimilitude' can be claimed by any artistic movement at the height of its influence. Controversy between conservative and radical critics arises when the former views any artistic innovation as a distortion of reality and the latter sees it as a necessary means of evoking the real. This confusion arises from a transformation of genres and in turn signifies that the artistic code is in the process of changing. For Jacobsen this transformation is the important artistic fact.

It lies at the heart of Juri Tynjanov's concept of literary evolution, that is an idea of 'the mutation of systems'.[3] Genesis of literary phenomena is to be sought in their evolution out of previous literary systems. While he uses his argument to postulate the interrelationship of literary facts and the futility of analysing texts in isolation, he simultaneously restricts analysis of the interrelationship of literary facts and social forces. 'The evolution of literature', he states, 'as of other cultural systems does not coincide either in tempo or in character with the systems with which it is interrelated.'[4] While he is justified in trying to protect literary evolution from deterministic explanations specifying particular social conditions, Tynjanov's schema presents difficulties for analysing the relation of novel and society. Changes in fictional themes, for example, can be partly explained as the outcome of a changing social world. There is an important distinction here between literary influence and fictional thematics. Conrad read Dostoevsky, and Thomas Mann later read both of them. In the history of the novel many chain reactions of this sort can be detected. Yet what each of these novelists writes about varies enormously, and is a variation which cannot be explained solely by mutations of form. Dostoevsky wrote about the Imperial Russia of the sixties, Conrad the British imperial world at the turn of the century, and Mann about the whole historical period of modern Germany through which he lived. In each case, themes differ despite influences, because the political systems are different, the forms of culture are different, the occupations and social class of the major characters are different. Literary evolution may explain the continuity of the modern novel; at the same time change and variation within different societies explain the difference. Very often the formalists merely substitute for the relativity of realism, a relativity of genres, exemplified by Jacobsen's concept of the dominant.[5] For the question as to what constitutes the dominant aesthetic function at any given time can only be answered by the artist, the critic and the audience. The formalists here are in the very dilemma which they ascribed to the realists. For these three groupings can and will differ over what constitutes the dominant just as much as they do over what constitutes the real.

The neglect of thematics was a common feature of early formalism, where it was usually considered inferior to the 'device' of the plot. Thus Shlovsky saw the main task in interpreting the novel as 'laying bare the device', that is, the literary technique of composition. Moreover his view that the task of criticism is to show how each novelist parades his own technique is seriously flawed. It is never clear whether the author lays bare the theme about which he writes or the form in which he expresses that theme. In his essay on Sterne, Shlovsky made the notorious remark that '*Tristram Shandy* is the most typical novel in world-history', because of the continuous self-conscious commentary of the author on his own narration. The remark is a naïvely ahistorical. For Sterne had in fact written a picaresque novel at the very beginning of the period of realism, when the degree of authorial intervention in the narrative was still a matter of artistic uncertainty. The subsequent history of the novel showed how untypical it was to be.

On the question of thematics, Shlovsky's work is vastly inferior to that of Tomashevsky. He denigrates it for a start by regarding plot-composition as being artistically independent of what he pejoratively called 'the story-stuff' of the novel. In this way he devalues the whole idea of the fictional theme. 'Art', he wrote, 'is the way of experiencing the artfulness of an object; the object is not important.'[6] Yet his remarkable analysis of defamiliarisation actually contradicts this statement. If we take just one of the many defamiliarisation devices which he finds in Tolstoy, the description of flogging[7], it becomes clear that such a device is a means of revealing the real by the very act of casting it in an unfamiliar light. Tolstoy was able to break down conventional perceptions of phenomena by this means. But such phenomena were indelibly social and the whole point about revealing to us in a different light is to alter our consciousness of them—in other words to change social consciousness. It is important to understand defamiliarisation as an artistic device precisely because of the phenomenon being defamiliarised. The question of how invariably leads back to the question of what. The formalist extrapolation of the question of how remains highly artificial and unjustified.

The later writings of the formalists are a distinctive response to the types of criticism which they faced from the more political writers' organisations in the Soviet State such as RAPP. The fetish of the device was soon relinquished in a spirited and more sociological attempt to counter fierce dogmatic criticism. Eichenbaum's idea of literary environment steers a middle course between a theory of instrinsic mutation and vulgar-sociological determinism. Tomashevsky's *Thematics* restores to formalism the concern with literary content. Eichenbaum's essay arose out of his critique of literary biography, but in refusing to allocate much importance to the writer's personality in the discussion of literature, he nonetheless conceded the importance of his cultural environment. What is important here is not the writer's social class or the stage of historical development his country has reached, so much as the milieu which engendered processes of mediation. The state of publishing, censorship, accessible audience, financial independence—factors which vary so much before and after the Russian Revolution—are significant factors of literary environment which mediate the writer's relationship to society as a whole. 'Literature', Eichenbaum warns, 'like any other specific order of things, is not generated from facts belonging to other orders and therefore *cannot be reduced* to such facts.'[8] The coincidence of class identity and literary output is a historically contingent, and not a necessary fact. Class struggle and literary struggle can coincide but not necessarily so, since they are two independent orders of facts. Eichenbaum concluded that the dogmatic attempt to derive a writer's ideology from his literary texts was a futile and meaningless exercise.

Tomashevsky's famous essay, though concerned with creating a formal aesthetics of the novel, has a number of important sociological insights. He considered more seriously than many other formalists the problem of readership, arguing that modern audiences demand plausible, and by implication realist, themes. 'General interest in a theme', he suggests 'is determined by the historical conditions prevailing when the work appears'.[9] The realism of a theme is therefore conditional upon an audience accepting it as realistic measured by their involvement in what they read. This deliberate repudiation of an objective criterion of realism is nonetheless an aesthetic requirement—the requirement of creating 'a realist illusion'. This is Tomashevsky's formula for a compromise between formalism and realism, but the way in which it is reached reveals some remarkable ambiguities. For he goes on to suggest that it arises from the psychological weaknesses of human nature which cannot live up to the stringent demands of the aesthetic laws uncovered by literary science. All audiences, naïve or sophisticated, demand some measure of realistic illusion:

> For more experienced readers the need for realistic illusion expresses itself as a demand for 'lifelikeness'. Although firmly aware of the fictitious nature of the work, the experienced reader demands nevertheless some kind of conformity to reality, and finds the value of the work in this conformity. Even readers fully aware of the laws of aesthetic structure may not be psychologically free from the need for such illusion. As a result each motif must be introduced as a *probable* motif in the given situation. But since the laws of plot construction have nothing in common with probability, any introduction of motifs is a compromise between objective reality and historical tradition.[10]

Tomashevsky is in effect making a distinction between aesthetic pleasure and aesthetic cognition. Pleasure consists in spontaneously entering into the illusion of the real, knowledge consists in knowing that the real is illusory. In a way, therefore, knowledge must invariably intrude on pleasure, which is seen as a weakness of human nature. The separation of pleasure and knowledge is in danger of becoming a distinction between naïve audience and experienced critic, and exemplifies the strange aridity which is present in all formalism. When art is dissected purely in terms of its technical problems, what human enjoyment can it actually create? Do those who know that the real is fictional frustrate their own experience of the real? The evidence suggests that the formalists actually did. Their failure to grasp the importance of the real *within* the fictional left them floundering in a literary desert of their own making.

One feature of Tomashevsky's work which undoubtedly redresses the balance is his observations on the conflict of interest in the novel. This derives from his study of plot structure, similar in many ways to Aristotle's analysis of dramatic structure, where he charts the different stages of plot development—conflict, intrigue, tension, climax and ending. The story has its own internal dialectic, nourished on a conflict of interest:

> The development of a story may be generally understood as a progress from one situation to another, so that each situation is characterised by a *conflict* of interest, by discord and struggle among the characters. The dialectical development of the story is analogous to the development of social-historical processes in which each new historical stage is seen both as a result of the struggle of social groups in the preceding stage and as a battle for the interests of the new social group constituting the new social system.[11]

Clearly we cannot see the novel as reflecting *the* class struggle of modern society in any transparent sense. But given the internal dialectic of fiction, and given the subject matter of the realist novel, there will be an important relationship between the internal conflicts between the characters, or within the characters, and the society from which they have been drawn. Whether it is the inner conflict of the hero or the social conflict of the major characters, conflictual elements in the novel refract conflictual elements in society. The difference lies in the contrast between the finality of a fiction which brings its action to a close and the openness of history in which life goes on, unendingly. In the political novel the complementarity of conflictual elements, in fiction and society respectively, is at its greatest. For here the selection by the author of conflictual elements is usually deliberate, although the internal dialectic of the novel's development gives these elements a fictional logic of their own, as for example in Dostoevsky's *The Devils*. As we shall see the way in which fiction imposes its own logic and constraint upon its historical subject-matter is itself a form of artistic liberation. The literariness of the political novel is as immense and indisputable as any other form of modern fiction. What the formalists failed to recognise was that there is no basic contradiction between the fictional and the real, for no one reads a novel on the assumption that everything in it actually happened. As for literary evolution, Auerbach, as we have seen, supplied the vital factor missing from formalism, a historical conception of how change in genre is related to change in society.

II

The influence of the Russian formalists has been at its strongest on the development of structuralist theories in post-war France. Lévi-Strauss's study of savage myth owes much to earlier work by Propp and Jacobsen on the tale. But so-called linguistic structuralism is a much more eclectic movement, owing more to Heidegger's theory of metalanguage as universal Being than to the formalist study of poetics.[12] In the writings of Michel Foucault, Jacques Derrida, Julia Kristeva and the magazine *Tel Quel*, the idea of *Literaturnost* has been discarded altogether. The separation of literature and language, writer and critic, fiction and society have all been dissolved in a variety of reductionist formulae viewing the world in terms of a primordial metalanguage which is self-generating and independent of human *praxis*. This militant anti-humanism had led the French structuralists to cease regarding literature as a phenomenon of human history or creative endeavour. Thus the elimination of the figure of the artist from the consideration of art is consonant with Foucault's nihilist vision of 'the abolition of man'.[13] The logical outcome of this attitude is one which the structuralists have already arrived at—the non-existence of art itself. What the Nazis attempted to accomplish by the burning of books, the structuralists have tried to achieve by actually writing them.

In genetic structuralism on the other hand, a serious attempt has been made to consider man and his history in the study of literature. Before linguistic and genetic structuralism went their separate ways, we must consider the relevant intellectual history which helped to give birth to them. In France the seminal work of structuralism was Roland Barthes' remarkable essay *Writing Degree Zero*, which at once promises a literary-sociological alternative to realism and simultaneously destroys its own promise. But it is impossible to understand Barthes, or linguistic structuralism, without considering the novelist and critic Maurice Blanchot. Blanchot's writings provided structuralism with an inspiration notably missing from Russian formalism. They are imbued with a strange metaphysical pathos of the limits of language which makes the forlorn separation of the signifier and the signified seem worse than the fate of Paul and Virginie. In *Literature and the Right to Death*, Blanchot attempts to give textbook grammar the status of a tragic myth. The connection of language and reality are conveyed by two terms which have since become a familiar obsession—absence and death. For Blanchot the act of writing is an act of dying and the naming of an object in the act of writing is a fasification of reality denoting its absence.[14] 'Before I can say: this woman,' he writes, 'I must take away from her her bodily reality in one way or another, must render her absent and annhilate her.'[15] In his novels *Thomas l'obscur* and *Amindanab* he fictionalises the pathos of destroying the object he names and losing himself in a kind of death by doing so. True to fiction, the grammatical object becomes a sex object with a female name, either Anne or Lucie, but with no more human qualities than the subject himself who, by degrees, is eliminated from his own subjective experience. Thus the task for structuralism has already been mythically stated—to make humanity the slaves of grammar. What we see in the work of Barthes, Derrida and *Tel Quel* is its scholastic demythologisation, that is the attempted elimination of that element of loss and pathos which tried to give it the semblance of a human fate. The fictional strand in Blanchot leads on to the radical anti-humanism of Robbe-Grillet whose *choisisme* is the elaborate articulation of the personal experience of a world of mute objects in which the person or hero whose experience it is might just as well not exist.

Blanchot is to linguistic structuralism what Kafka was to critical theory, the writer of fiction providing them with an origin for their analytical themes and who, at the same time, was analytically their own equal. Barthes's ideas of rhetoric, the novel as lie, and colourless writing, are all derived from Blanchot. His attack on the realist novel is an attempt to show its inherent falseness through a concern with history, which it betrays by turning into fiction. The lynchpin of Barthes's argument is the grammatical function of the narrative past tense, the preterite. Through the use of the preterite the novel repossesses the past but only by masking the real through the narrative it imposes on it. Equally Barthes sees the literary separation of form and reality in the novel as a linguistic function—the division between signifier and signified. Barthes claims that it is a division testifying to the cultural triumph of bourgeois society:

> The teleology common to the novel and to narrated History is the alienation of the facts: the preterite is the very act by which society affirms its possession of the past and its possibility. It creates a content credible, yet flaunted as an illusion; it is the ultimate term of a formal dialectics which clothes an unreal fact in the garb first of truth, then of a lie denounced as such. This had to be related to a certain mythology of the universal typifying the bourgeois society of which the Novel is a characteristic product; it involves giving to the imaginary a formal guarantee of the real, but while preserving in the sign the ambiguity of a double object at once true and false.[16]

This passage is an unqualified denunciation of the unity of the imaginary and the real which is attained in the novel. It leaves open only two alternatives; the denunciation of the imaginary as historically worthless or, conversely, the denunciation of the real as artistically invalid. Barthes and his followers take the latter option, hence their refusal to speak of the novel as fiction. For them the imaginary is a feature of all writing (*écriture*), none of which needs any 'formal guarantee of the real'. And writing, whether literary, critical or even political, is largely a matter of form. 'Writing' itself is a conceptual artefact deliberately intended to destroy the dialectic of fiction and history and create a severe rupture between language and reality. But its plausibility is contradicted by the analytical produce on which it is based. To call the novel a characteristic product of bourgeois society is to refer back to a historical reality which, without any formal guarantee of the real, would be utterly senseless. Barthes can deny history only by invoking it. In his own scheme of things the end of history is in fact historically conditioned.

This becomes evident in his remarks on the evolution of literary form. Here Barthes stands Lukács's historicism on its head and regards 1848 not as the beginning of the end for the novel, but its true beginning in a literature of pure form. The modern historical era is one in which the writer denies history. But unfortunately for Barthes 'the Flaubertisation of writing' only makes sense because history—and bourgeois society—actually exist, and continue to exist despite the increasing absence of any reference to them in the literature which Barthes admires. The evolution of form, and a very ethnocentric form at that, in the writing of Flaubert, Mallarmé, Proust, Gide, Blanchot and Camus, is a linear process which Barthes unwittingly transforms into a diachronic myth. History may not evolve but writing cannot cease to do so. Barthes is left with the *reductio ad absurdum* that the only form of human evolution is literary evolution, that is, increasing resort to a form of writing denying the dynamic processes on which it is based.

Just as critical theory has its myth of post-history in the writings of Kafka and the figure of 'one-dimensional' man, Barthes' myth of post-history resides in zero-literature, or 'colourless writing'. Such writing, he argues, achieves freedom from bourgeois domination through its total lack of signifying qualities. Being utterly devoid of social or historical meaning, it cannot 'lie'. By saying nothing, the writer remains 'irretrievably honest'. The result is 'innocence'. The equation of innocence and nihilism reads like a perverse inversion of the religious myth of the Fall. Barthes sees its practical realisation in the fiction of Albert Camus:

> The aim here is to go beyond Literature by entrusting one's fate to a basic sort of speech, equally far from living language and from literary language proper. This transparent form of speech, initiated by Camus's *Outsider*, achieves a style of absence which is almost an ideal absence of style; writing is then reduced to a sort of negative mood in which the social or mythical characters of a language are abolished in favour of a neutral and inert state of form: thus thought remains wholly responsible without being overlaid by a secondary commitment of form to a history of its own.[17]

The final sentence in this passage shows that Barthes thought he had found a solution to the problem of literary evolution immanent in form. In a literature of pure inertia and negation, form itself is eliminated. The Blanchotesque 'absence' in *The Outsider* is seen as the anti-eschatological consummation of modern fiction—an absurd assumption when one remembers the main theme of the novel. The hero, Mersault, a *pied noir* resident in colonial Algiers, impulsively murders an Arab without any moral compunction or subsequent remorse.[18] In reality the neutral style does not successfully eliminate the signified qualities of the historical setting, but actually gives them a sociological significance which Camus himself did not realise.

Barthes, like Adorno, has a negative vision of the literary refusal of contemporary bourgeois society. But instead of being based on shock and dissonance, his is based on inertia and nothingness. The escape from history and society is identified with this refusal and founded on the purity of an opacity without resonance. By denouncing the close relationship of novel and society as a conspiracy of falseness in which the real contaminates the imaginary, and the imaginary the real, Barthes unintentionally affirms the essential humanism of realist fiction. The separation of fiction and society is dialectical. But the subjugation of literature and life to the totality of metalanguage is totalitarian. In succumbing to the totalitarian vision of language present in the later Heidegger and Blanchot, his French apostle, Barthes and the structuralists have inaugurated a critical asceticism resulting in the self-censorship of literature.

Free of fascism or Stalinism, privileged mandarins in one of the most intellectually tolerant of the liberal-capitalist countries, they have accomplished a *trahison des clercs* which involves no deference to immediate political masters. There is perhaps no greater example in contemporary European culture of the absolute freedom to be utterly debilitating. By contrast the realist novel they repudiate has as its subject man and his chances of human self-fulfilment, chances that can be kept or lost but chances which exist through a vision of hope and a belief in humanity. In this sense it is not realism but structuralism which gives us greater clues to the stagnation of academic culture at the present time, though it remains merely one school of thought among many. Barthes's criticism has often been presented as an alternative to the didactic concept of engaged writing.[19] But in truth it merely uses didacticism as a pretext to repudiate realism in the interest of nothingness.

By contrast genetic structuralism attempts to restore reality to fiction but in a way which escapes the epistemology of a naïve realism. At the same time Lucien Goldmann and Michel Zéraffa are like Barthes in wishing to rescue modern fiction from Lukács's distinction between realism and naturalism. Their resort to structure as an explanatory concept is an attempt to illuminate the social and realistic nature of a fiction progressively retreating from society. Goldmann, a disciple of the early Lukács, is most famous for his study of Pascal, Racine and Jansenism in *The Hidden God*. Here his dependence on Lukács is at times slavish. While the study is generally a sociological success, his idea of Racine's tragic vision is curiously *spaetromantisch*, almost as if the young Lukács had written *Andromaque*. In his writings on the novel, Goldmann comes equally under the influence of the idea of the problematic hero. But he departs from Lukács in trying to outline his own sociological method. He rejects *mimesis* in favour of a procedure for establishing a homology of structures between literature and social consciousness. Here literature is no longer the mechanistic reflection of the consciousness of distinctive social groups, but a significant ordering of that consciousness which did not previously exist. The historical importance and uniqueness of great literature lies in its radical restructuring of the *conscience collective*. 'Thus the work', he writes, 'constitutes a collective achievement through the individual consciousness of its creator, an achievement which will afterwards reveal to the group what it was moving towards 'without knowing it' in its ideas, its feelings and its behaviour.[20] Goldmann's notion of structure here is dynamic and derived, epistemologically speaking, from Lukács's notion of the 'possible class-consciousness' of an emergent social class. Literature is similar in its restructuring function to other ideological phenomena but different by virtue of its completely imaginary nature. It does not refer to the real world in the same way as economics or philosophy.

The important relationship stressed by Goldmann's method is clear—the relationship of literary text and social consciousness. But in

Goldmann's actual studies of modern fiction, his use of this method is totally inconsistent. It applies to his interpretation of the revolutionary novels of Malraux, but not to his studies of the *nouveau roman*. In the latter he seeks out homologies between the literary text and the *economic infrastructure* of society. Here the relationship of fiction and society is no longer mediated by the problem of values. Rather it is a mechanistic reflection of the changing nature of the economic system, in which social consciousness, as the third element, plays only a secondary role. Having resorted to the idea of structure to avoid the problems of a mechancial materialism, Goldmann then resorts to a mechanistic theory of structures. He distinguishes between the classic period of capitalist society based on a system of market exchange, when the problematic hero of the novel stands opposed to all reification inherent in the commodity structure, and a modern postwar period, a stabilised reified world where objects themselves have eliminated the importance of human relationships. Here the problematic hero gives way to the text without a subject, and the imaginary character of the novel is no longer a human person. Like Barthes and Adorno, Goldmann conceives of a long intermission between the classic and the contemporary period, the time of a crisis of values between 1910 and 1945, when Malraux's revolutionary novels, setting out an alternative to Western capitalist societies, become highly significant.[21]

Goldmann sees the problematic hero in a Heideggerian light. His is the existentialist search for authentic values in a degraded capitalist world. The values he seeks, however, are less important than the authenticity of seeking them. The authentic is part of his existential nature and not of the values to which he aspires. Goldmann states a homology of two sets of oppositions. The first is that of use-value and exchange-value in the world of the market. The second is that of authentic values and degraded values in the world of the novel. But looked at more closely, the latter seems like an analogy derived from the former. Goldmann, it appears, has sought some *a priori* literary equivalent of the economic distinction that Marx saw in capitalist production. Here he seems to have artificially transplanted Marx's economic categories into his literary criticism. It is this same analogy, disguised as homology, which dictates his analysis of the *nouveau roman*. Here the problematic hero has gone, Goldmann states, and the main feature of the novel is 'a more or less radical disappearance of the character and a corresponding strengthening of the autonomy of objects'.[22] This directly reflects the economic change to a period of imperialism and the large-scale concentration of capital. Goldmann saw the stabilising and self-regulating mechanisms of advanced capitalism much as Marcuse saw advanced technological rationality. It was the completion of a long-term historical process: 'the suppression of all essential importance attributed to the individual and the individual life within the economic structures, and therefore, in social life as a whole.'[23] The *nouveau roman*, therefore, does not merely reflect the elimination of realist characters by its authors. It also reflects the total elimination of individualism by advanced capitalism.

Whereas Goldmann had previously devised literary categories to fit Marx's economic distinctions, it can be seen that he is now doing the opposite. He constructs a very crude version of advanced capitalism to fit the dehumanising features of the *nouveau roman*. The advantage of homology here seems to be a false means of demonstrating a necessary connection without, at the same time, postulating a causal relationship. When he talks of specific authors, Goldmann does point out the differences between them, between the *choisisme* of Alain Robbe-Grillet and the tropisms of Nathalie Sarraute. But he still discerns one vital common denominator—the similarity of attitude towards reification. Here the familiar Lukácsian problem of ideological attitude returns with a vengeance. The text is the literary transposition of the author's ideological attitude towards a reified world: knowledge of the reality of the unreal. But Goldmann's explanation cannot go beyond a certain point. It cannot say *how* advanced capitalism makes the world more unreal and equally it cannot say how this is reflected in the novel. Goldmann merely explains each, capitalism and the novel, in terms of the other, and his argument becomes circular. Reification is little more than a tennis ball being hit backwards and forwards from one side of the court to the other.

A more serious objection can be made. The sense of a reified world can be conveyed through the humanist vision of the realist novel. Nowhere does Goldmann demonstrate that this is no longer possible, merely that French novelists have abandoned it as a means of doing so. But in the novel of tragic realism, part of the element of tragic conflict has always been in the hero, or character's, opposition to a world which is an inert, external existence oppressing him. And only in the realist novel can the element of rebellion against such a world be suggested. For the characters of the *nouveau roman* lack any of the figural characteristics necessary to such action. Only the author, who is not in the novel, or better still, the critic who has not even written it, can smugly point out this alarming void. The character in the novel is powerless to do so.

A more masterly and more complex version of genetic structuralism can be found in the studies of Michel Zéraffa. Zéraffa follows more consistently the attempt to illuminate the relationship between literary text and social consciousness. His main objection to realism lies in his claim that the novel does not reflect reality, but reveals appearances—appearances in life which are nonetheless the basis of social contradictions. Radically revising the problematic of the realist novel, Zéraffa suggests that such contradictions can be sought in the difference between the values for which the character, or hero, seeks and the actual social relationships in which he becomes embedded. The novel is less significant for the reality it lays bare in any objective sense, than in the values which its narrative action explodes. What E. M. Forster had called the 'life-by-values'[24] is a focal point for any sociology of the novel. Zéraffa writes:

> It can be argued that the great realistic novelists betrayed the framework to which their work was fundamentally tied—provided the word 'betray' is read in both senses: to reveal and to repudiate. In fact their work revealed, first, that a 'world-vision' is really a vision which is partisan and applicable only to part of reality; secondly that the society which the writer believes himself to experience directly is really seen by him through a glass distorted by bourgeois culture. But the same work repudiates its own overall intention both through the death which awaits its hero and, more especially, because of the real substance of the novel, which, whatever the author makes of it, reveals the existence of insoluble contradictions, in the Marxist sense.[25]

This is a significant advance on the sociological vision of Lukács and Goldmann because it pinpoints that area of social reality which the novel portrays—the relationship between human values and social life from the viewpoint of the fictional characters who endure it. The 'life-by-values' is the significant focus of social reality in the novel. But Zéraffa is wrong to state that the writer of the realist novel invariably sees life 'through a glass distorted by bourgeois culture'. Even, and perhaps especially, the conservative values espoused in the realist novel are often in direct opposition to bourgeois culture. It is not bourgeois culture which distorts the writer's view of reality, but it *is* very often bourgeois culture which prevents the realisation of those values for which the anti-bourgeois character strives. This is the point significantly in which the serious problematic of the novel is elevated to tragedy.

Zéraffa's brilliant insight into realist fiction comes partly from his idea of it as an unconscious ideological product.[26] But this approach also seriously hinders the theory of the novel. While evading the pitfalls of intentionality, it is largely reductionist, seeing literature as a function of ideological production in general. 'In writing his book,' Zéraffa claims, 'the novelist inevitably becomes part and parcel of a system of ideological production which is designed to mask the real system of production with all its antagonisms and conflicts.'[27] Literature is practically reduced to the unconscious function of legitimating the teleological rationality of the bourgeoisie, a rationality which is itself false. Such an approach takes little account of the diversity of values in modern fiction, in Balzac and Dostoevsky, Conrad and Faulkner, Joyce and Lawrence. This diversity of values operates both in the attitude of the author and in the text, despite—or even because—attitude and text conflict. Zéraffa, and Pierre Macherey, try to impose a homogeneity of values on modern literature which simply does not exist.

Moreover, they overlook one significant feature of the realist text itself. The realist novel has its own internal dialectic of appearance and reality.

Appearances are undermined by the action of the novel itself. In tragic realism, revelation is intrinsic to the novel's narrative structure, of the text finally dispersing the illusions which initially appear in the story it tells. The idea that the Marxist reader alone cognises the disparity between the appearances in the novel and the real world which never appears there is only·true of a mediocre fiction not worth criticising in the first place. In particular it is meaningless to assert, for this reason, that the realist novel belongs to a wider system of ideological production. Either the statement is a banal truism, merely stating that literature is a part of the culture of its age, or else it implies the impossibility of fiction ever exploding the shibboleths of bourgeois ideology. The latter is precisely what tragic realism does. The text may transform the values of its author but, in different ways, both author and text are marginal to the bourgeois culture their values oppose. Amidst the immense diversity of tragic realism, there is one key unifying factor. It is opposition in both text and author to the most fundamental concept of bourgeois ideology—the idea of progress. This opposition is embodied in the fate of the tragic hero. Neither Prince Myshkin nor Joe Christmas, Heathcliff nor Adrian Leverkuehn are bourgeois heroes, nor could they ever be. The point of the hero's fate is not to reveal the real (i.e. economic) relationships of production—even though in *Germinal* it actually does. Rather it is to subvert those very values which attempt to mask them. The accomplishment of tragic realism then becomes clear. It unmasks false values through its failure to mask the real.

Compared with Goldmann, Zéraffa's genetic structuralism is remarkably eclectic. It attempts to interweave the arguments of the early Lukács with the productionist aesthetic of Macherey on the one hand, and Barthes's 'Flaubertisation of writing' on the other. For a sociology of the novel, such a task is genuinely difficult, and Zeráffa's argument becomes, at times, dense and elliptical. Such a synthesis creates a fundamental paradox. To deal with realist literature through the productionist theory is convenient because, unlike Barthes, such a theory does make reference to fiction's signifying qualities. On the other hand, it tends to be mechanical and ahistorical, deliberately excluding dialectic critique. The result is that Zéraffa has a very static concept of realist fiction. Inspired by Barthes, he sees anti-realist fiction, on the other hand, in terms of the progressive erasure of signifying qualities. Yet as we have already seen, Barthes's theory is involuntarily historical. The retreat into style is an evolutionary process. The result is that Zéraffa has two alternating theories of the novel. One looks at realist fiction in terms of its production and its content, but does so without regard to its historical evolution. The other looks at anti-realist fiction from an evolutionary perspective but with little regard to its production or its content.

It is not altogether true to say that Zéraffa ignores the content of the anti-realist novel. But in this genre he regards it as characteristically subordinate to form. The subordination of content to form is itself a sociological phenomenon. With the novels of Joyce and Woolf, Broch and Dorothy Richardson in mind, he claims that for the modern writer 'the concrete life of the oppressed is as inaccessible . . . as bourgeois life is contemptible'.[28] Instead he possesses the sensibility of the intelligentsia, which isolates him from all other social classes. As a result aesthetic form itself becomes a social object. What matters now, Zéraffa claims, is 'how to translate the *experience of the real* through *specific forms*'. By this means, the social rebellion of the realist novel is ultimately transformed into aesthetic affront. Form itself becomes the transgressor.[29]

Zéraffa seems to imply that this is a general feature of the modern novel, a function of historical necessity. But while the life of the oppressed may be inaccessible to a certain kind of writer, it is clearly not true of all writers. Such a generalisation is impossible to make. Proust, Woolf and Richardson are the contemporaries of Dreiser, Faulkner and Hemingway. The retreat to form is one historical option among many, and even here the question must be asked, Is such a retreat inseparable from the question of content? Here again Zéraffa changes the position he inherits from Barthes. The retreat to self is not purely aesthetic dissatisfaction with mimesis nor cultural isolation from other social classes. He gives a third reason—the retreat from metropolis. Unlike the other two, this is a negative response to a general social experience. The modern writer rejects the inhuman world of technology. By reintroducing a positive social content into his argument, Zéraffa is able once more to revert to a productionist position. For the response to the technological world is a response to the world of appearances. 'The great literary movement of the twenties', he asserts, 'confused capitalism with industrialisation.'[30]

What we see here is really a remarkable feat of juggling, in which the particular theory which Zéraffa employs at any given time seems to be the general sociological theory of the modern novel. In actual fact, each particular theory is related to whichever genre he happens to be considering. This is not the result of casuistry on the part of the critic, so much as a reflection of the intrinsic difficulty of constructing a general theory of the modern novel, from the sociological point of view. This becomes even clearer when he considers Kafka. For Kafka is seen to destroy simultaneously the novel of metropolis, of realism, and of *erlebte Rede*, in fact the whole of the modern literary tradition up to that point. Here Zéraffa attaches himself to yet another paradigm—that of critical theory. His interpretation of Kafka's work as putting 'liberalism on trial' is slightly different from that of Adorno or Benjamin. But his concentration on the unidimensionality of Kafka's narrative where the hero is reduced to a 'machine for living' treads a familiar route. As Zéraffa himself says, the road has been cleared for the arrival of one-dimensional man. Thereafter follows the familiar eschatology. Insofar as fiction continues to appear in the wake of Kafka, it seems like a postscript in the ruins of the holocaust, meandering on as 'the private experience of society' when its artistic force has been spent. Beyond Kafka lies 'the phantom society'.

The failure of Zéraffa to sew together these different paradigms into a general theory is a function of the diversity of modern fiction. It is not only a question of the diversity of literary movements but also of their co-existence. Where one literary genre has triumphed over the ashes of others, it is by political means alone. There is no Western equivalent of socialist realism. And though the critics of realism have pointed out some of its aesthetic inadequacies, they have failed to see just how much changes in the twentieth-century novel are transformations within a realist frame-work. Non-naturalistic speech, the stream of consciousness, the unresolved ending, the encyclopaedic display of scientific knowledge are features which separate the novel of twentieth-century realism from its nineteenth-century counterpart. But they extend the real rather than dissolving it. The dissolution of the real depends upon general features of narrative structure—the dissolution of character, the abandonment of time and place, the adumbration of private experience. These are the crucial points of difference.

It has always been difficult to draw the dividing line between realist and non-realist fiction. It will continue to be. But the very notion of betrayal which Zéraffa introduces presupposes the basic mimetic function of the novel. In this sense he has introduced a point which conventional realists have often overlooked and which, actually, has little to do with structuralism at all. The values portrayed in the novel are 'betrayed' by the life its characters lead there. The life-by-value and the fate of the literary character are interdependent. Through the fate of its characters the novel becomes a test of its own values. But it is a test precisely because for its reader the action unfolds in a context which is socially real. Despite the polemical objections from formalist and structuralist critics, this element of social reality cannot finally be ignored.

4 Tragic Realism and the Political Novel

Tragic realism is a literary affront to the rational solution of human problems. As a result, it is more subversive than ever before; but equally it is rarer. In liberal-capitalist countries the ideological techniques of moderation and consensus are used to patch over class differences and inequalities. In state-socialist countries the rational solution of human problems is the prerogative of dictatorial bureaucracies. The culture of rationality atrophies tragic fiction. More recently, it has discouraged a serious literary concern with politics. For the educated rationalist the political novel in particular must seem archaic unless it is a confirmation of his own prejudices. A variety of forms of communication have passed it by, more vital, more immediate and more relevant to the outcome of political issues—at least in appearance. In the West, the political novel can no longer compete with the investigative journalism of the media. In the East, it cannot usually be published, unless it ultimately reflects the superior wisdom of the Communist Party. Tragic realism in the political novel is the greatest cultural embarrassment of all. It portrays loss and tragedy at the political epicentre of modern rationality, that arena of human endeavour where the myth of total control over the environment is fabricated. The modern intelligentsia, whether liberal or Marxist, has increasingly adhered to one version or other of this myth. As a result it has ignored the novel for more immediate forms of cultural expression conserving the rationalist myth it has appropriated—the mass media in the West, the Party in the East. The vast increase of education in the post-war world which has brought a vast readership to modern fiction has also created the conditions for an antithetical attitude towards it—the attitude that knowledge is power and fiction is private fantasy, the assumption that in the public world fiction is redundant.

Over the past hundred years, however, the political novel has guaranteed the continuity of literary realism. As Irving Howe has remarked, it is concerned not only with the workings of society but with the *idea* of society operating problematically through the consciousness of its characters.[1] It has been a fictional correlative of classic sociology, exhibiting a profound concern with the perturbing dynamics of an abstract entity—society. Unlike sociology, it has transformed that abstraction into flesh and blood. It portrays the impact of politics on people at all levels of society. This universality distinguishes it from the parliamentary novels of Trollope and Disraeli. More recently the same factor has proved it superior to the Whitehall novels of C. P. Snow and the political thriller of espionage. Like journalism, the latter reduces politics to the secrecy in which its leaders operate. The political novel does the opposite. Its characters experience the unavoidable impact of politics in its widest possible sense.

This also separates it from the novel of private experience. The political novel cannot confine its themes to the limits of the solitary ego. It directly confronts the hero with the preformed experience of others, who exist in their own right as individual beings. It runs contrary to the evasion of social relationships seen in Woolf and Richardson, Beckett and Sarraute, Miller and Burroughs. So far, we have not fully considered the basis of characterisation in realist fiction. In the first chapter, the discussion of Auerbach provided us with a seminal vision of tragic realism. But this merely put it in the context of literary and historical development. Conceptually speaking this purely historical emphasis is inadequate. Auerbach himself realised this and sought to base his theory of realist fiction on the idea of *figura*. Before we consider the etymology of the concept, and its advantages, we might note in passing that it plays a similar role in his literary theory as the concept of type does in Lukács's later theory of the novel. But Auerbach avoids some of the difficulties encountered by Lukács in his attempt to juxtapose the typical, or realist hero, and the eccentric, or modernist hero. The very marginality of the tragic hero to bourgeois society can make him appear eccentric when his 'eccentricity' is in fact a profound sociological comment on the normality it disturbs. According to Lukács the rebellious hero saves himself from being eccentric by acting in an ideologically progressive manner. But in tragic realism this is the exception, rather than the rule, and the dichotomy of eccentric and type is hence inadequate.

For Auerbach, *figura* is a concept arising in Latin antiquity and finding its Christian expression in medieval Europe.[2] The *figura* is a specific feature of Judaeo-Christian prophecy in which the religious figure or prophet of the Old Testament 'prefigures' the Messiah whose arrival is anxiously awaited from generation to generation. Even within its religious context, Auerbach argues, the *figura* is historical and realistic. The Messiah will appear at a definite time and place and will be a human being, despite being the Son of God. This type of figural realism, which is radically opposed to all allegorical and mystical forms of thought, finds its greatest literary expression in Dante. The earthly figures whom Dante meets in the Inferno or in Paradise are real, not figments of his imagination and they do not represent abstract moral qualities. 'Thus Virgil is not an allegory of an attribute, capacity, power or historical institution. He is neither reason nor poetry nor the Empire. He is Virgil himself.'[3] The afterworld is the place where human beings find their genuine fulfilment, but they are still beings with the same identity which they possessed on earth. For Dante the world was only *umbra futurorum*, a prefiguration of the transcendent other-worldy reality in which it is destined to recur.

In a culture where direct contact with the supernatural has been lost, figural realism assumes instead a remarkable this-worldly dimension. The fulfilment of the *figura* can only take place on earth. This in itself does not mean a break with religious aspiration which is still so important, for example in Dostoevsky. What it does mean is that the moral aspirations of the characters in modern literature, the values for which they seek, have to be realised in the world in which they live. Once the break with the supernatural is complete, the *figura* has universal literary significance. It is the historical reason for the novel itself. Moreover it cannot be separated from the fate of the two most important belief-systems of modern Europe – Christianity and socialism. The fiction of realistic characterisation is inseparable from an emergent culture of indvidualism, from an awakening perception of people as individuals. Perhaps it was for this reason that Orwell called the novel a Protestant art-form. The character has a uniquely individual fate. But the figural nature of the character is more than this. It undergoes two distinct phases. Characters start off as portraits, either singular or composite, of real life models. Individual lives prefigure individual fates. Yet great fiction transforms them into something more than mere biographical passage through life. It fulfils them. This is what Faulkner meant when he said his task was creating out of the materials of the human spirit something which did not exist before. Figural realism works in the novel in two ways—the transposition of the figure from life into the text, and the subsequent development of the character within the narrative of the text. In the political novel, Bakunin has been the model for a variety of fictional portraits, but the character in the text who initially resembles him thereafter takes on a life of his own.

Figural realism stresses the life-by-value but in a radical and often disconcerting way. The fictional fulfilment of the *figura* in its two-fold sense is not purely utopian. It can be found in good or evil, in the extremes of heaven or hell. Tragic realism, with the loss or death which awaits its heroes, is the shipwreck of the figural prophecy. The sublime harmony of the fate which awaits Dante and Beatrice in paradise can never be attained by the tragic hero. For tragedy signifies a fulfilment attained only through the destruction of its ripest promise. Tragic fate is the denial of the promise which the novel has already revealed to us. In modern society which the novel reflects, that promise is socialism. Originating out of one system of belief, Christianity, figural realism has most bearing on that belief-system which is in the process of superseding it. Just as the literary problem of the *figura* is that of fulfilment, or realisation, the historical problem of socialism as belief is fundamentally the same—the authentic realisation of its values. Deriving from a common root in Judaeo-Christian prophecy, the novel and socialism confront each other most genuinely in tragic realism where politics is their common subject.

Figural realism, of course, is not always tragic. Following Auerbach's distinction between the tragic and the serious, we can justifiably distinguish between tragic and affirmative realism, between *The Idiot*, *Wuthering Heights*, *Light in August* and *Under the Volcano* and *Old Goriot*, *Middlemarch*, *Ulysses* and *Remembrance of Things Past*. Since the class distinction between the serious and comic has also vanished, affirmative realism embraces both serious and comic fiction, sometimes, as in *Ulysses*, in the same novel. Moreover the tragic or affirmative elements are a property of the text, not its author. Tolstoy wrote *War and Peace* as well as *Anna Karenin*, Melville *The Confidence-Man* as well as *Moby Dick*, Faulkner *The Hamlet* as well as *The Sound and the Fury* and Thomas Mann wrote *Felix Krull* as well as *Doctor Faustus*. Not even Dostoevsky, whose tragic vision was so immense, wrote only in a tragic vein. But figural realism, either tragic or affirmative, can be distinguished from two kinds of fiction evading the problem of characterisation: a documentary fiction where no serious characterisation is attempted, and a didactic fiction where characters are purely the mouthpieces for ideas. Tragic and affirmative realism are both critical but not in the sense meant by Lukács. Their critical element cannot be sought in the ideological attitude of the author but in the life-by-value of the characters he creates. The difference between the tragic and the affirmative hinges upon one key factor: eventual separation from or reconciliation with the world through which the characters live in the novel. Though each resolution differs from the other, both are responses to an alienation or disaffection which already exists, which contains within it the critical component of realist fiction. The ending of the novel is the final resolution of *figura*—where realisation is attained or denied.

Within a figural schema, the distinction between realism and symbolism is meaningless. Characters or events can be real and symbolic at the same time, existing concretely yet reflecting what lies elsewhere, what is already past or prefiguring what is to come. All fictional characters signify more than what can be stated about them empirically, and the reader of the novel instinctively realises this. He follows the character's fate as if it were real though knowing all the time that it is a product of the writer's imagination, and sensing instinctively that the movement of the character towards his fate is itself a process of realisation symbolising, as well as reflecting, a wider predicament of mankind.

Figural realism is essential to an understanding of the dialectic of the novel. The realisation of human hopes which it promises, often only to destroy, follows from the complex sense of loss motivating the writer in the first place. The novelist is conservative in his attachment to a world which is in the process of disappearance, but if he is a great novelist then his characters will possess the human capacities essential to the world which is to replace it. This is as true of the literary innovators who stand on the threshold of 'modernism' as it is of the nineteenth-century realists they superseded. Proust's Guermantes circle, Joyce's colonial Dublin,

Faulkner's poor yet aristocratic Deep South, even Durrell's Alexandria are sociological landmarks of modern fiction which celebrate a doomed world in the shadow of its own death. Both the break-up of the aristocracy and the breakdown of Empire, irreversible processes of historical change, produce fictional characters who outlast a world which finally perishes. What endures in Proust and Joyce, in Faulkner, Durrell and Djuna Barnes, is not form or experimentation but the characters whose fate and sensibility are crystallised by innovation in form, characters whose language and sensibility is the affront to convention which many critics have mistaken as form itself.

Conservative yet often prophetic, the great novelist of modern fiction invariably inhabits that 'border country' of which Raymond Williams has spoken.[4] The contribution of Irish and American writers to English fiction is well known. What seems to matter most is not a feeling of authentic ethnic identity but a constant double identity involving a double alienation: nominal adherence to a literary and cultural tradition from which the writer's personal circumstances distance him completely, but also alienation from the world which his novels portray. Joyce, Hardy and Lawrence are all alienated from an Establishment culture but also spiritually apart from the actual world their novels reveal to us. But their alienation from what seems unjust to them is inseparable from their attachment to what seems equally to be vanishing. The loss of community, that familiar conservative theme, points indirectly to a feeling for community as yet unrealised but often hinted at.

In the political novel, however, the possibilities for reconciliation, for an affirmative mode of writing, are drastically limited by the theme the writer is undertaking. In Austen and Eliot, Joyce and Proust, affirmative endings can be found through personal contentment or metaphysical harmony, whether it be achieved through remembrance or myth. But in Dostoevsky and Conrad, Zola and Solzhenitsyn, the head-on confrontation with society as a whole permits of no such reconciliation. In the social novel reconciliation is possible in spite of politics: in the political novel, politics denies reconciliation. Molly Bloom's final yes is never granted. In *Under the Volcano*, one of the last great works of tragic realism, the dialectical interplay of apolitical man and his political destiny brings the novel to an unpredictable but decisive conclusion. Geoffrey Firmin, drugged, alcholic, exiled and socially outcast, is the consummation of all those asocial qualities which Lukács claimed had destroyed modern fiction. But even then, politics invades his terrifying solipsism in the shape of a fascist Mexican policeman who catches up with Firmin's anarchist past. Spender has said that Firmin is not a genuine hero because he is permanently drunk, but his brutal murder is nonetheless tragic, a culmination of the factors of waste which have already destroyed him as a man. Politically helpless, the irony of his shooting as a political subversive gives the final shape to his life of poignant but shapeless degeneration. Firmin's hope lies in the past, his anguish in the present. His future is a void. Yet his death at the hands of an arbitrary and vicious authority gives the lie to the myth of private experience on which the novel is allegedly based. His death is a political act even if his life had ceased to be a significant fact. The final line of the novel, Firmin's epitaph, lingers in the memory: 'Somebody threw a dead dog after him down the ravine.' It might be an epitaph for all the tragic heroes of the political novel. For unlike the great men of history, they are not canonised as martyrs of causes, they are not honoured. Instead they are forgotten and the world goes on without them. Unable to do without history, the political novel portrays the death of those whom history will not remember—except as characters in a novel.

In the criticism of Kermode and Friedman, there is an argument which challenges the compatibility of the tragic and the real.[5] It relates to the sense of a novel's ending. Traditionally it has been seen as common sense to assume that a novel must end on a note of finality such as marriage or death, while life does not. Short of nuclear extinction, life goes on. The artistic re-appraisal of this idea from Hardy onwards suggests an increasing realism on the part of the modern author. The transition from a closed to a more open structure of experience involves some acknowledgment of the artificial nature of the ending. For the end begins to appear as the arbitrary limit upon the flow of experience which the novel has generated. In James and Conrad, Forster and Lawrence, there is a sense of the ending as unable to contain the human experience it has expressed, an experience which spills over the limits required by the psychological satisfaction of finality.

The more open an ending, the less conducive it might appear to tragic fiction. But the closed structure need not necessarily be tragic. The conventional nineteenth-century romance often ends in a happy marriage. Even the ironic ending of *The Age of Reason*, where Daniel is conveniently conjured up to solve the problem of Marcelle's pregnancy, has a closed and affirmative ring about it. The tragic ending, by comparison, often seems closed because its cathartic elements appear to exhaust experience. The loss of the hero's life, of the cause for which he fights, of the person whom he loves, all seem to the reader to stem the flow of experience which had preceded them. Often they stop it in its tracks. Forster even claimed that the endings of all great novels are disappointing because the author has already driven himself to exhaustion. In tragic fiction, these two separate elements, catharsis and creative exhaustion often merge into one another. But does that mean they are incompatible with an open structure of experience? I would suggest not. Tragic realism, combining catharsis and creative exhaustion, still resonates a sense of life continuing beyond the fictive limit it sets. Yet because it is cathartic, it undoubtedly takes more force away from Lawrence's 'wave which cannot halt'. Lawrence is not a tragic writer precisely because the open flow of experience in his novels is not vitiated by tragic loss. By this very token, he cannot crystallise the irreconcilability of his characters' lives and the values by which they try to live. The purely open experience merely defers what the tragic actually consummates. The great feature of tragic realism, from Tolstoy to Ernest Hemingway, is the expanding of experience amidst tragic loss. Unlike classical tragedy, catharsis here is counter-balanced by a deeply rooted sense of the real. As Robert Jordan's end approaches, the other partisans escape and the war goes on. Jordan knows this, acknowledges the existence of the future in which he cannot share, and the resolution of a war whose result is still in the balance.

It is true that tragic realism satisfies, in Conrad's words, 'the desire for finality, for which our hearts yearn'. Yet the tragic ending is never an apocalypse. Like Henry James, it imbues the reader 'with the sense of life still going on'.[6] If one takes the open structure of the novel seriously then Benjamin's idea of tragic finality seems highly sentimental. The reader should not be content with warming himself in the flames of the hero's death. He must actively juxtapose the hero's fate with the world that continues in his absence. Nowhere is this illustrated more clearly than in *Nostromo*. It is a novel which pushes itself beyond a number of possible endings. It could end when Nostromo and Decoud escape with the cargo of silver, or it could end when Nostromo returns triumphantly to the mainland. But Conrad forces his hero beyond the point which suggests finality to linger on in an afterlife of disillusion and futile obsession. The tragic ending, which comes with his murder by mistaken identity, comes about when the possible affirmative endings have been rejected. The very point at which Nostromo's deeds are sufficient to make him a mythical hero is also the point at which his disaffection grows ripe. Conrad stands the whole idea of heroic adventure on its head. Nostromo does not achieve a final and lasting unity with the world through heroic adventure. Such a unity is merely a staging post on the way to alienation and irredeemable loss. The stream of experience carries Nostromo beyond success to tragedy.

Another feature of contemporary realism which must not be overlooked is the importance of language. More than ever before in the history of the novel, language mediates the reflection of reality. Though the creation of a poetic language the modern writer makes inroads into the speech and consciousness of his characters in a way which violates all notions of a documentary fiction. It is not reflexive consciousness, as Adorno thought, but language which sets itself up in opposition to the cult of the fact. In secret monologue or public dialogue, consciousness or speech, the sensibility of the literary character achieves a new figural dimension. This should not be seen as an inner literary space protecting fiction against the cult of the fact. It is a literary development which transcends the cult of the fact in a culture which is becoming increasingly more factual in its obsessions, in which the separation of fact and fantasy is much wider than ever before. The point of the contemporary realist novel must be to ensure, in the words of Thomas Mann, 'that a voice is given the creature for his woe'. The writer must implant in the speech and consciousness of his

characters a language which is unique and irreducible without losing sight
of the reality he wishes to express. As the work of Joyce and Hemingway,
Mann and Djuna Barnes testifies, the problem is complex. But if it means
anything, originality in realist fiction refers to the creation of a language
appropriate to the reality it tries to express. The separation of style from
theme, of form from content, has been, and always will be, false.

The crucial relationship between language and figural realism lies in the
question of characterisation. More important than the language which
revolutionises the narrative of the modern novel is the speech which gives
the fictional character his authentic voice. This transformation can be seen
by comparing the account of Ivan Karamazov's conversation with the
devil with that of Adrian Leverkuehn in *Doctor Faustus*. While influenced
by Dostoevsky in his treatment of the demonic, Mann in no way imitates
him. The temptation offered Adrian is very different from the temptation
offered Ivan. But the language in which Adrian and his imaginary devil
converse is not that of ordinary speech. It is a medieval dialect, archaic yet
for that very reason suited to the archaic nature of demonic temptation.
But the context is contemporary, as contemporary as the music which
Adrian composes. The language *is* Adrian. It is the literary equivalent of
the music which, in the novel, can only be spoken of, never reproduced.
Adrian's secret record and, later, his tragic confession, are his authentic
voice. But they can only be expressed in a speech which defies both
conversational and intellectual convention. In adopting a speech which
defies conventional speech, Mann expresses in his tragic hero a sensibility
which defies conventional reality. Adrian's secret language mediates his
rejection of the public world of music and scholarship he finds incompatible with the real world of musical creation.

For all that, the major character of the realist novel cannot be reduced to
the voice which is given him. The reader must be able to imagine him as
real. The voice given the hero can heighten or expand the dimensions of
that reality, but cannot act as a substitute for it. Equally the reader must
continue to identify with the character about which he reads in some
significant respect. At the least he must be able, by the act of his own
imagination, to put himelf in that character's place. The originality of the
great novelist lies in extending the power of the reader's imagination. For
the reader does not identify himself purely and simply with the language
which is being used. What continues to distinguish the novel from the
poem is the creation of imaginary beings. The soliloquy of Molly Bloom is
more poetic than most modern poetry but only because it is read as the
nocturnal reverie of a character in a novel.

Voice and ending are merely two of the salient themes in the
transformation of the realist novel. In all tragic realism, however, there are
constants which go beyond changes in form. The novel of tragic realism is
about moral values and the failure to attain them in a fictive world which
impresses the reader as being socially real. This very achievement contains

within it an artistic vision of the transformation of modern society. In the fiction we have somewhat arbitrarily termed the political novel, this vision of transformation is often inspired, paradoxically, by the impulse to conserve present life from the onward march of history. Yet the effect of this has often been to reveal the new forces of history. Often conservative in its inspiration, the political novel of tragic realism is usually democratic in its achievement. Its sense of the new, its prophetic character, emerge from a sense of loss, and perhaps more decisively, a feeling of damnation in a secular world. For the first time in world-history, and perhaps the last, the tragic vision finds expression within the boundaries of the real.

Part II

5 Tolstoy and Dostoevsky: Passion and Russian Society

In studying the political novel, we may take the liberty of starting by looking at two major novels which are hardly political at all—*The Idiot* and *Anna Karenin*. Dostoevsky's novel was written towards the end of the 1860s, Tolstoy's several years later. These works represent, arguably, the pinnacle of creative writing in the novel form. Greater than any work which preceded them, they have not since been rivalled—except by the other major works of the authors who wrote them. This provides us with a sociological lesson which cannot be overlooked. World-literature achieved its greatest peak in modern times in a society which was more backward—economically, socially and politically—than nearly all the rest of Europe. Between them, Tolstoy and Dostoevsky destroy the myth of the novel as a bourgeois art-form. If we add Turgenev the third great writer of the period, more liberal and generous of spirit, but no match for the creative genius of the other two, we have a literature whose concern barely touches upon bourgeois life. Instead it focuses on two significant social groups in mid-nineteenth-century Russia—the aristocracy and the intelligentsia. The great Russian novels portray the complex relationship between these two groups, a relationship characterised by the social rootlessness of the critical intelligentsia and the political backwardness of the ruling aristocracy. This, in a nutshell, constitutes the problematic of the Russian novel. Implacably opposed to one another, both encouraged the Westernisation of Russia in different ways. The Russian gentry, never more than one per cent of the population, looked to the West for its manners, its dress and its language—French. The intelligentsia, a stratum of educated Russians from the priesthood and the *Raznochintsky*, looked to the West for the ideas which would destroy the aristocratic domination of Russian society.[1]

The abolition of serfdom in 1861 inaugurated the agrarian changes which were eventually to undermine the economic position of the gentry. In their collective support for abolition the intelligentsia found their greatest, but also their last, focal point of unity. After that, the radicals split from the liberal reformers and the conservative Slavophiles disowned both of them. The disunity was also reflected in the growing estrangement of writers and critics. The friendly relations of Belinksy, Turgenev and Herzen in the forties symbolised a unity of progressive attitude in art and politics. By the end of the sixties this had been irreparably broken. Dostoevsky, Turgenev and Tolstoy disassociated themselves from the great radical journal of the period, *Contemporary*. Its young critics, politically militant and uncompromising, in turn expressed their hostility towards the writers. Though fiction and criticism experienced the negative unity of being subject to the same forms of repressive censorship, this was no longer enough to hold them together. The irreconcilable division between literature and cultural criticism, later to reappear in Soviet Russia in a more sinister form, had now been established.

The paradox of radical criticism was this. Chernyshevsky, Dubrolyubov and Pisarev demanded a fiction of social and political utility, a literature which possessed constructive proposals for a future and more enlightened society. Yet their view of fiction was in part blinded by the political function which the censorship unwittingly bestowed upon it. For at that time writing novels, though subject to censorship, was still a less persecuted enterprise than writing political tracts. Both Herzen and Chernyshevsky wrote novels as a means of evading political censorship, but they adopted fiction without seriously reflecting upon the consequences of the evasion which they had undertaken. Herzen's *Who is to Blame?*, Chernyshevsky's *What is to be done?*, bear the mark of a political, not an artistic, consciousness. But the damage had been done. A precedent had been set to validate the notion that fiction is a continuation of politics by other means.

The most significant feature of the work of Tolstoy and Dostoevsky is that it ignores the aesthetic prescriptions of *Contemporary*. Indeed Dostoevsky reacted artistically to the radical critics in a different way altogether. The nihilists, as Turgenev called them, achieved literary notoriety through the character of Bazarov in *Fathers and Sons*. At first greeted with scorn by the radical critics, Turgenev's hero was later adopted by Pisarev as a true apostle of their ideas. With Dostoevsky's nihilists, however, such an inversion was not really possible at all. Their unintentional utility was minimal from the radical point of view. They simply could not be heralded as the positive heroes of a progressive fiction. Dostoevsky and the radical critics inevitably became implacable enemies during the period of great fiction after *Crime and Punishment*.

Another source of conflict between writer and critic was over the sociological dimensions of their literature. From a politically progressive viewpoint, many radical critics regarded the Russian aristocracy as an archaic and obsolete literary subject, a privileged relic of a social order near to the verge of collapse and hence unworthy of artistic attention. Yet *Anna Karenin* and *The Idiot* are both novels, from totally conflicting perspectives, about the life of the Russian aristocracy. For Tolstoy, as a prosperous landowner, this was a natural subject. But Dostoevsky, the son of an *arriviste* landowner, an ex-revolutionary calling himself 'a literary proletarian', such a subject was more of an exception to the rule. Though an ardent Slavophile, Dostoevsky knew little and wrote even less about rural life. The result can be seen in the differing themes of the novels. Tolstoy wrote of the higher circles of the aristocracy in both city and country; Dostoevsky about the lesser aristocratic circles in an urban context. While one author is at the very centre of upper-class life, the other is at its margins. Despite this difference, which is ultimately crucial, the common feature of the novels is their portrayal of a social class through its intimate personal relationships, relationships which centre around the public expression and awareness of passion.

Passion in Russian society reveals the strength and weakness of its ruling class during the nineteenth century. But these can only be seen by studying the minutiae of the social relationships within which that passion is embedded and where, like all the passion of tragic literature, it eventually dies. Tolstoy's vision of the aristocracy is of its enduring strength and nobility but also of its universality. For Dostoevsky it is ghostly and unstable, prophetically doomed to collapse. The lyrical and epic qualities of Tolstoy's narrative are eminently suited to Tolstoy's stable vision, while the quality of phantasmogoria in *The Idiot*, its poetic dissonance and this-worldly mysticism, convey most brilliantly the sense of a world on the verge of disintegration. Anna's death takes place in a world with enduring structures of feeling and behaviour, but that of Nastasyia Fillipovna seems almost to take the world away with it too. Tolstoy and Dostoevsky reveal the destiny of the class most significant to both in the structures of passion in which the major characters are enmeshed. The key to this passion is the key which unlocks the secrets of politics and society in a world whose nobility and backwardness are nonetheless a profound refraction of the crises of Western bourgeois society.

Anna Karenin, as a novel of passion with a tragic heroine, evokes immediate comparison with that great French novel written a decade previously, *Madame Bovary*. The central theme of both is adulterous passion engendered in the absence of marital love. Yet they differ by virtue of class where they are similar by virtue of sex. Anna Karenin's predicament is aristocratic, Emma Bovary's is bourgeois. The first significant feature of this is that the men Emma encounters are never of equal status. They are boring like her husband, idiotic like Homais, or perfidious like Leon. Her adultery is secretive, her disaffection with marriage something that she keeps to herself. Her married life is filled with monotony, the profit motive, and provincial respectability; her adultery is characterised by sensual pleasure. To that extent, Emma's passion is not an attachment to a unique person but to physical desire on the one hand and the principle of infidelity on the other. In this way she allows herself to be deceived by her lover, who shares in her pleasure but does not reciprocate her passion. Emma attains tragic stature precisely through the baseness and mediocrity of the men around her, none of whom can ultimately satisfy her. For they possess all the bourgeois qualities which Flaubert thought despicable.

The tragic predicament of Anna Karenin is on a totally different plane altogether. Throughout the novel her husband and lover are of equal stature as human beings. Most remarkable is the switching of the point of view by which Tolstoy enables us to see the action through the eyes of all the major characters, including Karenin himself, 'the coldest and most rational of men'. On equal terms with the men in her life, Anna also has the sympathy and friendship of other women. There is a remarkable equality of sensibility here which is lacking in Flaubert's novel, where the bourgeois are simply caricatures. At the same time, out of all those who suffer in their personal lives, as all do, it is only Anna's fate which is tragic. For hers is the fate, in a privileged class, of the exploited and subjugated married woman. We can identify the injustice of her position in spite of the sympathy which Tolstoy engages from us for all those others whose affliction is not as great. The tragic fate of Anna surmounts the problematic fate of Karenin and Vronsky, Dolly and Oblonsky, Kitty and Levin.

What distinguishes Anna Karenin from Emma Bovary at the level of feeling is the openness and intensity of passion. Emma's adultery is her secret refuge from a stultifying life, but Anna's affair with Vronsky becomes her life and she lives it openly, finally bearing Vronsky a child. And her passion has a purity which is only possible in a life encompassed by the sexual values of the aristocracy. Adultery was considered an acceptable pastime as long it was discreet, purely hedonistic and did not endanger the marriage. But Anna's passion for Vronsky is the opposite of hedonism. It is an enduring attachment in violation of sexual convention to which society gives no recognition. By violating the values of her class, Anna fulfils her heart. Passion in Tolstoy's novel is stranded tragically between hedonism and marriage. Anna's tragic fate is illuminated by the normal fate of her contemporaries. The suffering created by Oblonsky's adultery is overcome by his own remorse and Dolly's forgiveness. Kitty's unrequited feeling for Vronsky suggests the conventional path which the Russian officer should have trod had he not fallen in love with a married woman. The love within marriage of Kitty and Levin, their moderate devotion to one another, suggests a standard of normal happiness which Anna and Vronsky can never attain. Each of these relationships suggests, at crucial stages in the plot, the alternative to tragic passion. It is the great virtue of Tolstoy's novel that we can identify both with those who settle for personal happiness and those who are overcome by tragic passion, for they, and the choice between them, are elements of a common humanity shared by all. While Flaubert contrasts the tragic with the ignoble, Tolstoy sets tragedy against the warmth, the simplicity and occasional heartbreaks of daily life.

In his study of passion in Western Society, Dennis de Rougemont has claimed that the cult of passionate love, established in feudal Europe, has been so democratised in the modern bourgeois world that, dull and diluted, it has lost its aesthetic virtues together with its spiritual and tragic values.[2] The medieval myth of a passion which violates all moral and political convention, even the rules of courtly love, has its most powerful expression in the myth of Tristan and Iseult. In the medieval romance the invention of obstacles to fulfilment is usually an unrealistic device in the context of a myth. But in the modern novel, in the conflict between the legitimate marriage and the illegitimate passion, the social situation has to some extent to be realistic. At the same time, the bourgeois romance is a dilution of the medieval romance. It lacks that element of tragic nobility, which cannot be realistically rediscovered in a utilitarian money-conscious bourgeois society. Contemporaneous with the flowering bourgeois societies of the West, Tolstoy's Russian novel retains the element of nobility which characterises the medieval romance. But it does so realistically, for Russia is still a predominantly aristocratic society which has never experienced a bourgeois revolution. In *Anna Karenin*, nobility is both a class attribute and a quality of life. It is precisely this two-fold feature of nobility which *Madame Bovary* lacks. In transforming the medieval myth into fictional reality Tolstoy retains the element of nobility essential to tragic passion, but he can only do so through a vision of the stable and enduring nature of the ruling aristocracy of Russia.

In *Anna Karenin*, the love-potion of Tristan and Iseult is rendered realistically: the passion of Anna and Vronsky is a social event. Sparked off at the ball where, conventionally speaking, Vronsky should have conformed to his role by choosing the enraptured Kitty, it comes to fruition with Vronsky's sudden appearance on the train which Anna is taking from Moscow to Petersberg. The train is assailed by a terrible storm. The means by which Tolstoy links the human encounter to the adverse elements is a masterpiece of deceptive simplicity:

> She looked around and instantly recognised Vronsky. Putting his hand to the peak of his cap, he bowed to her and asked if she needed anything and could he be of service to her? For some time she gazed intently at him, making no answer, and though he stood in the shadow, she saw, or fancied she saw, even the expression of his face and eyes. It was the same expression of reverential ecstasy which had so worked upon her the night before. She had assured herself more than once during the last few days and again a moment ago that Vronsky was no more to her than any of the hundreds of identical young men one came across everywhere, and that she would never allow herself to bestow a thought upon him. Yet in the first flash of seeing him again a feeling of joyful pride swept over her. She had no need to ask why he was there. She knew as well as if he told her he was there in order to be where she was.
>
> 'I did not know you were travelling. What are you coming for?' she asked, letting fall the hand which was about to grasp the handrail. An irrepressible delight and animation shone in her face.
>
> 'What am I coming for?' he repeated, looking straight into her eye. 'You know that I have come to be where you are,' he said. 'I can't help myself'.

At that moment the wind, as if it had surmounted all obstacles, sent the snow flying from the carriage roofs and rattled a loose sheet of iron; while in front the hoarse whistle of the engine began to wail, plaintive and mournful. All the awfulness of the storm now appeared to her more beautiful than ever.[3]

The event Tolstoy depicts is a supreme example of figural realism, for it prefigures the event which tragically ends Anna's life. The two events are the most momentous in Anna's life—the moment when her passion for Vronsky becomes actuality and the moment when the passion she considers betrayed is finally ended. Both take place in the railway station with the departure of the train from its platform. But in the first instance Anna is a surprised and delighted passenger. In the second she is the despairing woman who throws herself under the wheels of the train. The passage is a premonition of the ultimate tragic event in which it finds its echo and the destruction of its own promise. Passion deserts her at the same railway station at which it had so unexpectedly flooded her heart. The significant feature of Tolstoy's novel is that these events are real and the experience of them is real. In one type of critical schema the snow blown suddenly from the carriage roofs after Vronsky's declaration of his unwavering devotion may seem symbolic, but it actually happens. What is important, however, is not that it does, but that Anna responds to it in the way that she does. After Vronsky's words, the storm she had felt as a terrifying threat becomes a source of beauty, as if passion and passion alone had conquered the adversities of nature. Through Anna's eyes, passion overwhelms all obstacles, dismisses all threats to the frailty of the human condition. When, in her final desperate hour, Anna feel Vronsky's passion to have ebbed away from her, that sense of frailty, of pure helplessness, returns to overwhelm and destroy her.

The realism of tragic passion is such that it cannot be confined to the personal feeling which is its indisputable source. It must also reveal its social context, and through its social context, its wider significance for society as a whole. Tolstoy does precisely this. Anna's predicament as a married woman who rejects her husband's and bears her lover's child is this: she is the exploited member of a privileged class, indeed *the* most privileged class. This element of exploitation, and discrimination, within the confines of privilege is a function of sex. In Tolstoy's vision of a noble aristocracy, his tragic realism entails that there is no tragic hero, only a tragic heroine. In this instance the dialectic of novel and society demands of necessity that a woman possess this function. In *Anna Karenin*, Tolstoy does not, and cannot, create a tragic hero. Prince Andrei has no tragic successor in the Russia which had long since overcome the threat of conquest from the West. In a stable, aristocratic, and no longer threatened Russia, the tragic nobility associated with the sufferings of war no longer exists. Tolstoy originally conceived *War and Peace* as a contemporary novel, but it was not to be. Prince Andrei is an indisputably historical figure, and while Pierre Bezukhov has his latterday counterpart in Konstantin Levin, both of them fictional portraits of Tolstoy himself, the position of Vronsky is radically different from that of Andrei. The noble officer hero cannot command the centre of the stage when the Russian Empire is no longer threatened.

The significant social consequence of Anna's affair, and the scandal it causes, is that neither her husband nor Vronsky are ruined by it. Both suffer severely. Karenin becomes ill and Vronsky awakes one night in a feverish state and tries to shoot himself. But the pursuit of their careers and the reserves of privilege on which they can draw, eventually immunise them from a state of affairs showing no prospect of resolution. Karenin conducts his inquiry into expenditure on irrigation with compulsive zeal. Even when Vronsky resigns his commission and moves with Anna to the country to escape the scandal of their relationship, he has sufficient resources to ensure material and political success. He becomes a landowner, the benefactor of a nearby hospital and a member of his local *Zemstvo*. Within the ruling aristocracy, the flowing stable mastery of life acts as a shock-absorber. It contains the destructive effects of a public passion for Anna's husband and her lover. As successful men of a ruling aristocratic class, they do not share the pain of Anna's growing isolation with anything approaching the same intensity. Both men remain pillars of strength within the community, one as landowner, the other as administrator. They remain men of practical action with the power to rule over others. If Karenin as a cold bureaucratic administrator lacks Vronsky's nobility of character, their respective social roles complement each other perfectly. The conflict over Anna is never a conflict between men of different social standing or a conflict of ideals.

Anna's dilemma, whether to divorce her husband and lose custody of her son, or stay married to the man she loathes even when he grants her the opportunity for divorce, makes her social position intolerable. Remote, like all wives of the aristocracy, from the practical world of their husbands, she is more vulnerable to the nuances of status operating at the level of ritual—within a class which cultivates it assiduously. One instance of this is the humiliating snub she suffers from Madame Kartosov at the opera. The incident, as Vronsky tells her, is trivial, for she has allowed herself to be upset by 'a silly woman's chatter'. Yet because of her compromised social standing, such chatter merely serves to open the deeper wounds of her position, the hurt and insecurity from which there is no respite. In her ensuing quarrel with Vronsky the incident becomes magnified out of all proportion, for it brings out what lies beneath it—Anna's feeling that no one can possibly suffer as much from the situation as she herself. Her final distraught words to Vronsky convey the immensity of this feeling and with it the sense that they are *unequal* in their capacity to sustain passion over months, then years of suffering: 'Yes, if you loved me as I love you, if you were tortured as I am . . .' she said, looking at him with an expression of terror.[4]

Anna spontaneously expresses a sense of *greater* passion than Vronsky because of the *greater* hurt she suffers at the hands of aristocratic society. It is Tolstoy's great talent to portray the lives of his characters over time, as they change and as they grow old. Here he portrays the development of their passion over time, and with it the sense of greater effort that Anna, as a woman, needs to sustain it, an effort of which she fleetingly thinks her lover incapable.

The contrast between Anna's situation and that of Levin is crucial to the development of the novel. Both are socially privileged and socially disaffected. But neither would understand the source of the other's disaffection. Anna makes the discovery that the fruits of privilege can never bring happiness, Levin the discovery that they can never bring justice. Neither is capable of the other's discovery. Anna may question the legal and practical privileges belonging to the men of her class which she herself lacks: but she never questions the privileges of her class as a whole. Levin, on the other hand, challenges in his reflections the whole basis of the agrarian system on which his personal wealth rests. Yet nothing brings him greater personal pleasure than a ritual for the privileged he takes for granted—a summer day's shooting. Though Levin is perplexed and conscience-stricken by the unjust anomalies of his position, its very security makes his fate at best problematic. It is a predicament amenable to the promise of rational solution in a way that Anna's can never be.

It is symptomatic of this impasse between the sensibility of Anna and that of Levin that the novel has two endings: the first when Anna throws herself under the train and the second, official ending when Levin eventually finds the justice he is looking for in a special type of Christianity. Having led separate lives, which barely intersected, Anna and Levin have separate destinies. But Levin's glowing statement of religious conviction cannot expiate the tragedy of Anna's suicide. It actually seems artificial. Tolstoy had intended it didactically as an ideal attitude of mind towards the problems of the society he was writing about. But it is an attitude of mind which cannot obviate the cruelty of Anna's fate or Vronsky's feeling afterwards on his way to the Turkish front that he is 'a broken man'. The tragic events preceding it render it myopic. While Tolstoy is masterly in demonstrating how life goes on after the individual tragedies which stamp their mark upon it, the note of affirmation on which the novel ends is slightly flawed. Beyond the authentic domestic happiness of Kitty and Levin lies Levin's constant restless moralising which is certainly *not* 'the positive meaning of goodness' he claims to have discovered for his life.

The precondition for tragic nobility in *Anna Karenin* is the aristocratic mastery of life. But Anna attains that nobility only by taking her own life, by subverting the very foundations of the seemingly natural order on which the ruling power of the men around her is based, and in which she does not share. For women of the ruling class share in its mastery through compliance with its sexual and social mores—a compliance which enhances their personal esteem. Aristocratic culture bestows upon them a graciousness, dignity and charm lacking in the culture of other social classes. As part of a cultural artifice built upon landed wealth and inherited title, they are the rewards of its weaker sex, refracting the longstanding political mastery of its men. By compromising her social position, by overtly rejecting marriage in favour of passion, Anna violates the subtle sexual relationship of mores and power. By faithfully following her own feelings, even into the confusions and contradictions to which they led her, she becomes socially ostracised and so in opposition to the values of her own class without consciously wishing to subvert them.

By contrast, Vronsky, his spirit broken by her suicide, leaves for the Turkish war to share a fate which is communal rather than solitary, where the death which possibly awaits him is the death of any other soldier who has not suffered his personal bereavement. Despite the sympathy which surrounds her throughout, Anna's fate is solitary of necessity. Her involuntary subversion is a challenge to the exercise of power of the class to which she belongs, while Levin, whose reformist ideas are superficially iconclastic, points the way to the type of enlightened compromise which saved the British aristocracy but, for one reason or another, did little to help their Russian counterparts. Being reformist is the luxury of a privileged landowner but being passionate is the sin of a fallen woman.

The relevance of Anna's plight to the contemporary world seems diminished by the changing laws of marriage and divorce. But to say that her fate is a fate which could not befall a contemporary woman is too isolated a statement. If the divorce laws have changed, and the social position of women changed, class situation has changed also. In all modern societies the political power of the aristocracy has practically vanished, hence the relationship between sex, class and that elusive quality of nobility which pervades Tolstoy's novel has also been lost. But its universal appeal remains. In an artistic medium which is distinctly modern, whose theme of the conflict between marriage and passion is a cultural commonplace in thousands of instantly forgotten romances, the noble becomes universal. The nostalgia for the noble qualities of a vanishing class is transformed into a search for the universally noble qualities of all mankind. Unlike the characters of Trollope or Henry James, Tolstoy's characters are identifiable as universally human was well as being distinctively members of a specific class. The classlessness of great Russian literature, and its superiority to much Victorian fiction, proceeds from a unique class-rootedness which is pre-bourgeois and non-Western. Where Marx, historically speaking, saw the suffering of modern mankind centred in the suffering of its proletariat, Tolstoy saw human nobility centred in the class of which he himself was a member. But whereas the universality of the proletariat is premised on its future rise to power, that of the nobility is based on its historical eclipse. The difference between Marx and Tolstoy is that between historical prophecy and artistic fact. The aristocratic universal is preserved not in life, but in art, for the class which inspired it has vanished.

Tolstoy's aristic accomplishment was to create the aristocratic universal precisely through the lack of prescience about the future annhilation of the class from which he derived it. The same is not true of Dosteovsky. In *The Idiot* he destroys the Russian aristocracy in the very process of fictionally recreating it. Unlike Tolstoy, Dostoevsky's experience of the Russian aristocracy had been more or less from the outside. In his own travels, lacking access to the highest circles, he saw it crumbling around the edges. At the gaming tables in Germany and Switzerland, he saw the fortunes of the Russian gentry brazenly squandered, fortunes greater than the advances on his latest novel which he was in the process of squandering himself. He also saw the parasitical and unprofitable use of money by members of a class in the process of making themselves destitute. Tolstoy had a view of the aristocracy as a stable and enduring class, even if it was socially unjust. But Dostoevsky saw it in the process of imminent disintegration, a prospect he exaggerated in *The Idiot* because of his personal distance at that time from the centres of aristocratic power. His vision nonetheless was thoroughly prophetic. Another fact must be noted. In his fiction, Dostoevsky came to the aristocracy having written *Notes from Underground, Poor Folk, Crime and Punishment* and *The House of the Dead*. He had portrayed the poor, the petit-bourgeois, the criminal and the destitute of urban life, and he had drawn in a harrowing way on his prison experience in Siberia. Chronologically speaking his fiction appears to reverse almost completely Auerbach's evolutionary schema. Dostoevsky started from the lowest social strata in his early novels, then proceeded to work his way upwards. His literary career almost defies explanation. Almost, but not quite, for Dostoevsky's life as a revolutionary sentenced to the firing squad and reprieved at the last moment, as a convict in Siberia who developed severe fits of epilepsy, and finally as a destitute writer with Slavophile beliefs, provides us with *The Idiot's* embryonic pattern. His own desire to mix in the highest social circles, a desire he did not finally achieve until the end of his life, is reflected in Prince Myshkin's desire for acceptance in aristocratic circles. His political conservatism was the ideological key to possible success. Yet his fiction belied his reactionary social aspirations. *The Idiot* is the supreme example, where Dostoevsky's feeling of non-acceptance by those superior circles to which he aspired is transformed into a remarkable novel.

The focal point of *The Idiot*, as with Anna Karenin, is the passion of its central characters. But here passion is more complex than in Tolstoy. The social alternatives to passion are all there—hedonism on the one hand, marriage and respectability on the other—but Dostoevsky's vision of passion is much deeper and more shattering. For unlike Prince Andrei or

Count Vronsky, the noble prince of his novel is an idiot. Epileptic, mentally deranged and recently returned from Switzerland where he had been receiving treatment, Myshkin represents the realisation of a totally different type of myth from the medieval myth of passion. Myshkin's return to Russia is a fictional realisation of the myth of Christ. Forced to live in the realistic world of the novel and not the mythical world of the New Testament, Christ appears as a naïve simpleton, whose insight into the feelings and aspirations of his fellow beings is nonetheless remarkable. His spontaneous mercy, his unconditional forgiveness of others make them gasp with admiration. But his naïvety, his total lack of cunning and malice, his indifference to the power he can exert over others prompt everyone to think that he 'is not all there'. He is Christ born at the wrong time, returning to the wrong place, forgiving those who do not wish to be saved.

What complicates the formula of passion against society is Myshkin's spontaneous compassion. He is not passionate but compassionate, and the development of the story hinges upon this crucial division, a division which is never truly complementary, which can never be healed or reconciled. Dostoevsky places passion and compassion side by side in the real world with an intensity which is truly tragic. But it would be wrong to see Myshkin and Rogozhin as abstract symbols of passion and compassion. The reality of the relationships in which Myshkin becomes involved are more complex. As in Tolstoy's novel they hinge upon the tragic heroine. Nastasyia Filippovna, the woman they both love, herself falls in love with the compassionate Prince and not the passionate Rogozhin whom she finally and fatally chooses to run off with. In the figure of Nastasyia, the mutuality of passion which characterises the relationship of Anna and Vronsky is actually torn apart. She loves the Prince for his Christ-like qualities, the qualities of purity, of mercy and of forgiveness which are never those of carnal passion. In loving Nastasyia, Myshkin actually forsakes, for the first and only time, those very qualities for which she loves him. Rogozhin, whose passion for Nastasyia is jealous, brutal and unconditional, does not elicit passion in return but only the sensuality which Nastasyia gives to those who are passionate for her. In loving Nastasyia passionately the Prince violates the meekness of his universal compassion. In loving the Prince passionately Nastasyia violates the sensuality of the courtesan she has been up until that time. But their mutual passion is doomed. Because their passion does not derive, as it does with Anna and Vronsky, from what they are; it derives from the destruction or the betrayal of what they are. Passion is the abandonment of everything that each of them stands for. It is as if Dostoevsky extracted from the New Testament what is only hinted at in the relationship of Christ and Mary Magdalene. By loving each other carnally, they would forsake themselves, abandoning themselves to a passion which, for diametrically opposed reasons, was not in the nature of either of them. Between the compassionate nature of the saintly prince and the sensuality of the self-willed Nastasyia, stands the passion whose fulfilment is beyond attainment.

But the context of this tragic denial, which results in Nastasyia leaving the Prince for Rogozhin on the morning of their intended wedding, is indisputably social. The authentic passion of the novel is the active, dominant passion of Rogozhin, as jealous as that of Othello, as absolute as that of Heathcliff for Catherine Earnshaw. Yet Rogozhin's passion is not noble. In the pre-bourgeois Russia of the 1860s, Rogozhin surfaces from underground, inheriting a fortune from his father who, though a successful businessman, is a member of an obscure Patriarchal sect. Coarse, boorish, dissipated and brutal, he is the antithesis of Tolstoy's noble hero, the incarnation of all those qualities which aristocratic *ésprit* seeks to banish. Possessing the social title to nobility which Rogozhin lacks, the Prince comes from a background of social destitution. But even then, he lacks the conventional qualities of aristocratic nobility just as much as Rogozhin. Emanating the quality of princely compassion, that remarkable contradiction in terms which is the extraordinary strength of the novel, he cannot, as Rogozhin tells him, love without pity. For pity is the catalyst to his passion for Nastasyia, a necessary catalyst without which he is incapable of passion at all. Passion, in the novel, comes from below, from the prodigal son of an obscure merchant and from a fallen woman orphaned in childhood and seduced by her ward. Yet the connection between passion and nobility is maintained precisely when it is in danger of being destroyed. For Nastasyia identifies the compassionate qualities of the prince as noble virtues, as genuine features of a nobility grounded precariously in the almost worthless title attached to his name.

The most immediate and striking feature of Myshkin in that he is completely unrecognisable as a nobleman of any sort. His social manner is, quite unintentionally, an affront to the formality and hierarchy of aristocratic life. Waiting for his interview with General Yepanchin, he confesses at great length to the servant in the anteroom his horror of the guillotine, bestowing on his embarrassed listener the status of a social equal. This facet of his personality is poignantly echoed a moment later when Nastasyia Filippovna enters unexpectedly on the scene. She fails to socially identify him:

> Nastasyia Filippovna looked bewildered at the prince. 'A prince? Is he a prince? Fancy that, and I took him for a footman just now and sent him into announce me! Ha! Ha! Ha!⁵

Yet very soon afterwards she falls absolutely in love with him. For at the famous convocation where she considers the marriage proposals of Ganya and Rogozhin, she sees and feels Myshkin's pity for her transform itself into passion. His pity lies in his desperate plea to her not to marry either of her suitors. His passion reveals itself immediately afterwards in the scandalous confession that the Prince himself desires her. Nastasyia is swept away by the pity she has transformed out of all recognition. She falls in love.

The choice of marriage partners confronting Nastasyia is one belonging to the literary conventions of the romantic novel, a choice between the respectable Ganya and the passionate Rogozhin. But here the comparison ends. Nastasyia is not the innocent heroine morally entitled to such a choice. Ganya, financially greedy and hypocritical, seeks only the dowry offered by the embarrassed Totsky to establish a career in the civil service. In some ways he is the test case for the *embourgeoisement* of the lesser aristocracy, and consequently one of the most unsympathetic characters Dostoevsky ever created. In contrast Rogozhin, whose inheritance gives him all the money he could ever have wished for, regards it as intrinsically worthless. He is willing to squander his whole fortune to gain Nastasyia, and the scandalous scene where he rudely interrupts Ganya's marriage proposal and turns it into a public auction is the very antithesis of the conventional confession of passionate devotion. But Rogozhin's quasi-criminal existence and Nastasyia's notoriety are nothing compared to the role of Myshkin. For his intervention compels her to reject both respectability and passion. In doing so, it compels her into a new and necessary passion from which she can never escape. To reject Ganya for Rogozhin shocks the assembled company. But her subsequent acceptance of the prince's offer is utterly profane. In this respect there is a partial restoration of normality when she capriciously rejects the prince again to go off with Rogozhin. But the tossing of Rogozhin's money into the stove and the humiliation of Ganya testify to an extraordinary power in Nastasyia Filippovna. She possesses a terrible cruelty and capacity for wounding of which most modern heroines would not be capable.

The portrait of Nastasyia, far more compelling than Chernyshevsky's Vera in *What is to be Done?*, shows us a remarkable feature of Dostoevsky's realism. Totally independent and self-willed, Nastasyia is not, from an intellectual standpoint at least, an emancipated woman. Though one suspects that Dostoevsky wished to create a Russian equivalent of George Sand, he thankfully failed to do so. For Nastasyia, in constantly violating the rules which govern her life, dispenses with intellectual rationale. Disregarding the conventional role of her sex, she practises an un-principled anarchic pride. After a fashion, therefore, she is emancipated, but only through a supreme effort of personal will. Yet that effort is founded on the necessity of her being, *ab initio*, a fallen woman. For instead of taking the conventional route to respectability by putting her depraved life behind her, she uses it as a springboard for an emancipation which ends in death. Indeed that emancipation merely projects her into a more fundamental necessity of her being—the impossible choice between a passion she receives but to which she cannot give and a passion she wants to give but from which she cannot truly receive. Choice, in this sense, freed from social constraint by her effort of will, is impossible. For either way the loss is insuperable. Wishing passion without pity, she can only show passion for that very pity whose passion is flawed.

But the provisional emancipation of Nastasyia—emancipated in a way that Anna Karenin was not—has an even greater importance. It is this which secures the Prince's passion. Nastasyia does not suffer passively like most exploited women but actively in course of socially establishing the right to that freedom which ultimately founders on necessity. To this aspect of her life, the prince has no resistance. His passion for her is predicated on her active being in relation to his own meekness and passivity. Rogozhin's passion is one of jealous and frenzied possession of the object he loves; but Myshkin's is a yielding of innocence to experience. If Dostoevsky has realised the myth of Christ and Mary Magdalene, he has also inverted it. The Christ-like Myshkin looks on grief-stricken and helpless while his liberated Mary Magdalene is crucified. Yet, at the same time, his very compassion is one of the causes of her crucifixion. Without possibility of resurrection, her death finally breaks his spirit, as if the destiny of the passive Christ was irreversible madness. Having intensified the suffering of others through his absolute compassion which has the intention of alleviating it Myshkin ultimately suffers a fate for which all compassion is superfluous. Returning to Schneider's clinic in Switzerland, he fails to recognise the overbearing Mrs Yepanchin who has 'a good Russian cry over him'. Having avoided crucifixion and performed no miracles, the prince lives out his days in total insanity.

Side by side with the tragic failure of passion lies the social failure of arranged marriage. Aglaya Yepanchin, the complete opposite of Nastasyia, young, innocent and totally dependent on her family, is the ideal marriage match. Mrs Yepanchin, who seems to pledge her life on organising the successful betrothal of her daughter, has almost absolute control over her future. But in the end Mrs Yepanchin succeeds in organising nothing. Myshkin breaks off his engagement to Aglaya to marry Nastasyia, realising at the end that he loves both women with, as Radomsky puts it, 'two different kinds of love'. Aglaya is as jealous of Nastasyia as Rogozhin is of the prince. But her jealousy springs from a precocious awareness of Myshkin's passion for the older woman and reveals itself in her mocking recital of Pushkin's ballad of the poor knight. She senses intuitively that his passion for Nastasyia violates his compassionate nature. It is only through marriage to Aglaya that Myshkin has any prospect of finding conventional love and happiness, and in her delirious letters to Aglaya, whom she has never met, Nastasyia recognises the purity of their relationship, its purity of innocence. 'I knew without words you were a light for him. I've lived near him for a whole month and I understood that you too love him; you and he are one and the same to me. . . . You are innocent and in your innocence lies all perfection.'

But the perfection of innocence is not to be. In a novel where all the characters seem to be assembled together for every significant event which takes place, Aglaya and Nastasyia do not meet until near the end, when Aglaya has read the other woman's letters and rejected them. Seeing the two women together, their mutual hatred and scorn, the prince, unwilling to choose between them, is forced to do so. When Aglaya accuses her rival of torturing and jilting him, her open confession of her own feelings are, though she does not realise it, also those of Nastasyia whom she wrongfully accuses. So different in temperament and background, both women love Myshkin for the same reason:

'I must also tell you that never in my life have I met a man like him for noble simplicity of mind and for boundless trustfulness. I realised after what he had told me that anyone who wished could deceive him, and that whoever deceived him, he would forgive afterwards and that is why I fell in love with him. . . .'[6]

But of the two, it is Nastasyia who has 'pierced his heart for ever'. It is she who can say to Agalaya in his presence that she will order him to leave the younger woman and stay with her for good, and it is she whose side the prince takes as the confrontation reaches its bitter climax. As Aglaya rushes from the room and Nastasyia falls unconscious in the prince's arms, the prince hesitates, as significantly as Hamlet on seeing his uncle at prayer. He does not run after Aglaya when she is finally humiliated and at that moment she knows their relationship is finished, that Myshkin has forsaken his Christian heart by refusing her the compassion she demands of him. The novel ends in a denial of everything it promises. No marriage ceremony is performed, no happiness attained, no passion requited. One by one, all the options are destroyed. Nastasyia deserts Myshkin at the church door to run off with the jealous lover who stabs her through the heart. Aglaya, who 'had always sat at home, corked up in a bottle', waiting 'to be married straight out of a bottle', leaves for Paris where she lives with a Polish revolutionary whom she finally marries in contravention of everything which her parents had tried to attain for her. Rogozhin for his murder is sentenced to fifteen years hard labour in a Siberian labour camp. Myshkin goes back into exile and renewed madness, having failed to redeem Russia amidst the personal tragedies of his life.

The tragedy of passion is linked to Myshkin's failure to become the redeemer of Russia he so dearly desires to be. For instead of redeeming the poor and oppressed he tries to redeem their leaders. But treated as an idiot, he becomes a plaything of the aristocracy, laughed at for his guileless spirit, yet marvelled at for his irreproachable honesty. Like a well-subscribed charity, he becomes the conscience of the aristocracy but never its consciousness. In search of a lost nobility which he finds in its very opposite, the humble and suffering figure of Christ, he confuses quite fundamentally the whole nature of modern Christian civilisation. For the authentic values of the New Testament can never be those of a ruling power. As the pathetic

General Ivolgin tells him, to extend sympathy to men of high rank when they lie and delude themselves is an insult to their nobility. The fact is, none of Dostoevsky's high-ranking officers show much trace of Tolstoyan nobility. They fume, ramble and prevaricate. And it is for this reason that, to their utmost embarrassment, Myshkin pities them. Dostoevsky shows the vulnerability of the aristocracy where Tolstoy shows its strength. Myshkin reveals the very weaknesses of those he is urging to reclaim their nobility.

His first and last introduction to the very highest of aristocratic circles reveals his own dilemma. He wants to reconcile himself to the class to which he belongs in title but from which social circumstances have long estranged him. But his efforts merely throw into relief the vast gap that exists. At the Yepanchins', where he is paraded before the highest circles as Aglaya's future husband, his insight is inseparable from his mental affliction. Leonid Grossman has claimed that his dramatic speech to them is an apologia for the aristocratic classes. But it is precisely the opposite. His missionary zeal is accompanied by the clumsiness which results in the smashing of the Yepanchins' Chinese vase. His prophetic vision of the ruin of those he addresses culminates in an epileptic fit leaving him unconscious on the floor. But just before his seizure he makes the climactic speech revealing his fear for the future of the class he is misguidedly pledged to save:

> 'I came here with anguish in my heart', went on the prince, with ever-mounting agitation, speaking more and more rapidly, more strangely and animatedly. 'I – I was afraid of you, I was also afraid of myself. Of myself most of all. On my way back to Petersberg I decided that I must see our foremost men, men in high places, men belonging to the oldest families, to which I belong myself, men among whom I am the foremost by birth myself. For I am now sitting among princes like myself am I not? I wanted to get to know you, and that was necessary, very, very necessary! I have always heard a great deal more evil than good about you—about the pettiness and exclusiveness of your interests, your backwardness, your inadequate education, your absurd habits—oh, so much is being written and talked about you! I came here today full of curiousity, fear and confusion. I had to see for myself whether the whole of this upper crust of Russian society is really worthless, has outlived its time, has exhausted itself by existing too long. . . .
>
> 'Just now, as I was coming here, I was thinking: "How on earth shall I talk to them? How shall I start so that they may understand at least something?" Oh, how I was afraid, but I was more afraid for you. Awfully, awfully! And yet how could I be afraid? Was it not shameful to be afraid? . . .
>
> 'You're laughing, Ivan Petrovitch? You think that I was afraid for the *others*, that I am *their* advocate, a democrat an upholder of equality?' he

laughed hysterically (he kept interrupting his speech every minute by short rapturous bursts of laughter) 'I am afraid for you, for all of you and for all of us. For I am a prince of ancient lineage myself, and I am sitting among princes. I am saying this to save you all, so as to prevent our class from vanishing for nothing into utter darkness without realising anything, abusing everything and losing everything. . . .

'Listen', the prince went on, 'I know that it's no good talking, that it's much better to set an example, much better simply to start—I've started already and—and can one really be unhappy? Oh, what do my grief and my troubles matter if I have the power to be happy? You know, I can't understand how one can pass by a tree and not be happy at the sight of it! To talk to a man and not be happy in loving him? Oh, it's only that I'm not able to put it into words but—but think how many beautiful things there are at every step, things even the most wretched man cannot but find beautiful! Look at a child, look at God's sunset, look at the grass how it grows, look at the eyes that gaze at you and love you. . . .'[7]

His audience see the speech as the tirade of a madman. The whole catastrophe confirms Mrs Yepanchin in her opinion that the prince is 'impossible'. As for the content of the speech we do not need to know Weber's sociology of world-religions to realise that the prophecy of Christian redemption would be alien to almost any ruling aristocracy. Myshkin's attack on Catholicism, his Slavophile dogma, his simplistic view of Christian virtues fall on embarrassed ears. Earlier, the prince had been the object of public attack by Ippolit's radical friends as a wealthy superfluous man undeserving of the fortune he had inherited. The passage in which the denunciation is read out has all the reflexivity of the Shakespearean play within the play. But in the context of tragic realism, this reflexive passage is Dostoevsky's artistic defence of his tragic hero against his radical critics—the criticism that his hero is too wealthy, simple-minded and ineffectual to be of any social use or interest to the progressive reader. The tragic ending shifts the ground from under that criticism by shifting the ground from under the aristocracy which cannot understand, let alone heed, the delirious warning of an epileptic madman. In the eyes of his privileged audience, Myshkin might just as well belong to Ippolit's own circle of nihilists. For he remains a rootless ideologue, a strange subversive who arouses animosity where he craves acceptance. The relationship between aristocracy and intelligentsia is the very opposite of that in Tolstoy. Tolstoy's aristocratic heroes, with their intellectual leanings, absorb new reformist ideas and try to put them into practice. Dostoevsky's intellectuals are trapped in a permanent alienation from the ruling order from which simple good-natured intent can provide no escape. Dostoevsky's fiction is therefore closer in nature to the historical alienation of the Russian intelligentsia from its masters. The ineffectuality of Myshkin involuntarily betrays the ineffectuality of the Slavophile ideal to which Dostoevsky himself clung so tenaciously.

Dostoevsky nonetheless possesses a vision of community beyond tragic conflict. Needless to say it has little to do with Slavophile ideals. It lies in the image which gave rise to the novel in the first place, and actually completes it—the image of the prince and Rogozhin side by side watching over Nastasyia's dead body. Earlier the novel had echoed the strange, wonderful sisterhood and brotherhood which passion bestowed upon its protagonists. There were Nastasyia's wild strange letters to Aglaya, the scene where Myshkin exchanges crosses with Rogozhin who nonetheless tries to murder him. But at the end the most poignant scene of all unfolds. After finding his runaway bride murdered by the knife which earlier had nearly been plunged into his own heart, the prince lies down, side by side with the murderer who comforts him in his distress and horror. Out of tragic conflict springs briefly a poignant harmony which is ultimately doomed.

Myshkin's failure to convert the aristocracy to his simple Christian virtues is only partly a function of his 'idiocy'. In addition he is unfaithful to them himself. In tragic realism passion undermines the values by which its heroes live, and the Prince's uncontrollable passion for Nastasyia compels him to an unchristian rejection of Aglaya. But Dostoevsky's novel goes even further. It completely severs the relationship between Christian and noble values in a ruling aristocracy whose religion is indisputably Christian. Myshkin's tragic life is like an experimental invalidation of his deepest principles. In Tolstoy's last novel *Resurrection* we witness the very opposite. The relationship of Christianity and nobility remains intact, but only through an escape from passion. The Christianity of Nekhludov, the nobleman hero, is based on improving the conditions under which people live, in all spheres of life. But the source of his reforming impulse is a guilty conscience. As a well-established judge presiding over the criminal trial for murder of a prostitute he once loved, it is guilt over his own part in her ruination which prompts him into action. But that guilt itself is ambiguous, for not only is it guilt over Natasha's suffering but also over the consequences of his own passion. Henceforth reform replaces passion as the dominant feature of Nekhludov's life. His reminiscence of the passionate affair with Natasha is like a nostalgia for literature itself. For in his present life passion is no longer possible, and Tolstoy seems to be announcing the expiration of one of the great themes of his fiction halfway through the novel. In a last desperate attempt to expiate his guilt, Nekhludov visits Natasha in prison and offers to marry her. But the woman's embarrassment, and subsequent contempt, tells all. Defunct relationships cannot be resurrected any more than the creative talent of the author which is in the process of dying. The title of the novel, therefore, is false in two senses. Passion and the artistic power to create it vanish almost in the same breath.

With passion only a memory in the mind of the hero, nothing can intrude upon the reforming Christian spirit which Tolstoy transposed directly from his own life. Penal reform, agrarian reform, endless petitioning of authorities in high places, are all grist to the mill. As reform replaces passion, didactic fiction replaces tragic realism. Starting off with the potentially tragic ending to Natasha's life, Tolstoy proceeds to rescue it from tragedy. Passion is resurrected as personal care carefully circumscribed by the respective roles of penal reformer and prisoner—these replacing the roles of nobleman and serving girl which made the original seduction possible. But personal care is in turn transformed into a abstract care for all humanity. Nekhludov uses the predicament of Natasha as a springboard for an investigation of the conditions of all prisoners. Passionate as a lover, then guilty as a judge, Nekhludov ends up with the sterile objectivity of an impartial journalist whose only emotion is occasional moral indignation. His Christian values are never put to the test through personal involvement, because his involvement decreases as the novel continues. True, his conscience is more involved, but as such it is detached from his personal fate which is unaffected by the terrible prison conditions he witnesses. Similarly his plea for redistribution of land remains a suggestion to his peasantry which has no narrative consequences. His estate is never expropriated and his life consequently does not change.

This contrast between Tolstoy and Dostoevsky, the differing role of Christian values in their fiction and the differing role of passion, is maintained in Dostoevsky's last novel *The Brothers Karamazov*. Whereas the importance of passion here is nowhere near as great as it is in *The Idiot*, the concern with Christ remains. In *Resurrection* Tolstoy had offered an artificial and didactic formula for Christian redemption. In Dostoevsky's novel, in the celebrated story of the Grand Inquisitor, Christ returns to earth but is reduced to silence. But his is a silence which speaks volumes. As the Grand Inquisitor lectures him on the history of the church founded in the intruder's name, we come to witness a testament to the enduring power of orthodoxy in any system of belief, an orthodoxy whose practice violates what it preaches at every opportunity. The same orthodoxy blesses the Grand Inquisitor with the gift of speech and reduces his opponents to silence. Were all the great prophets of history to return to see what history had done to their prophecies, they too would be reduced to silence. In the case of Christianity the process took place over many centuries. In the case of socialism in Dostoevsky's own country it was to take place within less than a decade. The silent dignity of the mysterious figure in Ivan's story was something of a luxury. People were forcibly reduced to silence, and allowed to speak publicly only to a rehearsed script of false confession. Critics have argued that it is not realistic to present a story of the Second Coming in which the Messiah is reduced to silence. But in the eyes of the Grand Inquisitor, the truth of the Messiah's message has already become stale, weary and unprofitable. Already knowing what Christ might say, his speech, like all orthodox speech, preempts the message and renders its tellers superfluous. 'I went back', he proclaims 'and joined the hosts of those who have *corrected your work*.' The parable of Christianity, at a time when it was beginning to lose its universal sway, has since become a parable of the rise and betrayal of socialism. The Inquisitor's final words are words which no one but Dostoevsky could have written:

> I repeat, tomorrow you will behold the obedient flock which at a mere sign from me will rush to heap up the hot coals against the stake at which I shall burn you because you have come to meddle with us. For if anyone has deserved our fire, it is you. Tomorrow I shall burn you. *Dixi!*[8]

6 Dostoevsky: the demonic *Tendenz*

The Devils is the most politically controversial of all Dostoevsky's novels. It contains a vicious caricature of Russian liberalism, and open condemnation of the revolutionary ideas of its epoch. Many Marxist critics have preferred to concentrate on Dostoevsky's other work rather than risk the task of condemning it in terms of their own theory. Lukács is no exception to the rule. Apart from some brief remarks on Nicholas Stavrogin, he ignores the novel almost completely.[1] The fact remains that the novel is written in a realist tradition and fulfils all the criteria of Lukács 'critical realism' bar one—and that one of course is crucial. The novel does not champion an ideologically progressive attitude.

The text therefore has a basic difficulty for all partisans of revolution. While condemning revolution, it is not a purely reactionary polemic. It transforms into creative fiction a bewildering complex of social and political ideas of the period. As an *Ideenroman* it takes seriously the very ideas it was the author's intention to reject, and its very seriousness in this respect outlives Dostoevsky's original intention. Dostoevsky attacks the liberal and revolutionary ideas of the 1860s, yet at the same time these ideas are indispensable to his creative achievement. Intrinsic to the literary worth of the text itself, they cannot be dismissed as an alien external force to which the author reacts out of ignorance and fear. For the novel reveals a totalising perspective on Russian politics and society drawn from the ideologies of its respective protagonists but yet surpassing them. What Dostoevsky hated as a person was necessary for his success as a novelist. Needless to say, this vital feature of his writing has often been conveniently overlooked.

Because Dostoevsky took a topical terrorist outrage of the time as the main theme of the novel, it has been dismissed as a piece of journalistic sensationalism, or at best a patchwork of documentary fact and hysterical fantasy. As is well known, the theme is based on the assassination of a student, Ivanov, by fellow-members of his secret revolutionary circle acting under the order of their leader, Sergei Nechaev. The murder took place in 1868, towards the end of a turbulent decade in Russian intellectual life. Nechaev justified the creation of the revolutionary group as a part of a network of world-wide groups secretly pledged to revolution. Although Nechaev was an emissary of Bakunin, the claim was a total fiction. In the novel the villain, Peter Verkhovensky and his victim, Shatov, are based on Nechaev and Ivanov respectively. The actual incident became a scandal in revolutionary circles. Bakunin disowned Nechaev and Marx expressed his disgust at the whole affair. In a rather barbarous manner Nechaev had inaugurated the style of the professional revolutionary without its substance—absolute secrecy and ruthless terror but no popular support among the masses. Dostoevsky himself seemed to sense this quite clearly. The virtue of his literary talent was to locate this phenomenon within a remarkable vision of the changing culture of Russian society, and of the role of the radical intelligentsia within this process of change. He did not extrapolate the incident as a sensational issue, but rather used it as a springboard for a creative quest, part sociological, part metaphysical, into the nature of a new and sinister evil bearing an organic relationship to the society from which it had sprung.

He cannot be accused, as Lukács accused Zola, of the naturalist fallacy of descriptive journalism which strips literary characters of their authentic subjectivity. The process of characterisation in *The Devils* is complex, but has a relatively simple starting point. Most of the major characters have their model in real life and can actually be compared with the people on whom they were based. But the actual criterion of literary realism can never be based on such a resemblance, and it is pointless to ask how alike Peter Verkhovensky and Nechaev, Stepan Verkhovensky and Granovsky the Russian liberal are. And despite the scandal it caused at the time, there is little use in comparing Karmazinov with the real Turgenev. For the relationships between the characters within the novel do not remotely resemble the relationships, if any, between the real persons on whom they are based. The importance of the characters is therefore determined by their relationship to the setting of the novel and its plot. The disparate figures on whom Dostoevsky based his major characters are thus thrown together in a way which in real life would have been improbable. But given this initial improbability the eventual outcome of their relationships within the novel is no less credible. This is the logic of the imaginative act of literary recreation, a logic involving political and sociological validity. The question posed is, what might happen if such characters are thrown together in the way that they are? Only the finalised text can give the answer.

There is an experimental logic attached to all literary creation, but in the case of *The Devils* it is quite clearly circumscribed by a feature of Dostoevsky's personal life—his earlier involvement with revolutionary circles in Russia. The first-hand experience of revolutionary activity artistically motivates him even though that experience is long since past. For the contemporary setting of the novel, Dostoevsky drew on experiences of twenty years previously—his involvement with the Petrashevsky circle in St Petersberg for which he was arrested in 1848. As a reactionary outsider to the Nechaev conspiracy which is no more than a story in a newspaper, Dostoevsky feels himself to be witnessing a very familiar world. This is crucial to the interior viewpoint of revolutionary activity the novel portrays, in for example the masterly account of the meeting at Virginsky's. Through his literature Dostoevsky actually re-establishes contact with a world he had forsaken. The intensity of his writing is such that distance and irony, those great weapons of political disillusionment, are practically impossible. At the same time this same first-hand experience prevents Dostoevsky from idealising political activity in the way that Turgenev did in *Virgin Soil*. In *Virgin Soil* the populist impulses of Lavretsky are inseparable from Turgenev's own nostalgia for the countryside from which he voluntarily exiled himself. Hence the hero's greater ease among the gentry he theoretically repudiates and his ineffectuality among the peasants his principles demand that he supports. In rejecting a superficial sympathy with his major characters, Dostoevsky actually gives them a power and intensity which is lacking in Turgenev's sentimentalised portraits of the young Russian populists.

It should not be overlooked, however, that one writer chose populism as a subject for a political novel and the other fratricidal terror. The opposition to the critics of *Contemporary* that both novelists felt very deeply expressed itself in different ways. Turgenev feared for the sanctity of art; Dostoevsky for the future destiny of Russia. The paradox is revealed in Dostoevsky's own estimation of Turgenev's work. He saw Turgenev's most positive literary creation in Bazarov, the nihilist doctor of *Fathers and Sons*, the militant progressive whose utilitarian repudiation of art contained everything that Turgenev hated. Otherwise he came to regard Turgenev's writing as superficial and sentimental, the product of the gentry upbringing he despised, but in some ways envied. Dostoevsky's Slavophile opposition to revolution was inextricably linked to an equally intense hatred of Westernised liberalism of the kind espoused by Turgenev and David Granovsky. As a political novel, *The Devils* was intended as a polemical attack on both liberals and revolutionaries, who in turn were forces adamantly opposed to each other. Yet the significant feature of the novel is that, despite its political tendency, it stands head and shoulders above all the other anti-nihilist literature proliferating during the period. But it does so precisely because of the vast disparity between initial intention and ultimate achievement. *The Devils* is not the crystallisation of a reactionary political attitude, as many Marxists seem to think, but a text which passes over into artistic impersonality. Indisputably Dostoevskyan, artististically unique in one sense, it transcends the constricting attitudes which Dostoevsky in vain sought to place upon it. Instead it conforms to the necessity of great art. In writing something about which he thought, *a priori*, he knew everything, Dostoevsky actually writes about something whose nature is not yet known to him, until he actually completes it.

Dostoevsky's response to the politics of the day is mediated in the text by a response to other preceding literary works expressing some aspect of that politics. Two novels in particular are important for their negative influence—*Fathers and Sons* and *What is to be done?*. Dostoevsky took from each its central theme and proceeded to transform them out of all recognition. From Turgenev he took the theme of generational conflict and from Chernyshevsky the idea of the novel as the expression of a correct political tendency. *The Devils* incorporates both by subverting them, by denying the possible reconciliation of different generations and by subjecting political tendency to circumstances which destroy its rational utopianism. As a writer Dostoevsky experienced the tension between *mimesis* and *Tendenz* which Chernyshevsky had vainly tried to eliminate in his writings on aesthetics. *What is to be done?* is a didactic novel which jettisons *mimesis* in favour of *Tendenz*. It tries to faithfully answer the question posed in its title, but does so without creating a truly resistant social world with which its utopian ideas might conflict. Chernyshevsky's message is clear: the realisation of ideas which are correctly formulated is unproblematical. Thus the rational freedom of Vera Pavlovna to change marriage partners at will is annulled by the fact that Lopukhov and Kirsanov are themselves interchangeable as personalities, differing from each other in no significant way whatsoever. The seamstresses co-operative, meant to be a rational experiment in economic justice, is in reality a paternalistic experiment in petit-bourgeois socialism. Rakhemtov, the novel's positive hero who sleeps on a bed of nails, does possess formidable qualities. But as 'a new man' he arises in a complete social vacuum, possessing little organic relationship to the rest of the novel. The rational programme for living which Chernyshevsky designs so artificially occurs in the absence of social constraints and of social conflict.

Dostoevsky claimed that he too was writing a tendentious novel, but a negative one, one which would repudiate the revolutionism of his enemies. Yet his demonic vision of political tendency, of what we can call demonic *Tendenz*, remains faithful to the mimetic functions of the novel. 'Having taken an event', he wrote, 'I tried only to classify its possibility in our society and precisely as a social event, not as an anecdote, not a description of a peculiar occurrence in Moscow.' In his portrayal of revolutionary conspiracy as a social event, he tries to avoid being purely descriptive on the one hand, or purely tendentious on the other. The novel focusses on the collision of values and reality and in one way or another reality resists the attempt Dostoevsky's heroes make to put their beliefs successfully into practice.

There are two major criticisms levelled against Dostoevsky; the first that his characters are social misfits and psychopaths, the second that his religious ideas are archaic. The former criticism originates with Mikhailovsky the populist writer in his famous reference to Dostoevsky's 'cruel talent'. But although much of the behaviour in the novel is abnormal, it is the behaviour of the socially alienated in abnormal circumstances. Dostoevsky's vision of the moral relativity of all human behaviour is never greater than here. But it arises from a base of social normality which is subsequently violated with ever-increasing intensity. The revolutionary conspiracy and the subsequent debâcle only make sense as a breakdown of community. As for Dostoevsky's Slavophile ideas, they may well have been extinguished by the Russian revolution, but even in his own novels they lead a very precarious existence. The characters who champion them do not possess the rabid, dogmatic certainty of the author of *Diary of a Writer*. Often they are hesitant and uncertain. As human beings they have their distinctive flaws. Alyosha Karamazov remains the intellectual inferior of his brother Ivan. In *The Idiot* the epileptic Myshkin is mistaken for a nihilist and in *The Devils* Shatov, the devoted follower of Christ, is tormented by his failure to assert an unconditional belief in God. By comparison both the social darwinism of Shigalyov and the metaphysical egoism of Kirilov present more compelling ideological visions of the world. In this novel, as much as all the others, Dostoevsky failed to achieve his great ambition—to create the great Slavophile hero whose positive tendency was beyond question. But this very failure in *The Devils* leads to the very opposite consequence. The heroic and tragic stature of the novel revolves around those revolutionary ideals which Dostoevsky by now despised. Specifically the novel is concerned with those who refuse them and those who betray them, and this combination of refusal and betrayal gives the novel its sense of tragic loss. For it is this which lies at the very heart of the demonic *Tendenz*.

Despite Dostoevsky's hatred of revolution, it is socialism which constitutes the absent centre of the novel. The major characters of the novel, Shatov and Kirilov, Shigalyev, Stavrogin and Peter Verkhovensky develop forms of deflection from a socialist ideal they either refuse or betray. The exception is Stepan Verkhovensky whose erratic liberalism is nonetheless consistent with a political ideal. His consistent liberalism within a weak personality contrasts with the revolutionaries who draw their strength from the very perversion of ideals. An insipid liberalism is too malleable to betray: but a visionary socialism is too demanding not to. Dostoevsky's revolutionaries are metaphysical casualties of a demand for the unity of theory and practice whose rigours are impossible to sustain. What the novel reveals is the subsequent disunity of theory and practice. This is the basis of Dostoevsky's tragic vision. For the realisation of that tragic disunity is more than the terrorist shambles we see at the end of the novel. It is the outcome of the dogmatic intensity of men whose failure has put them beyond all hope, but who nonetheless live that failure through to its bitter end.

It would probably be wrong to interpret this purely and simply as the triumph of Dostoevsky's unconscious mind over his conscious attitudes. Clearly the unconscious, that absence of conscious life always present in artistic creation, is a cogent factor in his writing. But creation itself involves a conscious struggle to unleash the forces initially unknown to it.

Dostoevsky's notebooks reveal to us something of this complex relationship in the craft of fiction.[2] They reveal the alternative events or outcomes which he has imagined and rejected, the inevitable process of selection which takes place before the final text is produced. But they also reveal his method of creation. To start with, his characters do not even have names, or if they do, these are the names of real people whom he then fictionalises. In *The Devils*, where Dostoevsky knows the central incident of the novel before he knows anything else, the characters begin as abstract social stereotypes—a student, an engineer, a prince. The ideas and sentiments they are meant to embody are written out in advance of the narrative. But the narrative transforms them. When the characters become flesh and blood, when they are named as Shatov, Kirilov and Stavrogin, they also transform the abstraction behind their imaginary being into an actuality which Dostoevsky himself had not foreseen.

This is the crux of Dostoevsky's creative method, the juncture at which the unconscious intervenes and is then disciplined into fiction. Initially the ideas lack context and the characterisation is flat. The characters become *realistic* in the very process of being *fictionalised*. Collectively they begin to take on a life of their own in the context of the developing narrative. The contrast between Chernyshevsky and Dostoevsky is nowhere clearer. Chernyshevsky uses plot and narrative as clumsy contrivances to enable characters to express the right ideas and perform the correct and appropriate actions. In Dostoevsky narrative action *is* the realisation of sentiments and values. The notebooks actually provide the key to the author's figural realism. They set down all the possibilities for the character, many of which are missing from the final text. This disparity between intention and achievement, between possibility and actuality, is fundamental to the dialectic of the imaginary and the real. The raw figure of the notebooks, closer perhaps to the real-life person or persons from whom he is taken, is transformed imaginatively into the character of the novel where he becomes more realistically convincing. The variety of unformed alternatives in the writer's mind prefigure the direction the character finally takes. But even here the novel has an open structure, for the actual character one reads about suggests a variety of alternative possibilities *within* the novel which remain absent from it. What actually happens also conveys what never does.

In *The Devils*, the fictive betrayal is twofold; betrayal of authorial ideology and tragic loss of human potentiality. We have already mentioned Shatov, the ex-revolutionary whose Slavophile yearnings are closest to Dostoevsky's own. Yet the uncertainty over God and the humility before Christ which characterise Shatov's values are also weaknesses of his personality. Overawed by Stavrogin, the father of the child to whom his wife gives birth on the morning of his own assassination, his humility is transformed into a vulnerability towards the charisma of his fellow-men. He acts like the victim Peter Verkhovensky has designated him to be, for humbled, he is also masochistic and passive, barely resisting the fate imposed upon him by terrorist logic. Dostoevsky's fictional self-portrait lacks heroic stature. By contrast the weakest figure in the whole novel achieves it at the very end. Stepan Verkhovensky, whining, conciliatory, afraid, comes to a poignant realisation of his lifelong failings on his deathbed. But his citation of the biblical parables, the parable of the swine and the passage from Revelations, is more than this. It is a means of reaffirming his commitment to his fellow-men after all the calamitous events in the town. In his hour of death, he refuses to abandon hope.

The major betrayal of moral values comes from the two central characters, Nicholas Stavrogin and Peter Verkhovensky. Stavrogin, the formidable aristocrat whom Dostoevsky had modelled on Nikolai Speshnev, a fellow member of the Petrashevsky circle in Petersberg, has the potential qualities of an all-conquering hero.[3] Proud, imposing, physically feared by his enemies, he is the *alter ego* of Myshkin. Still the potential aristocratic saviour that the earlier hero was, he nevertheless radiates nobility at the expense of compassion. But unlike Myshkin, he does not even try to use his redemptive powers. Instead he repudiates them out of scorn for his fellow-beings. Cloaked at the outset in the mystique of a proto-Nietzschean superman, he is gradually revealed as a symptom of aristocratic decay. His 'rational malice' shows him to be the master of the calculated insult. The biting of the Governor's ear, the ridiculing of the duel with Gaganov, the courtship of a crippled girl are all instances of a nonchalant scorn of respectable society. But Stavrogin also scorns the role of Messiah in which Peter and Shatov try to cast him. His unfulfilled charisma leads to atrophy and waste, and finally to the rational despair of cold deliberate suicide.

Peter Verkhovensky deviates even more from Dostoevsky's original intention. The notebooks are dotted with references to him as a blunderer and a political amateur, blind to the consequences of his own action. In fact, he turns out to be almost the opposite. His cunning and manipulative powers enable him to orchestrate the whole development of the revolutionary debacle. His talent for intrigue sustains the narrative momentum of the novel. The plot comes to life through the political energy of the novel's arch-villain, who has that remarkable dominating presence conventionally reserved for the hero. To the extent that the expected hero, Stavrogin, refuses to materialise as one, Peter's villainy comes to reign supreme.

The fictive 'betrayal' is equally evident in event and setting as it is in character. Ivanov's assassination took place in Moscow but the setting in *The Devils* is a large provincial town based upon the northern city, Tver, where Bakunin himself had actually spent some time. Intuitively, Dostoevsky realised that a large anonymous city was too atomised to convey the interdependence of the political establishment and the revolutionaries, whose actions mutually reinforce their respective political positions. He had a vision of the organic interdependence of the community as a whole in relation to the single event of Shatov's killing, a vision of the intertwining of social hierachies and classes all the way from von Lembke, the governor, to Fedka, the convict. In the big city, this would have been impossible. The provincial setting is at once more claustrophobic, but also more alien to the revolutionaries and visionaries of the novel. The expression of ideas which would be extraordinary and controversial in the intellectual circles of Moscow or Petersberg seem even more anomalous in the provincial setting Dostoevsky chooses. But by doing so, Dostoevsky creates a portrait in cameo of mid-century Russia itself, of provincial chauvinism and cosmopolitan *Weltschmerz* improbably co-existing. Ironically, slavish fidelity to the actual history of the outrage would have undermined the quest to portray its social relevance. For Dostoevsky constructs a chain reaction of events to which terror as an isolated incident could never be a catalyst. It must also be remembered that the actual source of agitation—an authentic agitation—is the strike by the Spigulin workmen. It is only by implanting a suggestion of the link between the strike and the fire following the governor's fête that Verkhovensky can involve the whole community in a panic and distress serving as a camouflage for his own terror. Instead of using terror to spread disaffection, Verkhovensky does the opposite. He foments disaffection in order to create the conditions for the act of fratricidal terror.

The close interdependence of all sectors of the community is reinforced by the actual blood relation between Stepan and Peter Verkhovensky. The archetypal liberal and the archetypal revolutionary of the sixties are literally father and son. It is a bolder step than either Turgenev or Chernyshevsky had taken. But it was not gratuitous. The relationship remains a concrete symbol of the conflict of generational ideologies while at the same time containing a profound insight into the psychology of the weak father and the contemptuous son. The relationship operates on two levels simultaneously—that of the clash of ideas and that of the clash of personalities. There is little evidence of the formal conflict of balanced arguments prevalent in the confrontation between Pavel and Bazarov. Instead there is a clash of garbled attitudes cast adrift from their intellectual moorings, vulgarised by personal obsession. Stepan's gibbering weakness, his desire not to give offence, is answered by Peter's amoral contempt. Because his father is so ineffectual, rebellion is no longer necessary and scornful manipulation becomes the order of the day. Stepan tries to ingratiate himself by offering his son a copy of *What is to be done?*, but Peter casts it contemptuously aside, his indifference to doctrine so great as to deny any call to action which remains doctrinal.

Peter's great talent is for the orchestration of social collapse, a grandiose task before which all theory becomes superflous. The fiasco of the governor's fête, the workers' strike, the arson of Fedka and the final assassination of Shatov are disparate events he synchronises almost to perfection. In doing so, he produces in microcosm the phenomenon of communal disintegration. Such a feat is in no sense a result of collective revolutionary activity. Virginsky's revolutionary circle is amateurish and consumed by internal strife. Were it not for Verkhovensky, they would have no importance at all. Their active role commences only when Fedka's arson which Peter also instigates has done its damage. When the fire and the murder of the Lebyatkins has thrown everyone into a state of bewilderment and panic, Verkhovensky bullies the revolutionaries into protecting themselves from incrimination by an act which is even more incriminating—Shatov's assassination. The killing is an organisational master-stroke of collective self-destruction. The group is arrested for a crime it did not need to commit, but which it had committed to avoid arrest for the others of which it was innocent. It thus finds itself implicated in a self-fulfilling prophecy by default. For it did not become part of a revolutionary conspiracy that it was too impractical to undertake on its own, until it was actually accused of already having done so. This is Peter's major achievement, apart, of course, from his own escape back to Switzerland.

Another remarkable feature of his technique is the double standards which surround his intrigue. Secret and conspiratorial with the revolutionaries, he is open and brazen with the establishment. His flattery of Julia von Lembke, the governor's wife, is totally ostentatious. But the end result is the same. He traps the governor into that same dependence as the circle at Virginsky's. Lembke relies on Peter to assure him that fears of a revolutionary conspiracy are exaggerated, while the revolutionaries rely on him to assure them of their own importance. His growing manipulation of events is matched only by their growing helplessness, until they are all demoralised by the distrust he sows with such malevolent energy. For the Governor and the revolutionaries share a common fate; Verkhovensky has set them on to parallel roads of destruction. His effectiveness suits neither conservative nor revolutionary orthodoxy. His famous claim—'I am not a socialist but a rogue'—cynically subverts any belief in political principles, while his personal manipulation of an ill-defined chaos can hardly be accommodated to a conspiracy theory of revolution. Dostoevsky's vision is one of nihilism resulting from chaos where there is, in addition, a moral vacuum which none can fill. Peter brings the town 'to the point of collapse' at the same time as all his own schemes end in disaster.

But Peter's radical cynicism, which so ruthlessly subverts all forms of revolutionary idealism, is itself undermined by the perversion of the only ideal which touches him—the idea of a Russian Messiah. Nicholas Stavrogin is the only man who can fill the role, but he actually resists the consequences of his charisma upon those who are in awe of him. Whereas Peter is the catalyst to human fallibility, Stavrogin is the personification of human hope. But his indifference is as devastating as Peter's militant destructiveness. Just as the amoral principles of Ivan Karamazov

precipitate Smerdyakov's confused homicide, so Stavrogin's indifference
to moral standards is a catalyst to the final debacle. It would be wrong to
see the relationship of Peter and Stavrogin as a mirror of the actual
affiliation of Nechaev and Bakunin. But Stavrogin's refusal to be shocked
or truly outraged by any of Peter's villainous schemes is a type of knowing
complicity which the scornful aristocrat cannot shed. Dostoevsky trans-
lates a political relationship back into a personal one. Moreover Stavrogin
is not like Bakunin, a distant authority, but a first-hand observer of the
catastrophe he does nothing to prevent.

Stavrogin is the most rigorous anti-hero of the realist novel, influencing
the course of events largely by virtue of what he does not do. Contemptuous
of Peter's conspiracy, he makes no attempt to alter its consequences, or save
the life of the unfortunate Shatov. Failing to honour his duel with
Gaganov, he cannot sustain his passion for Lisa. His hypocritical
involvement with the lame Mary Lebytkin is a calculated insult to
respectable society. Where Peter resorts to blackmail to impose his will,
Stavrogin possesses the forbidding attributes of sensuality and power. But
he withholds them completely. The sense of loss, of non-fulfilment, is sealed
by his refusal to accept the role for which Peter has prepared him and for
which he has directed the whole revolutionary conspiracy. Stavrogin
spurns the offer of becoming the new revolutionary Tsar whom Peter can
worship with impunity. But the nature of Peter's pleading, in a novel
which has so many extraordinary incidents, leaves the reader breathless:

> 'Stavrogin, you're beautiful' Verkhovensky cried almost in ecstasy. 'Do
> you know that you are beautiful? What is so fine about you is that
> sometimes you don't know it. Oh, I've made a thorough study of you! I
> often watch you without your being aware of it. You're even simple-
> minded and naïve—do you know that? You are, you are! I suppose you
> must be suffering and suffering genuinely too because of your simple-
> mindedness. I love beauty. I am a nihilist but I love beauty. Don't
> nihilists love beauty? The only thing they do not love is idols, but I love
> an idol. You are my idol! You don't insult anyone, and everyone hates
> you; you look upon everyone as your equal and everyone is afraid of you.
> That's good. No one will ever come up to you to slap you on the
> shoulder. You're an awful aristocrat. An aristocrat who goes in for
> democracy is irresistible. To sacrifice life—yours and another man's—is
> nothing to you. You're just the sort of man I need. I—I especially need a
> man like you. I don't know of any one but you. You're my leader, you're
> my sun and I am your worm.'[4]

Peter's frenzied admiration is echoed in Shatov's despairing question:
'Stavrogin, why am I condemned to believe in you for ever?' But his
adulation is something more. It is the quasi-erotic worship of 'the aristocrat
who goes in for democracy', who commands fear and respect from those

who are, in principle at least, his equals. A historical echo of this strange rapture can be found in the diary of Joseph Goebbels, where he records his first meeting with Hitler. The tone, the eroticism, the desire for submission are practically identical. Yet Hitler is no aristocrat, nor is he interested in democracy or equality. Stavrogin's charisma is the promise of something very different. It is the chimerical hoped-for link between the aristocratic and the democratic which never materialises. Stavrogin stands at the threshhold of the modern era, the era demanding the relinquishment of those very qualities which promise so much yet come to so little. Nobility is an anachronism in any revolutionary movement, but it is still a quality whose inevitable rejection leads to subsequent impoverishment. Conceived as a prelude to his great mission, the revolutionary conspiracy becomes meaningless without Stavrogin's participation. Not only does it become meaningless but it turns itself into a terrorist conspiracy with no real purpose. The relationship of Peter and Stavrogin at this time brings to mind the famous lines of Yeats: 'The best lack all conviction, while the worst are full of passionate intensity.' Peter's demonic activism scales new heights as Stavrogin's capacity to act decays.

At the same time, Yeats's idea of the 'best' is not truly appropriate. For Stavrogin makes no attempt to struggle against the fate which history offers him. By spurning the democratic, he ignobly consents in the doom of the noble, and shares complicity in the Nietzschean devaluation of values which Peter carries through so ruthlessly. The alternative to the impossible marriage of the socialistic and the aristocratic is organised nihilism. Verkhovensky is not an embryonic Leninist but the prototype of the fascist revolutionary. Despising the political establishment with whom he attempts to ingratiate himself, he sees revolution as a conscious means to dishonour and a force for permanent destruction. Nowhere else in the modern novel is there a person with the same talent for making revolutionaries betray their own principles. The sense of the demonic in Dostoevsky's text is actually twofold: it is a feature of revolutionary sensibility but also lies in the temptations which Peter offers to those already demonised. It implies, therefore, that all of them are capable of redemption until Peter finally and absolutely corrupts them.

Stavrogin is the only person Peter cannot persuade to act in accordance with his plans, yet the correlative of failing to act in accordance with Peter is a complete failure to act at all. But it is Kirilov, not Stavrogin, whose fate demonstrates that withdrawal from the world one despises is totally impossible. An ex-revolutionary recluse who contemplates suicide as the ultimate expression of human licence, his actual suicide provides Peter with a foolproof alibi for Shatov's assassination. In signing, at Peter's instigation, a false confession to Shatov's murder, Kirilov signs away the whole nature of human freedom, even the freedom to take his own life which he then does. Having forfeited all moral principles, Kirilov has no resistance left to the proposal which Peter thrusts upon him. Indeed he has no conception of the betrayal of principles, for the signed statement is as meaningless as any other act in this life other than the act which ends it. In Kirilov there looms the ghost of Max Stirner, but Dostoevsky transforms human self-mastery into last-minute capitulation, so that even the act of self-annihiliation is flawed by what precedes it. 'All man did was to invent God so as to live without killing himself,' Kirilov claims. But once God has been destroyed, the pure act of suicide is impossible, for it is tainted by the life it abandons. Kirilov becomes an accomplice in the murder of his former comrade.

Dostoevsky was not so much a prophet of revolutionary terror, a claim he would have to share with many lesser writers, but of revolutionary fratricide. It is this aspect of his vision which is most remarkable, the way in which the death of Shatov touches upon everyone. The fatalistic predictions of the sedentary Shigalyov, who maps out his scheme of a modern industrial slave state, provide the future context in which the fratricide of the novel becomes an institutional reality. If Dostoevsky prophesied the Russian revolution, he also prophesied its betrayal. For the agents of the transformation of Russia into a slave state were members of a revolutionary intelligentsia who, in Nadezdha Mandelstam's words, 'have burnt everything out of themselves except the cult of power'. While Verkhovensky is fascist in his own attitudes, his manipulation of others is always in terms of an appeal to a common revolutionary ideal which his actions then betray. In other words his cultivation of power through manipulation is the forerunner of the Stalinist methods which corrupted bolshevism even before Stalin's accession to undisputed dictatorship. By appealing to common values which he himself does not hold, Peter ensures the betrayal of those values by those who do hold them or, like Shatov and Kirilov, have held them and cannot forget them even when they have no more use for them.

The generational conflict in the novel also presents us with an immense vision of the failure of bourgeois society in Russia. Stepan Verkhovensky and Mrs Stavrogin epitomise the European influence of learning, respectability and civilised manners. But there is no culture of pecuniary self-confidence, of middle-class *largesse* which can act as a stabilising factor against the events which bring the town to the brink of total de-moralisation. The episode of the fête confirms this. The guests, not all of them invited, quickly transform themselves into a rabble whose sense of social occasion is sharply at odds with their besieged hosts. Their uncivilised manner is exacerbated by Karmazinov's literary recital which, precious and ineffectual, highlights the gap between the Russian middle-classes and the liberalised westerner. The recital should not merely be seen as vicious caricature of Turgenev, but of the powerlessness of what he represents, and the ridicule to which it is so easily exposed. The recital, based upon one of Turgenev's most sentimental stories, is as artificial as the ball itself. The cultivated sensibility and civilised manners of the West take root only among the Russian aristocracy. Outside it, they fall on stony soil. The specific social vulnerability in the novel reflects that of mid-nineteenth-century Russia as a whole. The social fabric rests on economic backwardness and political repression, yet as modernisation progresses it becomes increasingly vulnerable to a disaffected intelligentsia who try to exploit the widening gap between the ruling-classes and the Russian people. Peter Verkhovensky impatiently anticipates the proletariat who do not yet exist in Russia as a major social class. But the nature of his anticipation reveals them to be merely one possible means among others to the goal of a totally destructive revolution. The familiar reversal of ends and means which later came to characterise a world-communism in which partly rule was supreme, is here suggested in the text. The idea that revolution should spring from the oppressed, or even that it should be conducted on behalf of the oppressed, is reversed. A more familiar theme is implicit in Peter's mentality. The role of the oppressed is to conduct themselves on behalf of the revolution, and the whole point of their historical emergence is to satisfy the role that is already preordained for them.

It is possible to criticise Dostoevsky for never showing the true nature of Tsarist oppression in the novel. But such a criticism has to be qualified if we look at Dostoevsky's insight into the familiar incompetence of authorities faced with a terrorist outrage. Before the assassination the revolutionaries seem to be working in an atmosphere which is remarkably liberal. Afterwards, it is Stepan Verkhovensky's house which is raided. The weak vacillating liberal, totally without influence over his son, is finally humiliated by being treated as a potential conspirator when the truth is the absolute opposite. Having tried to escape from political life altogether, he nonetheless finds himself the victim of guilt by association. While Dostoevsky clearly exaggerates the degree of openness possible for rev-olutionary activity, that openness is part of his vision of an autocratic order provisionally in abeyance, represented by the weak liberal-minded von Lembke. What the novel gives is a picture of an autocratic order in microcosm beginning to disintegrate or effectively disintegrating in advance of its time. For the modern reader this process conjures up the breakdown of Tsarism and the setting up of a provisional government, events which Dostoevsky's own death preceded by several decades. *The Devils* shows what happens when the latent divisions of a society start to become manifest. If it does not reveal the class hatred which accompanied the Russian revolution, it still hints at the cataclysmic effect such hatred could have. At the end of the novel when von Lembke had been discredited, when Verkhovensky has escaped back to Switzerland, the guidelines are set for further conspiracy, further confrontation and further terror.

While the demonic *Tendenz* pervades the novel, the real message of the text contradicts the parable on which the title is based. Dostoevsky believed that the sickness of the Russian people would enter into the westernised intelligentsia, the swine who would plunge headlong into the abyss at the exhortation of Peter Verkhovensky. Completely cured, the Russian people would return to their faith in the Orthodox Christ. What actually happens is precisely the opposite. The 'sickness' of the intellectuals infects the behaviour of the whole town, which comes close to destroying itself. In an age of political ideology, whose effects Dostoevsky realised were irreversible, the sick man no longer sits at the feet of Jesus, and Dostoevsky's vain religious hopes are lost for ever.

The polarities of Dostoevsky's work, aristocracy and democracy, Christianity and communism, are reinforced in their symbiotic relationships by the dialectic of his writing. From a conservative view, lived and felt as well as thought, he created a radical thematics, a fictive world in which the demons of his imagination achieved extraordinary actuality. The connection between the real and the imaginary is further exemplified by the figural aspects of his writing. Aristocratic promise prefigures democratic reality: Christian yearning is transformed into communist ideal. What might be gained for humanity, but actually never is, is prefigured by what has been lost and can never be redeemed. The Christian promise of Myshkin, the aristocratic promise of Stavrogin, founder on the realities of a history which outruns them and which they cannot bring themselves to follow. Those who tread the road they have abandoned are all the poorer for doing so, for they suffer that loss which cannot be otherwise. But the power of the forces of human darkness which Dostoevsky evokes, reveals another type of relationship. The failure of goodness, once it is promised, once it is viewed as the basis for a better life, makes it all the more at the mercy of the evil which shadows it. Rogozhin shadows Myshkin, Peter shadows Stavrogin just as Iago shadows Othello. Dostoevsky's fiction is no more a rejection of socialism than it is of Christianity. But it is a constant reminder that its real possibility in the modern world hangs by the slenderest of threads. The power of tragic realism to date has been in visualising what happens when the thread actually snaps.

7 Zola: *Germinal* and Tragic *Praxis*

Marxist literary critics have long been wary of Zola's work. There seems to be an abiding suspicion that his fiction has never possessed the high seriousness typical of the bourgeois novel. Yet in terms of thematics, Zola seems to have fulfilled all the necessary criteria for a perceptive and committed writer. His famous cycle of novels *Les Rougon-Macquart* attack the bourgeois hypocrisy of the Second Empire, condemn the environmental conditions of the urban masses, and highlight the misery and exploitation of the poor through generations. For his pains Zola has been branded a naturalist, and presumably would have wished it since he used the term himself. But he never imagined just how pejorative the label was to become. Lukács in particular analyses Zola's fiction from the perspective of the author's pompous theories on literature, and finds no difficulty in proving the case against him. With slightly more sophistication, Zéraffa sets Zola forth as the forefather of a type of documentary realism attempting to shame the social conscience of its readers. In other words it is the forerunner of the type of naturalist fiction prevalent in the United States which later degenerates into a socially conscious soap opera suitable to any social democracy.

The truth about Zola is more complex than either of these suggestions. In his best fiction, Zola certainly goes beyond the descriptive and journalistic techniques of which he was fond. Moreover his sense of injustice, or the injustice which his fiction suggests, is free of the cloying sentimentality of later writers. One thing is certain. His writing, in particular *Germinal*, is at its best when it contradicts his self-proclaimed scientific theories. Indeed his exaggerated claim to scientific impartiality was partly a defence against the more obvious features of his work, its sensationalism, its potential for literary and social scandal, and its overt shock tactics. Today Zola's pseudo-rationalist theory of heredity seems utterly absurd. The whole intellectual tradition of modern psychology stands ranged against it and no one takes it seriously.

Translated into literary terms, Zola's primitive rejection of the complexity of human nature has damaging consequences for his claim to realism. For in many of his novels, it is the figural aspect of realism which is vitally lacking. If we look at his defence of an early novel *Thérèse Raquin*, it is not difficult to understand why:

My aim has been to study temperaments and not characters. That is the whole point of the book. I have chosen people completely dominated by their nerves and blood, without free will, drawn into each action of their lives by the inexorable laws of their physical nature. Thérèse and Laurent are human animals, nothing more. I have endeavoured to follow these animals through the devious working of their passions, the compulsion of their instincts, and the mental unbalance resulting from a nervous crisis. . . . There is a complete absence of soul, I freely admit, since that is how it is meant to be.[1]

The passage expresses a physiological reductionism which would have impressed Bazarov of *Fathers and Sons*, but for that reason also casts doubt upon the literary enterprise itself. For what is the use of fiction if it merely illustrates a determinism in human life which a science of heredity can already reveal to us? Human action, as action, seems in Zola's terms to be almost meaningless. Its maximal purpose seems to be a primitive need-satisfaction. Writing before Freud, Zola lacked the necessary word in his ear that a theory of human instincts is compatible with the device of sublimation.

   In some novels this approach has a disastrous effect on characterisation. In *L'Assommoir*, for example, Zola conceives of his characters as average social types with abnormal physiological impulses. Thus the Marxist criticism that Zola portrays working-class people here as moral degenerates is partly valid. The main fault is that Zola gives no sense of any alternative to a life of moral degradation. Nor does he convey convincingly how the descent of his characters ensues. It is instinctually predetermined that Coupeau, Lantier and Gervaise should sink into the utmost squalor, but for that very reason the means by which they do so within the plot is arbitrary and artificial. There seems to be no good reason why Coupeau should want to marry Gervaise after Lantier has deserted her, no good reason why Lantier should come back with Coupeau's approval, and no good reason for the triple descent into drunkenness or the polygamous household which ensues. Things merely happen without reason because they are preordained to do so. Zola's dogmatic determinism creates an arbitrary plot which in turn destroys any pretension to realism. If degeneracy is inevitable, then environment counts for nothing. Zola's own explanation of the novel sounds very hollow. 'I wanted', he writes, 'to portray the inevitable downfall of a working-class family in the polluted atmosphere of our urban areas. The logical sequence to drunkenness and indolence is the loosening of family ties, the filth of promiscuity, the progressive loss of decent feelings and as the climax, shame and death.' The discovery of such a formidable social problem is due largely to Zola's journalistic flair. But with the exception of a few outstanding passages, such as the fight between the two women at the start of the novel, he fails to give the work any figural dimension.

One of the central problems for Zola is that of the point of view. A common fault among many novelists is their failure to go beyond the purely autobiographical in their work. Zola's weakness is the opposite. He cannot project himself into his fiction at all. The resulting poverty of characterisation does not result in the elimination of the point of view, but its indiscriminate interchangeability. Zola turns his gift for entering into the heads of his characters at will into a nightmare of confusion. He flits from one to another with little or no rationale. In novels like *Nana* and *The Debacle*, the fault is accentuated by his fondness for large gatherings where opportunities for such self-indulgence are unlimited. Here his talent fundamentally betrays him. In his portrait of people *en masse*, in crowd scenes, battle scenes or social gatherings, there are few writers to equal his powers of description. But his narration suffers accordingly. The characters who witness, and are part of, such scenes seldom assimilate them to their own experience. Events such as these usually appear independent of those who participate in them, because they are also witnessed by an independent observer. This is the author himself.

In his predilection for public spectacles, weddings, feasts, fairs, funerals or political meetings Zola's fiction satisfies an obvious sociological criterion—the portrayal of collective behaviour. But the experience of the event by its participants is undifferentiated. In much of his writing there is no *felt* experience. To the extent that the individual is part of the mass, he loses his individuality. Zola's naturalist anti-phenomenological dogma at times unintentionally satisfies Nietzsche's vision of mass action as the behaviour of the human herd. In *L'Assommoir*, where the narrative as well as the dialogue is written in the Parisian argot which Zola regards as the seal of authenticity, one may speak of a collective proletarian narrative in which there is only a minimal separation of story and dialogue, of language and speech. In this respect it has features similar to those Goldmann detects in *Man's Estate*, but for this reason actually invalidates Goldmann's argument. Whereas Goldmann saw the collective and problematic hero as a feature of revolutionary community, in Zola it is the feature of a passive herd, degenerate and apolitical. Literary virtues which could possibly offset these faults are also lacking. The genealogy of the Rougon-Macquart tends to constrict in any single novel its spatial and historical dimensions. In producing a 'slum' novel, a 'courtesan' novel, an 'artist' novel, a 'miners' novel, and a 'war-and-commune' novel, Zola contributed quite substantially to the naturalist cliché of the work of fiction as a slice of life. For despite his concern with heredity, most of Zola's major characters have no past, except the formal one outlined in his genealogical table and to this the author does little more than pay lip service. In truth the mythical coherence of the Rougon-Macquart is maintained by accident of birth alone.

Germinal is the most notable exception to the general shortcomings of Zola's fiction. It is the one book on which his claim to undisputed literary greatness rests, in which he transcends the inadequacies marring the Rougon-Macquart as a whole. Initially Zola set out to compensate for the absence of proletarian politics in *L'Assommoir*, but *Germinal* is more than this. It is one of the great landmarks of tragic realism which violates naturalist convention in practically every respect. The main liberating factor in Zola's preparatory work for the novel was its setting and its theme. By intending a novel of the conflict between capital and labour, and by setting it in a very close mining community of north-eastern France, Zola freed himself of the shackles of heredity and physiological constants. The deterministic aspects of the novel are the material and historical conditions under which the miners' strike at Montsou takes place. But the strike itself is an attempt to make history on the basis of those conditions. The mining environment suggests both the possibilities and the constraints of human freedom. It is also true to say that Zola intuitively detected the tragic elements for his novel in the Marxian theory of capitalist development. This is not because he was a true scholar of Marx but because, generally, he was sensitive to the most socially and intellectually significant currents of his time. His appreciation of Marx was largely mediated by secondary socialist accounts of the time from writers like Yves Guyot, Emile Laveleye and Paul Leroy-Beaulieu, all of whom provided him with invaluable historical material. But the fact remained that Zola had uncovered an economic foundation for his tragic realism. The working people of Montsou were not the victims of evil employers but of the system to which employer and worker alike were subject, and which imprisoned them both in a trap of its own making. The strike is a tragic and heroic attempt to break out of the trap of history. But it is an attempt which is doomed to fail. Zola alighted upon an idea which was to become the dominant literary impulse of the novel—that class struggles within a relatively stable capitalist society are inconclusive and can have tragic consequences for those who participate in them. It is similar in many ways to the tragedy of premature revolution which Marx detects in Ferdinand Lassalle's drama *Franz von Sickungen*. It is significantly different by virtue of the fact that it is consciously derived from Marx's theory itself.

Henry James has suggested that the experience necessary for writing fiction can be gained from as little as a momentary glimpse at a group of people through an open door. Zola's method is exactly the opposite. Stranded in a kind of no-man's-land between journalism and sociology, he displays a voracious appetite for collecting as much raw data as he possibly can. But whether attained through conversations, interviews, or technical treatises, the cumulative details of mining are merely the point of departure for the imaginative act which transposes them into literature. While Zola's first description of the descent of the mine could not be accomplished without expert knowledge of the procedures involved, it is the vision of the descent into a subterranean darkness which is the important factor in the writing. Zola's method is similar to that of Melville in *Moly Dick*. Just as the accumulation of details about whaling heightens the tension surrounding the final encounter between Ahab and the white whale, so the varied descriptions of different aspects of the mine are the foundations upon which the portrayal of the final disaster is erected. Zola's technical and sociological accuracy does not preclude the imaginative endeavour of the artist. For the novel never aspires to being faithful documentary description. The strike and the events which follow from it are part of a composite portrait of various agitations within the mining communities of north-east France. Specifically, Zola combines in his novel two separate historical events within two different communities. Many of the incidents of the strike, including the massacre, are based on a strike at Aubin in 1869, while the duration of the strike is based upon a general strike at Anzin, the very area which Zola was at that time studying for purposes of his novel.[2]

The action at Montsou is created out of a series of historical incidents but at the same time out of a contemporary incident as well. Thus Zola's realism is only documentary up to a certain point. For he had to combine two separate purposes, firstly to write a novel about the Second Empire but also to arouse his readers' feelings about mining conditions which existed at the time of writing in 1884. Deliberately anachronistic at times, *Germinal* is both a historical *and* a contemporary novel. The reader could envisage it, not only as novel of the Second Empire but as a work concerned with the existing state of affairs in the mid-eighties. Zola draws both on works such as that of Simonin which depict mining conditions in the 1860s but equally on his own investigation of the Anzin mines. Fact remains the starting-point for fiction. What distinguishes Zola from other modern realists in this respect is the degree of factual material which he accumulated. In his case it is quite clear that documentary evidence is not a constraint upon his literary imagination but, on the contrary, its most important catalyst.

The problems caused by the point of view, which in some of his other novels are insuperable, are dealt with here by the device of hero as outsider. Étienne Lantier comes to the mining community to find work there, but ends up as the miners' leader. The development of the novel, and Lantier's fate, is concerned with his increasing participation in a life to which he was initially external. The detailed descriptions of mining life in the first part of the novel, both in the pit and the Maheu household, only make sense as events witnessed by a newcomer. To him they are fresh, strange and unjust and seen through Lantier's eyes the life of the community is defamiliarised. What the mining families are accustomed to, what over years and generations they have taken for granted, are procedures which Lantier treats with revulsion and which he desires to change. The reader shares with him the process of revelation, the 'opening of his eyes' to the real social conditions of the miners. But placed in the situation, Lantier then becomes one of them, participating to the full in the life which he views with a critical eye. What Lantier brings to the situation is not his psychological past but his political past, his previous work for the International. In this way the complexity of his character does not derive from his prior psychological development, of which we know nothing, but from his response to a series of complex events which take place with alarming swiftness. Despite Zola's concern with heredity which prompts him to give Étienne a drink problem and lack of self-control, the hero's personality actually develops in the course of the novel itself. For Lantier has to endure a cruel political *rite de passage* in which all his mental and physical capacities are stretched to the limit. It is the experience of Montsou, not the experience of childhood, which leaves an indelible mark upon Lantier's personality.

Significantly, the mining community is fundamentally conservative in its attitude towards its living and working conditions, trying desperately to hold on to, or literally conserve, the little that it possesses. At the level of poverty at which the Maheus live, this becomes an obsession. The effective lowering of wage rates which arises from changes in payment in the timbering system is a wrench to ingrained habit simply because it makes subsistence that much more difficult. It is thus the company which in effect disrupts the community before the reverse, in the form of a general strike, actually takes place. While Étienne acts on principle, the miners respond to him initially out of a sense of desperation, and only later, once the momentum of discontent is under way, do his principles transform themselves into promises in which they can fervently believe. Zola traces in completely human terms the emergence and the overreaching of working-class consciousness. What interests him is not the abstract formula of solidarity but the human dilemmas which are contained within it. Where Zola, in his treatment of poverty and industrial life, is superior to the affirmative realism of the Victorian novel is in his perspective on force of circumstance. Whereas Dickens, Eliot and Gaskell all imagined that class reconciliation was possible through the moral reform of the individual, and through the elimination of callousness towards suffering, Zola's tragic vision portrays just how marginal the impact of the good intention and the change of heart can be. The evils of the economic system generate circumstances which betray the good intentions and break the spirit of all those implicated in the struggle. The result is a catastrophe which cannot be blamed upon anyone in particular, though, at crucial stages, the way to disaster is paved by specific human failings. The employers, managers and engineers—and their families—can actually change little by personal kindness. Such kindness involves little sacrifice since they are materially protected from the worst consequences of the strike anyway. The result is that the failing to live up to specific values or moral standards is only significant among the miners themselves. For they alone are put to the test of gross material deprivation and suffering. Morality, not in itself bourgeois, is appropriated by Zola's bourgeoisie since they alone are in a position to abide by its standards. For that very reason it is in constant danger of becoming meaningless.

The limits of moral sensibility are shown in the case of the Grégoires. Caring employers who give their miners free lodging and fuel, they are also prepared to make occasional gestures of charity. But as the begging visit of Maheude shows, where charity endangers the principle of wage-calculation it is no longer permissible. In the adverse economic conditions affecting the mining companies at the time, suffering springs from financial necessity. Étienne puts it to Hennebeau that 'if the company wants to economise, it acts very badly in economising only on men'. But the manager can truthfully reply: 'Nearly half the mining companies in France are bankrupt. Besides it is stupid to accuse those who succeed of cruelty.'

Zola's portrayal of the capitalist families is rather sparse, and lacks the complexity, and the ambivalence, necessary to contrast them with the miners whose brutal simplicity is sorely tested by the demands of the strike. The flat unidimensional psychology of Zola which falls down badly for example in the infidelity of Madame Hennebeau with Négrel is actually suited to the dialectic of strike action where everything is at stake. *Germinal* must be one of the few major novels where the personal and sexual relationship do not provide an infrastructure for the novel as a whole; where, for example, the rivalry between Étienne and Chaval for Catherine is an offshoot of the conflict, rather than one of its sources. The truth is that Zola was ill at ease with personal relationships founded on sexuality, for their psychological dimensions were beyond him. *Germinal* succeeds where his other novels fail, because the priority of collective action frees it from the necessity of a sexual infrastructure. Where he attempts to fuse politics and sex, by making Chaval a blackleg as well as a blackguard, the effect is stereotyped and melodramatic, one of the weak links in the novel.

The crucial psychological element in the novel is that of collective *praxis*. The strike is not only a test of endurance but also the basis for the development of the miners' class consciousness. For what continues to motivate the strikers in the face of the company's intransigence to their demands is the feeling of fighting for more general and more abstract principles of justice. This involves a choice between the alternative strategies and alternative ends offered them by Étienne and Rasseneur, a choice between incompatible beliefs and promises which characterised fundamental differences within European socialism at that time. The contrast between Étienne and Rasseneur is not merely ideological, however. It also reveals a difference in political psychology which complements their difference of opinion. Etienne brings with him a freshness and determination lacking in the community, while Rasseneur has already suffered defeat and disillusion over a previous strike resulting in his expulsion from the mine. Étienne is bold and utopian; Rasseneur cautious and pragmatic. Embittered by the new wage system, angered by the mine disaster which nearly kills Jeanlin, it is Étienne's approach which sways the community. In the meeting at Bon Joyeux, they pledge themselves to join the International before the police break up the meeting. The ensuing strike is not only a test of their resilience but of their political consistency. It is a test of whether the community can maintain the severe discipline and accept the drastic sacrifices which the strike entails. Rasseneur's argument for caution is in part a plea to the meeting not to place themselves in a position where they might fail in their objectives and suffer in the process. But he is shouted down. The collective feeling of injustice is so strong that it can only find its objective correlative in the most militant strike action.

Étienne's early utopianism, which had seemed somewhat out of place, now becomes totally appropriate. His vision of socialism had seemed to the Maheus at first to be little more than a fairy tale. But in the clearing of the forest at Plan-des-Dames, 'the dazzling fairy vision' of a 'kingdom of equality and brotherhood' becomes more concrete, more compelling and more precise:

> But already Étienne was speaking again, in a different voice. He was no longer the secretary of an Association, but a leader, an apostle bringing the gospel of truth. Were there any cowards among them who would break their word? Why, they would have suffered for a whole month in vain and go back to the pits hanging their heads, back once again to face the never-ending agony! Wouldn't it be better to die at once in an attempt to destroy the tyranny of capital starving the workers? Wasn't it a stupid game that they had had quite enough of, this business of always submitting under the lash of hunger until it came to the point when once again hunger drove even the meekest of them to revolt? He showed how the miners were exploited and were the only ones to suffer from these disastrous crises, reduced to starvation whenever the exigencies of competition brought down prices. No! the timbering scale was unacceptable, it was only a disguised economy, they meant to rob each man of one hour of the working day. This time it had gone too far, and the time was coming for the downtrodden worms to turn and see justice done.
>
> He paused with arms outstretched. The word justice shook the crowd and a burst of applause passed over it like the rustle of dry leaves. Voices shouted:
>
> 'Justice! it's high time. . . . Justice!'
>
> . . . 'The wage system is a new form of slavery', he went on in a still more ringing voice. 'The mine should belong to the miner, like the sea to the fisherman and the earth to the peasant. . . . Do you understand? The mine is yours—yours, for you have all paid for it with a hundred years of blood and misery!'[3]

The tragedy is that the promise is never fulfilled and its failure is interpreted as a betrayal. As the strike prolongs their misery, the miners come to feel betrayed by Étienne, just as Étienne comes to feel betrayed by them. As a leader he cannot control the violence of the mob, which ends in the brutal death and castration of Maigret. As followers, they feel betrayed by his failure to gain the concessions he had promised them. After the massacre of the striking miners by soldiers guarding the other mines, their venom is deflected away from their employers towards him as the leader who failed them. Lantier returns in kind the contempt the community feels for him, almost as if their revolutionary hopes had never existed.

Inside the bar Étienne felt sick and his heart was full of bitterness. He remembered Rasseneur's prophecy in the forest when he had warned him about the ingratitude of the mob. What stupid brutality! how abominable to forget all he had done for them! They were like a blind force constantly feeding on itself. But underlying his indignation at these stupid brutes who were wrecking their own cause was chagrin at his own collapse and the tragic end of his own ambition. So it was all over already! He recalled how under the beech trees he had heard three thousand hearts beating in time with his own. On that night he had grasped popularity with both hands, these people had belonged to him and he knew he was their master. At that time he had been drunk with grandiose visions: Montsou at his feet, Paris beyond, returned to Parliament perhaps, blasting the bourgeoisie with his oratory, the first speech made in Parliament by a working man. All over now! This was the awakening, to find himself miserable and ostracised—his own people had driven him off with brickbats.[4]

The people betray themselves by degenerating under conditions of hunger and despair into an aimless brutal mob, but Étienne in turn betrays them, and himself, with his grandiose ambition. Zola does not shirk from portraying the disaffection between leader and followers nor from portraying the irrational violence which stems from extreme situations. Indeed the collective undertaking of the strike actually erodes the solidarity of the community which it initially cemented. The children, free of parental control, turn into vandals and live wild like animals. The women, unable to get the food they need for their families, act hysterically in the forefront of the rioting, attacking Cécile Grégoire and castrating Maigrat after his fatal fall from the roof. Éitienne's feelings of horror and revulsion are ambivalent. He hates to see the settlement betraying itself but also feels the ebbing of his own power over them. He is as corrupted by the power of leadership as they are by the power of violence. Socialist fulfillment, in the figural sense, is denied to all of them. Lantier is blamed for the ensuing massacre by soldiers goaded beyond endurance by the desperate strikers. But it was a confrontation which he at first had lamely tried to prevent. When finally attacked by those who had been his followers, he realises the consequences of the type of leadership he had dreamed of so ambitiously. The leader who exploits the success of his own policy must suffer the unpopularity of its failure. The initial distance between Lantier as a political outsider and the miners as an uneducated apolitical community is never finally broken down. Lantier had gambled everything only to lose. When Rasseneur repeats to the crowd the advice for which he had once been shouted down, that 'violence has never succeeded', he is cheered with enthusiasm.

The strike is not a total failure because for the owner of the Vandame concession, Deneulin, it was a pyrrhic victory. As a small capitalist he is its sole casuality, forced through financial ruin to sell his concession to the Montsou company. The strike had hit most the enemy that mattered least, and the economic recovery which ensues 'sounded the knell of small private enterpirse, of proprietors soon doomed to disappear, devoured piecemeal by the insatiable maw of capital, lost in the rising tide of great combines'. Yet this small crumb of comfort cannot atone for the suffering which the community has undergone. Zola's tragic vision stems from the realisation that the advance of the working-classes only came about in the long term through actions whose benefit was not reaped by those who committed them but future generations who had not participated in them. Lantier has to convince the settlement that their own circumstances will improve through their action, a conviction which proves unjustified. Yet were it not for this type of burning conviction, long-term gains would never be achieved. Every strike which has to be suppressed by soldiers, every riot which ends in massacre, is an erosion of the powers of the state acting in the interests of the employers. What subjectively means loss, suffering and betrayal to Étienne and his followers has an indiscernible effect which can only be believed in, not felt. The movement fails by deluding itself about the ease with which the mine can be taken over by the workers and by failing to adopt the ethic of self-sacrifice. But in the immediate anger which sparks off the agitation, the expounding of such an ethic would have produced no response. What the situation requires is utopian promises even if they cannot be attained.

This is the core of Zola's tragic realism, and one which sets him apart from the conservatism of other great novelists. His creative vision went straight to the heart of the dilemma of socialist *praxis*. As a writer, it put him in a position of grand isolation. Many conservative novelists such as Conrad and Mann were more adept at portraying the old order in the process of disintegration than the new order in the process of germination. Many socialist novelists were either utilitarian or romantic in their portrayal of working-class revolt, ignoring the very dilemma which Zola had illuminated, or even denying that such a dilemma existed. Zola neither glorified nor sentimentalised the collective problematic hero of his novel. Instead he was concerned with the high standards which authentic socialist values demand of the individual personality, and where those values are not met, where they are betrayed, the novel expresses the tragic pity of that failure.

Unfortunately, Zola's tragic vision, and its realism, are flawed by the ending of the novel. Zola transformed a realistic portrayal of natural disaster and collective violence into a Gothic horror story. The first blot on his literary copybook is Bonnemort's strangling of Cécile. What is even less convincing than the act of murder is the Grégoire visit to the settlement after all the troubles which caused their daughter's fatal end. But even worse is to follow. While Zola's portrayal of socialism and working-class life are excellent, the figure of Souveraine, the anarchist, is a disastrous failure. The disparity between his role in the community and his nihilistic beliefs is too great ever to be resolved. As an engineman at the pithead, he has the cosmopolitan background of a Russian anarchist forced to flee after an attempted assassination of the Tsar. His position in a small French mining village, after a previous life which would have flattered even Bakunin, is anomalous. His decision to stay at work and play no part in the strike is even more so. Zola artificially imported into a very local context the grandiose features of cosmopolitan rootlessness which characterised many Russian anarchists. Souveraine in this sense is a failed transplant and his final destruction of the mine after months of passivity has a total lack of conviction about it. It violates the reader's sense of what is possible even in a novel which is clearly concerned with the most extreme forms of political violence. In graphically describing the collapse of Le Voreux after Souveraine's sabotage, Zola abandons the disciplined form of his earlier writing for a sensationalist melodrama which heaps effect upon effect.

This is even more apparent in his treatment of passion. The triangular affair of Catherine and her two suitors is resolved in the flooded cavern of the mine where Zola attempts to give it a significance it clearly lacked above ground. Zola abdicates realism by making the destroyed mine a symbol of life itself. The relationship of Étienne and Catherine is finally consummated in the unlikeliest of circumstances, on the verge of exhaustion and death. It constitutes not only a resort to pretentious symbolism but a retreat from the portrayal of erotic passion within the social context of the novel. Thus they celebrate 'their wedding night, at the bottom of this tomb, on this bed of mud' loving each other 'in despair of everything, even death'. Above ground the only sexuality which Zola portrayed was the sexuality he had witnessed at first hand—the copulation of adolescents among the mine cuttings. The only way Zola could attempt to convey the uniqueness of passion was to give it a unique setting, but since the setting is so ridiculous the attempt most clearly fails.

The final apocalyptic destruction of Le Voreux finds its echo in the ending of *The Debacle*. The burning down of Paris as the Commune is finally defeated is the most convincing section of an unconvincing novel. From it one retains a feeling of primeval horror at the total destructiveness attendant on the failure of socialism. In *Germinal* perhaps, Zola intended to show something of the same disastrous process embodied in the sinister person of Souveraine. But whereas the description of the last days of the Commune is horrifyingly realistic, the destruction of Le Voreux enters the realm of fantasy. The mine, as well as being a crude symbol of hell on earth, becomes an infernal subterranean machine more suitable to science fiction. Despite this, however, the compelling realism of the miners' strike lives on in the memory. Zola was probably the first and quite possibly the last of the modern realists to portray the real relationships of production in a capitalist society from the viewpoint of the exploited, and not only that, but to convey the hope and the promise embodied in their doomed heroic revolt against it. Without recourse to complex individual psychology, failing in his quest to portray his hero's erotic passion, he nonetheless added new dimensions to the figural realism of the modern novel through his portrayal of collective action. It is an achievement which has rarely been repeated.

8 Conrad: the New Meaning of Tragic Irony

It was probably all to the good of literature that Conrad was an exiled seafaring Pole who wished to become an English gentleman. His travels made him a roving witness of the British Empire at its height. But he bore witness as an outsider and his literary portraits have an irony foreign to most natives of the island he so revered. His immensely subtle eye recorded the limits of Empire. For the masters of civilisation, his work points in only one direction, the very direction they were loathe to go. That direction was downward. Conrad's work is subversive in spite of itself. For it creates an alternative fiction to the myth of Empire.

His political fiction, however, goes beyond the mere exploration of the colonial impulse. But generalisation about its nature is difficult. One is tempted to suggest that Conrad's greatest work, *Nostromo* and *Heart of Darkness*, lies in an intermediate zone between land and sea, where the expanse of water is small but its significance immense, where the width of a narrowing river or the distance from port of the islands of the Archipelago are a matter of life and death. Certainly in *Under Western Eyes*, where the sea is abandoned for a landlocked country, some of his worst writing occurs, almost as if distance from reality was identical to distance from the sea. *The Secret Agent*, however, completely invalidates this supposition. It is one of the very few great novels of tragic realism to be set entirely in a Western city. And it is London itself which is one of the constituent elements of the tragedy.

Conrad's political fiction inevitably faces comparison with that of Dostoevsky. This was not merely because of the similarity of theme but also because Conrad's writing was a direct response to the major works of the Russian. In *Under Western Eyes* he tried to restore a sense of 'the lawlessness of autocracy' he mistakenly thought to be absent from Dostoevsky's work. And Stevie Verloc in *The Secret Agent* is intended to pay the real price for political innocence in an age of terror, a fate Conrad thought the Russian writer had sidestepped in the creation of his own saintly heroes. But one area where Conrad cannot rival Dostoevsky is in his portrait of revolutionaries. Where they are not loosely and mushily drawn, like Sophia Antonovna, they veer towards caricature, like Karl Yundt, Ossipon or Michaelis. The only exception to this consistent defect is Haldin, in the first part of *Under Western Eyes*.

Why is this so? A comparison of Haldin's situation with that of the anarchists in *The Secret Agent* is very instructive. Haldin is a political assassin on the run in his own country. The revolutionaries of London and Geneva are *exiles*, individuals cut off from the system of injustice which has nourished their revolutionary will. While Haldin is a subject for the tragic, Conrad's exiles are the object of satire or ineffectual melodrama. But while despising the revolutionary exiles of Europe, it is probably true that Conrad was attracted by their fate because it was similar to his own. He, too, had left Poland partly because of revolutionary connections within his family. He, too, felt some cultural alienation in his life in Britain. But the issue is even more complex. Conrad despised the revolutionaries for two totally opposed reasons. Like Dostoevsky, he saw them as possessed, deluded, insane. And he clearly saw the incompatibility of the revolutionary temperament with his own gift for irony. 'Remember', Sophia Antonovna tells Razumov in *Under Western Eyes*, 'that women, children, revolutionists hate irony which is the negation of all saving instincts, of all faith, of all devotion, of all action.' But Conrad was also contemptuous of the revolutionary exiles for the very opposite reason. They had become political fossils, living in the past. Now, like fish out of water, their energy had dried up, and they deluded themselves with memories of former days. Conrad's irony is dependent upon the device of exile, and on justaposing the conditions of exile with a revolutionary will which has been unwittingly abandoned by the exiles themselves. Faced with a real revolutionary situation, as in *Nostromo*, Conrad's irony transforms itself from satire into tragedy.

The defects of Conrad's portrayal of revolutionary exile are not as great, however, as many critics have suggested. For, by and large, the revolutionaries are the minor characters in his novels. Conrad's real gift is for showing how bystanders and ordinary people, the non-committed, are caught up in revolutionary events against their own will. Into each of his three political novels can be read a literary parable of the Tree of Knowledge in which, however, the fated apple is thrust straight into the victim's mouth. Just as Razumov has to react to the presence of a revolutionary assassin in his room, Nostromo has to come to terms with his cargo of silver and Winnie Verloc respond to the news of her brother's horrifying death. The premise of their life hitherto has been irreversibly undermined. Their fate must alter. For Nostromo, for Decoud, for Winnie and Stevie Verloc it does alter. They embark upon the voyage of discovery characteristic of figural realism, and their voyage ends in tragedy. Human self-fulfillment is revealed on the road to death.

Razumov, by contrast, merely goes through the motions of embarking upon this voyage. By accepting the role Mikulin offers him as a double-agent, his heroic stature is compromised from the very beginning. It merely confirms the amorality of the act of betrayal. Since Conrad's novel was such a direct response to Dostoevsky, it is interesting to compare

Dostoevsky's answer to the moral dilemma of informing with Conrad's fictionalisation of it. Near the end of his life when his political opinions were at their most reactionary, the Russian author had asked himself whether he could in all conscience report an assassin or terrorist to the authorities upon witnessing their outrage. He decided he could not. Razumov has no such scruples. He is resentful of Haldin's intrusion, not because he hates his politics, but because the assassin has destroyed his peace of mind and threatened his future career. When Haldin tells him of the assassination Razumov's response is spontaneous and explicit:

> Razumov kept down a cry of dismay. The sentiment of his life being utterly ruined by this contact with such a crime expressed itself quaintly by a sort of half-derisive mental exclamation, 'There goes my silver medal!'[1]

Conrad had already used the device of the double-agent in *The Secret Agent*. But Verloc, indolent and amoral, is really the villain of the story. Here Conrad is trying to attempt the opposite. He wants to make his double-agent the hero. But although Razumin is a problematic character who does have doubts about each moral compromise he makes, he is little more than the passive instrument of the Russian authorities. While he is never as brutal or dehumanised as Verloc, he is under orders just as much as Verloc is controlled by the Russian ambassador. The real hero of the novel is Haldin but his heroism is suppressed by the author in favour of the man who betrays him. Yet even in the second half of the novel in Geneva, Haldin's presence is still felt. Razumov's status amongst the revolutionaries rests on him being a surrogate version of the real hero. The ghost of Haldin pervades the becalmed narrative of events seen 'under Western eyes'. It is a reminder of the heroism Razumov has already betrayed. When discovered by the revolutionaries to be a Tsarist agent, his punishment at the end is not purely political. It seems to be symbolic of the author's failure to invent a genuine hero, a kind of political chastisement which has a literary parallel in the writing of the text itself. Razumov is cruelly deafened by Nikita, one feels, not merely because he was a spy but also because he never became a hero, because in the political context in which his author placed him, such a status was impossible. The fate of Razumov is not to find himself but to be found out—as a fraud.

In Razumov's duplicity we find a total denial of the life-by-value. This was the very opposite of what Conrad intended. He wished to give his hero the compromising temper of the western liberal but at the same time suggest in him elements of a mystic Slavophile spirit, of the quintessence of Holy Russia. But Dostoevsky had already shown such an unlikely combination to be impossible. Such values were irreconcilable, and Razumov could not bring himself to live by either of them. His life in Geneva is a vacuum of deceit shadowed by Haldin's ghost. It totally undermines the hollow sentiments placed in the mouth of Natalie Haldin towards the end of the novel:

> I believe that the future will be merciful to us. Revolutionist and reactionary, victim and executioner, betrayer and betrayed, they shall be pitied together when the light breaks on our black sky at last. Pitied and forgotten; for without that there can be no union and no love.[2]

The novel shows no evidence of unity or compassion. In fact it testifies to manipulation, ruthlessness and duplicity. In this respect Haldin's betrayal is significant, for it can be read as a betrayal of the novel itself. Deprived of all idealism, of all values, the novel must proceed without the life-by-value terminated with Haldin's death. The vapid Anglo-Saxon merely confirms this by narrating a story devoid of significance. Seen under Western eyes, the events preceding the Russian revolution have very little resonance.

It is significant that in this novel, Conrad's irony is very subdued. Where the political issues are cut and dried, there is little opportunity or point. But in his other novels, irony is not merely the dynamic element in Conrad's narrative. It is also the basis of his tragic vision. The tragic rests upon the ironic, since the fate of the hero is embedded in events actually being the opposite of what they seem. Here, as a master of realism, Conrad gives a new meaning to tragic irony. It is not merely an artistic device, as in drama, to let the audience know what the hero cannot see. The fusion of the ironic and the tragic arises from the author's feeling for a specific social reality. In Conrad's novels the complex dialectic of appearance and reality is invariably social. By unmasking appearances, his tragic hero discovers a social or political reality to which he was previously blind. The irony becomes tragic because the process of recognition results in the hero's damnation.

This can be seen very clearly in the fate of Stevie Verloc. Like Razumov, the character of Stevie was Conrad's artistic response to the inner anxiety Dostoevsky's work had caused him. More important than the similarities of Stevie and Prince Myshkin is the difference between them. Myshkin is the child-like adult trying ineffectually to preach and practise sainthood in a world grown indifferent to it. Stevie is a precocious child responding to the ideas of an adult world he can never control nor fully understand. Myshkin has his own ethereal morality but Stevie must copy the dubious morals of others—of Verloc and his foreign friends. And he takes seriously the values they have reduced to tired polemic and nostalgic fantasy. His soul is the seismograph of fading anarchist dreams. They live on in the imagination of a boy who does not fully understand them. The frenzied circles he draws in accompaniment to extremist conversations in the next room are symptomatic of a madness whose moral sensitivity is not shared by the men plotting to blow up the meridian line at Greenwich. In Stevie's moral rage, the violent anger which afflicts him when he sees the cabman beating the horse, in his realisation that the choice of a lesser evil does not lead to goodness, we see an extraordinary phenomenon. It is the revaluation of values which the anarchists themselves have destroyed, but, at the same time, a revaluation which results in Stevie's own conversion to terrorism, and his grotesque death. He is both a defenceless child coerced into committing a terrorist outrage and a person whose craving for moral purity leads him in exactly the same direction. Conrad's irony here is devastatingly effective. The terrorist act the anarchists would never commit is carried out by the double-agent contemptuous of all of them and a child who takes their pronouncements at their face value.

Stevie's fate, the by now familiar terrorist fate of being blown up by his own bomb, is tragic without being heroic. But the heroic element in the novel is actually inseparable from his fate to which it is a spontaneous response. It lies in Winnie Verloc's murder of her husband. Unlike Stevie, whose distraught mind cannot fail to question all moral values it collides with, Winnie's subservience to the conventional values of Victorian marriage is impeccable. In exchange for security and domestic stability, she is compliant, uncomplaining and refrains from showing any curiosity about the strange meetings except in connection with her anxiety over her brother. But Stevie's death destroys in an instant the whole convention on which her married life is based. For Verloc, the cold alien protector for whom she feels nothing, has destroyed the one person that she cherished. Even after she has stabbed him to death, the depth of her scorn allows no remorse:

> Her mental state was tinged by an austere contempt for that man who had let himself be killed so easily. He had been the master of a house, the husband of a woman, and the murderer of her Stevie. And now he was of no account in every respect. He was of less practical account than the clothing on his body, than his overcoat, his boots—than that hat lying on the floor. He was nothing.[3]

The murder is not only an act of revenge. It is a partial liberation, and a genuine act of passion of woman who has lived a largely passionless life. But Winnie Verloc's freedom is transient. It plunges her into a world without any sort of values at all. The alternative to the world of marriage, domestic security and male domination is anomie and chaos. Starting to feel horrified by the deed she has committed, Winnie once again seeks the security and protection she has relinquished. Her predicament is tragic, not only because of what she has done, but how she reflects upon her deed. Conrad's interlocking of the ironic and the tragic reveals itself in the consequent passage where he shows the limits of her vision and her courage. Desperately she tries to foist herself upon the unsuspecting Ossipon, who does not realise she has murdered Verloc and accepts her for his own selfish purposes. But her murder now stands between her and the traditional submissive role of her sex to which she tries to restore herself. Ossipon promises to take her to Europe but on discovering Verloc's body, immediately thinks of how he can desert her. When he does, by jumping from the train at Victoria Station, she has nothing left to enable her to cling to life.

Her subsequent suicide, the 'act of madness and despair', is an ironic gloss upon the anarchist folly which permeates the book from beginning to end. After Ossipon has read of Winnie's death, the Professor tells him that 'madness and despair are a force' in a world which is limp and mediocre. Yet it is not the anarchists, only Stevie and Winnie, who actually experience it. In the original Greenwich incident it was the fate of the brother and sister which had inspired Conrad to write his novel in the first place. Not the outrage itself, but the fact, learnt unexpectedly from a friend, that the bomber blown to pieces was half-mad and his sister later committed suicide.[4] That was the inspiration which drew the novel out of a projected short satire of anarchism. Conrad's tragic heroes are the unpolitical innocents, the anonymous oppressed, living in the underbelly of the great metropolis. Only as the victims of the fruitless end-game taking place between anarchists, police and double-agents do they come to life.

The predicament of Winnie and Stevie cannot be isolated from Conrad's infernal vision of the city in which they live. As the ironic ending of *Heart of Darkness* makes clear, London is the *Citta Dolente*, the city of desolation, which in Dante constitutes the sixth circle of hell. Winnie and Stevie live in the same city of the dead as Kurtz's Intended, and are its true victims. The anarchist plot, seen conservatively by Conrad as the cause of their suffering, is no more than its catalyst. Their predicament is preformed. By contrast the comic features of the political conspiracy arise from its artificial nature. It is the meaningless political artefact which alone can rise above the city of desolation Conrad had discovered in his 'solitary and nocturnal walks'. The novel in fact reverses the whole convention of Western literature prior to the rise of the novel. It is the upper classes who provide the basis for satire, the underclass which provides the basis for tragedy. Each anarchist plotter has his necessary tie with the Establishment, Verloc with the Russian First Secretary, the Professor with Inspector Heat, Michaelis with his distinguished lady patroness, but Winnie and Stevie have connections with no-one. The failure of anarchism in the *Secret Agent* is a function of its relationship to diverse aspects of the Establishment, a failure which is comic, and genuinely comic, rather than tragic. The tragedy of anarchism, whether or not Conrad intended to see it in this light, lies in its complacent betrayal of the anonymous and the desolate who have no voice to express their suffering and no-one to whom they can express it. It is the class underlings who bear the tragic burden of the clashes within modern history.

The same is true of Nostromo. While never as anonymous as Winnie and Stevie Verloc, he is forced to respond to a conflict whose source is both exterior and superior to his own life, but which he then internalises and all but masters. Yet *Nostromo* is not just the story of Nostromo. Its range and vision are remarkable in their magnitude, far greater, as Conrad knew, than anything attempted in *The Secret Agent*. It has the same totalising perspective upon society in which the great novelists rival the great social theorists. But since the predominant concern of the novelist is with the values of a society and the social theorist with its material conditions, Conrad confronts history in a way which is different from Marx or Weber, Comte or Spencer. He confronts history as myth without, at the same time, neglecting the material conditions contributing to the mythology. The whole novel and the way it is written, the shifts in time perspective, the chronological looping, the switching of the point of view, bring to perfect fruition this process of history transforming itself into myth. Strategically placed at the beginning and the end of the story, Captain Mitchell's glowing eulogy of Nostromo's role in the founding of the Occidental Republic is the mythical boundary within which the real and forgotten history of the event is related. But it is not until the end, until the reader returns to the beginning with the truth which he initially lacked, that he realises the victors have retold the history of the events which almost brought their ruin.

Steadfast and myopic to the last, Mitchell's praise for Nostromo reveals the blindness necessary to myth. For 'our man Nostromo' had held his masters in splendid contempt during that very period when his actions had saved them. If Mitchell treats him like a hero suitable to be played in a Hollywood epic by John Wayne, then it must be added that he is a Latin John Wayne, a servant of superior interests, superior people and a superior Anglo-Saxon race. As a 'man of the people' his charisma has a distinctly ethnic tinge. It is charisma among his own people, not among those he serves. The ethnic and class distinctions are interwoven. Apolitical, outside the indigenous élite, indifferent to privilege, Nostromo can never become the social equal of the Anglo-Saxon imperialists. He remains 'a universal factotum—a prodigy of efficiency in his own sphere of life'. His action in dispersing the rebellious mob in Sulaco, in Mitchell's eyes a heroic act, would earn him a more pejorative epithet from other quarters—lackey of the counter-revolution.

In truth, the man whose resolute action helps to make history is also history's victim. For the circumstances under which he is called to act are circumstances outside his personal control. Whose control, then, are they not outside of? The one man in the novel whose decisions are more far-reaching than that of any other is Charles Gould, owner of the San Tomé silver mine, the concession inherited from his father who had let it go to ruin. A solitary Englishman among the Spanish élite with whom he is on amicable terms, Gould's vision of progress permeates the political and economic fabric of Costaguana. For the mine is intended to be both reality and symbol of the new success of a country stricken by countless years of misrule. The key to Gould's crusade is the silver itself. Decorative, often aesthetic, silver is nonetheless as intrinsically worthless as it is financially invaluable. As an incorruptible metal it takes on a value in people's minds which it does not have in benefiting their material lives. To use more abstract Marxian terms, its exchange-value is out of all proportion to its use-value. Gould does not exactly worship silver the way that frenzied gold-diggers worshipped gold. But he idealises the production of an abstract material wealth he himself owns. His philanthropic aspirations are not based purely upon the idea of a token redistribution of wealth but on the idea that a certain frame of mind and a certain way of life beneficial to all can result from people's acceptance of it as the source of their own well-being. He sees his moral materialism as being simultaneously a series of actions and a frame of meaning in which the truth of the mine is a truth which men can hold as self-evident. Such a 'truth' accords with 'his voiceless attitude towards the world of material things'. It is the alternative to the previous bloodstained history of the mine when 'whole tribes of Indians had perished in its exploitation'. His father's death had finally decided him. 'The mine had been the cause of an absurd moral disaster; its working must be made a serious and moral success.'

Gould's attempted atonement for his father's mistakes is also the beginnings of a working relationship between economic progress and enlightened parliamentarianism. In that dovetailing pluralist relationship typical of capitalist democracies the confidence of the politicians is reflected in the buoyancy of the economy and in turn their open admiration for the man whose success they regard as the cause of their own. Yet Conrad's vision takes us back yet another stage to where the extraction of a vital source of capital is itself dependent initially on capital which cannot be obtained from a willing government. The regression of the narrative backward through time, from Nostromo to Gould and then from Gould to Holroyd, is the apposite stylistic for the search for the historical causes of the events transforming Nostromo into a hero. The search for reality behind appearance is a backward search, and Conrad's gift for distancing himself from events through shift in perspective is admirably suited to his task.

Holroyd, the rich Christian industrialist in San Francisco, possesses economic interests vast enough for him to regard the financing of the San Tomé mine as his 'great man's caprice'. He epitomises two things, the remote control of capital in its imperialist setting, and the growing supremacy of American over British imperialism in the twentieth century. Conrad's prophetic vision of imperialism is as explosive as Dostoevsky's prophetic vision of revolution. Holroyd has an unashamed vision of world-domination in which, by comparison, Costaguana 'is the bottomless pit of ten percent loans and other fool investments'. In his speech is contained a remarkable revelation of the sequel to the decline of the British Empire, and an almost indolent sense of historical necessity:

European capital has been flung into Costaguana with both hands for years. We in this country know just about enough to keep indoors when it rains. We can sit and watch. Of course some day we shall step in. We are bound to. But there's no hurry. Time itself has got to wait upon the greatest country in the whole of God's universe. We shall be giving the word for everything: industry trade law journalism art politics and religion from Cape Horn clear over to Smith's Sound and beyond too, if anything worth taking hold of turns up at the North Pole. And then we shall have the leisure to take in hand the outlying islands and continents of the world. We shall run the world's business whether the world likes it or not. The world can't help it and neither can we, I guess.[5]

Holroyd casually spells out the reality behind the Monroe Doctrine. But in doing so, he puts into perspective Gould's vast ambition as a specific obsession 'definite in space and absolutely attainable within a limited time'. It is an obsession which is nonetheless utterly dependent on 'the temperament of a puritan and an insatiable imagination of conquest'. Gould's materialist idealism is thus a drop in the ocean which can still determine the whole fate of a backward nation. And by now Nostromo himself, the man of the people whose memory Mitchell had fawned upon, is reduced to an insignificant speck on the horizon. Conrad's feeling for distance and irony, which sometimes makes him shirk from the heroic dimensions of the characters he creates, is in this instance fully justified. For it is a distancing not in terms of impartiality but in terms of revelation, a revelation of the vast complex historical immensity against which the single-minded heroism of Nostromo pits itself.

In the novel, the rank and file of the Montero rebellion are distant figures. Recruited from the poor blacks and *Indios* in the hinterland of the country, they are those furthest removed from the civilising mission of privileged foreigners. They are the 'damned of the earth' to whom the strange symbolism Gould saw in his silver mine would be meaningless. They stand in the wings and Conrad, his conservative instincts hostile to them, cannot bring them on to the stage. Instead he shows us only the leaders who betray them, the cruel Sotillo and Pedro Montero, a brutal buffoon who tries to emulate Louis Napoleon. Yet it is only through the 'damned of the earth' that the military opportunism of the Monteros proves possible. They are the permanent shadow which lies across the brief enlightenment of the Sulaco republic. Characteristically Gould overrates the advantages of the mine for these people and underestimates the resentment it provokes. Ironically, he does so by expounding the virtues of material interest. But he does so by putting an empty materialist myth in the place of all other values:

What is wanted here is law, good faith, order, security. Anyone can declaim about these things, but I pin my faith to material interests. Only let the material interests once get a firm footing and they are bound to impose the conditions on which they alone can continue to exist. That's how your money-making is justified here in the face of lawlessness and disorder. It is justified because the security which it demands must be shared with an oppressed people. A better justice will come afterwards. That's your ray of hope.[6]

Later, when the first silver ingot is turned out from its mould, Mrs Gould remembers her husband's words and symbolically affirms his misconceived hope. Laying her hands upon it 'she endowed it with a justicative conception as though it were not a mere fact, but something far-reaching and impalpable, like the true expression of an emotion or the emergence of a principle'. In Costaguana where there is no stock exchange to sew together the economic and psychological aspects of human confidence, the confidence the silver generates inflates itself through the political machine. The mine finances the Ribiero dictatorship with its reforming mandate. It acts as a lifeline to harassed businessmen throughout the country and the key to political advancement for ambitious government officials. The true antidote to the 'indolence of the aristocrats' and 'the political immaturity of the people', it becomes 'an institution, a rallying point for everything in the province which needed order and stability to live'. Yet it provoked sufficient hostility to bring it to the point of disaster and failed to break Costaguana's vicious circle of misrule. Gould, whose idealism is devoted to the measure of influence he can have over people, is reduced to condoning the force necessary to suppress their revolt. Believing the mine was a form of pacification of its own accord, he has to give his blessing to Ribiero's army of pacification as it sails off to quell the Montero uprising in the south. Discreetly, however, he avoids attending the patriotic embarkátion, concentrating doggedly on keeping the flow of silver coming out of the mine.

From then onwards in the story, Gould is a spent force. He reappears only briefly to confirm the final corrosion of his idealism, his grim surrender to self-interest and corruption. With the onset of the rebellion the whole premise of his existence is shattered, and whatever the outcome of the war it cannot be resurrected. The hiatus between Gould, the prime mover of the nation, and Nostromo, the practical man of action, is filled by Martin Decoud, sceptic, dandy, Parisian intellectual, who lacks commitment to either warring faction. Equidistant from both Gould and Nostromo, Decoud's appearance is the means by which the perspective eventually shifts back to Nostromo himself. Decoud is, however involuntarily on his own part, the link between theory and practice, thought and action. He has an intellectual aloofness from the machinations of the Ribiero camp which Nostromo could not possibly possess, yet also comes to share Nostromo's fate as guardian of the precious cargo of silver. It is through contact with Decoud among other things that Nostromo comes to reject his stereotyped role as the faithful Capitaz de Cargadores. Or rather, Decoud paves the way for it. His shrewd mind penetrates the moral delusions of Gould and the political delusions of the Ribierists, where previously the triumphant advance of the Monteros at their expense had seemed nothing less than a grotesque act of historical injustice. When at first we see the Riberists on the verge of defeat they appear valiant and morally un-assailable compared with their contemptible foes. By the time we hear of them being rescued by General Barres in the third part of the book, the morality of their system has been totally undermined. One is tempted into sympathy for the system of imperial enlightenment in its moment of apparent defeat. Thereafter the novel extracts from the reader a cold irony towards its unexpected survival.

One interesting feature of Decoud is the anti-intellectual scorn which Conrad showers upon him. A journalist and dilettante who prefers writing about Costaguana in the Parisian Review to actually living in it, his remoteness from the world of political action is held up to ridicule. Yet one feels that Conrad here confuses two very different types of failure of the intellect. The first is the pretentious omniscience of those who in practice lead totally ineffectual lives. But the second, which actually characterises Decoud, is more complex. It is the failure to *feel* the impact that one's intellect and one's actions make upon the surrounding world. While Decoud regards the smuggling of the silver as a vainglorious farce, he nonetheless dutifully plays his part. While he sees the framing of a liberal constitution as a hopeless gesture in the final hour of defeat he nonetheless proceeds to disseminate his idea of an Occidental Republic. The fatal flaw in his chacter is not his incapacity to act but his ironic detachment from those very deeds he had no hesitation in performing. For the world which he attempts to change remains unreal for him. Describing the tumult and confusion in Sulaco in a letter to his sister, he remarks 'all this is life, must be life, since it is so much like a dream'. Despite Conrad's intention, Decoud's participation is decisive. After Montero's downfall, his idea of an Occidental Republic yields fruit in the more practical methods of Doctor Monygham. His suggestion that the silver must be prevented from falling into Montero's hands is shrewd politics, and proves itself to be correct. Decoud's ideas are infinitely more effective than Gould's idealism, but where Gould takes to heart the whole question of success or failure, Decoud remains numb to it. He has, instead, a studied aversion to the personal realisation of the ideas he produces.

Conrad has thus tried and failed to make Decoud the superfluous man characteristic of the early Russian novel. The dialectical necessity of the novel disallows this form of stasis. Decoud's unwavering scepticism is dynamic in its implications. The inclination to distance oneself so radically from one's own actions presupposes the inclination to act in the first place. When the chips are down, Decoud tries to apply liberal-democratic standards he reveres to the country of his birth which he mocks. His fate is consonant not with his failure, as Conrad would have us believe, but with his incapacity to recognise his ultimate success. The test of solitude he has to endure on the island after leaving Nostromo and taking the cargo of silver, is a test of self-conviction when no one is present to reassure him. As a result Decoud dies from 'want of faith in himself and others'. While the reader, benefiting from the chronological shift of the narrative, already knows that Nostromo has become a living legend, Decoud can only believe in Nostromo's failure and death. The architect of Sulaco's future republicanism 'believes in nothing', beholding 'the universe as a succession of incomprehensible images'. Conrad claims that Decoud lacks the urgency of a man of action to match 'the audacity of his intellect'. But what he really lacks is some principle of hope to enable him to endure solitude and adversity.

The contrast between Decoud and Nostromo is a crucial one, and Conrad's deliberate formulation of it is only partly accurate. The 'victim of the disillusioned weariness' due to 'intellectual audacity' is contrasted with 'the victim of the disenchanted vanity which is the reward of audacious action'. But the contrast also lies in their respective reputations. Decoud's suicide denies him any recognition for his actions, while Nostromo's saving of the silver, which he then secretly hoards on the island, is mythologised out of all proportion. One, falsely, becomes a hero; the other, equally falsely, becomes forgotten. But Nostromo's tenacity, his will to survive which Decoud does not possess, also brings out a fatal flaw which would never have affected his intellectual companion. He becomes fixated on the silver he has saved from the hands of the Monteros, and his obsession makes him strangely blind to the relativity of its value. When he returns to Sulaco history begins to leave him behind. Still fiercely possessive of the silver he has left behind, Nostromo lacks the perspicacity of Gould or Decoud. He cannot see that once production restarts at the mine under the new republic, the value of his hidden cargo is already worthless. For 'Sulaco had outstripped his prudence, growing rich swiftly on the hidden treasures of the earth'.

The silver is the key to a rejection of the existing order by Nostromo which does not lead to a search for a new one. It is the limit to Nostromo's scornful rejection of his former masters. He keeps the silver for himself thinking them undeserving of it. But the silver which had been their lifeline loses its value as its quantity is more than replenished. Only in Nostromo's obsession does the cargo retain the value, both real and symbolic, that it briefly possessed. Its heroic guardian is thus incapable of betraying it because of the relativity of its value in a constantly changing world. Nostromo's revolt is stillborn, despite his change of heart. For in his imagination germinates the misplaced seed of Gould's idealism—the idea of the silver as the universal secret of the earth. After he has been accidentally shot by Giorgio Viola, Nostromo reveals his defeat in his dying breath. 'The silver has killed me', he tells Mrs Gould. But it is as if she already knows and does not wish to hear. 'I, too, have hated the idea of that silver from the bottom of my heart.' His final words to her reveal the tragic limits of his audacity:

> 'Marvellous! that one of you should hate the wealth that you know so well how to take from the hands of the poor. The world rests on the poor, as old Giorgio says. You have always been good to the poor. But there is something accursed in wealth. Senora, shall I tell you where the treasure is. . . . Shining! Incorruptible!'
> 'No, Capataz', she said. 'No one misses it now. Let it be lost for ever.[7]'

The silver of course is never lost since the mine continues to function. But the idea of it is exhausted. For in some degree it has corrupted everybody. Montero betrays his promise to expel foreign capital because of it, Sotillo tortures because of it, Decoud dies with four silver ingots weighting him down in his pockets and Mitchell lives off his shares in the mine. The obsession it creates is also a denial of erotic passion. It destroys Mrs Gould's love for her husband, betrays Nostromo's promises to Giselle, and Decoud's passion for Antonia cannot endure his solitary exile with the precious cargo. The silver is a masculine passion, and each love-affair suffers its curse. It is not so much a sign of the fetishism of commodities as the fetishism of the visible substance underlying all wealth, and, by implication, all power. The fact that Antonia Avellanos is a dedicated patriot who persuades Decoud to take sides is not as striking as Conrad would have wished. Decoud's avowed motive for supporting a separate republic—so that he would never be parted from her—is in fact artificial. The paradox with Decoud is that he actually displays the passionate involvement in politics which he verbally condemns. Conrad is unable to create the legendary woman he aspired to, for Decoud already contains within himself the motives for action to which Antonia is merely a catalyst. The portrait of Mrs Gould is more convincing since it reveals a woman whose stoicism is matched by her perspicacity, a woman 'who resembled a good fairly, weary with a long career of well-doing, touched by the withering suspicion of the uselessness of her labours, the powerlessness of her magic'. In truth the women in the novel are the victims of the absence of a passion which is exhausted elsewhere.

The new republic, whose saviour can find no virtue in it, creates no binding principle to replace Gould's misguided idealism. The position of those who supported the Monteros has not altered, while the very settlers and Cargadores who had helped Nostromo fight off the mob, themselves start forming revolutionary secret societies to challenge the new order. The pattern is set for further disasters of corruption, misrule and revolt. The future generation of intellectuals become more strident and revolutionary than Decoud, the future generation of businessmen more corrupt and ruthless than Charles Gould, and the future military leaders more consistently repressive than their predecessors. The poor and the under-privileged remain poor and underprivileged. But that is outside the scope of the novel, a feature of more recent history. What Conrad had done was to show the ineffectiveness and inappropriateness of an imperial enlighten-ment trying to improve the moral and material condition of a more backward nation.

His response to the worship of material interests is fundamentally conservative. He repudiates it because it fails to bring any ordering principle into the affairs of Costaguana. In fact its effect is the opposite. His characters live out the tragic contradiction between beliefs with no material foundation and actions with no moral justification. As an institution, a process of production and a political event, the mine displays the figural characteristics of great realist fiction. As Charles Gould realised, it is the source of a potential way of life. The destiny of Conrad's characters is to discover it, for good or evil. The companionship of Nostromo and Decoud in the cargo of silver is a partnership in exploding the myth created around the mine. But in exploding the myth, they are doomed to a tragic end. Through them, Conrad explores the relationship between *figura* and the liberal idea of progress. Their evolution as characters parallels the progress of their country away from the impending evil of barbarism and misrule. But as each is transformed, Decoud by action, Nostromo by thought and obsession, each rejects in his own way the idea of progress as a consequence of their heroism. In terms of the dialectic of the novel this is precisely what gives each of them a heroic stature, namely tragic refusal. For even though they become its means, the very embodiment of its promise, progress for them can never be the truth. For Decoud, progress is unreal and for Nostromo, on his deathbed, it is a form of deceit.

The novel betrays the idea of progress in Zéraffa's double sense of the word—by revealing and repudiating it. But the gap between revelation and rejection is an immense chasm which cannot be bridged, and that very hiatus constitutes the tragic space of the novel. Decoud and Nostromo founder on the disparity between the idea of progress and the actualtiy of its realisation. The more their actions attempt to realise it, the more their minds begin to reject it. The specific feature of Conrad's tragic space is isolation and solitude, where the two tragic heroes are each unaware of the other's fate. Thus the unique feature of the novel, its dual heroism, is annulled by the very context in which it is enacted. Decoud in solitude on the island believes Nostomo dead, and when Nostromo discovers the empty lighter and the silver on the island with four ingots missing, he in turn assumes Decoud to be dead but cannot guess how or why. The fate of each remains unknown to the other, and in a profound sense unrecognised. The double tragedy is thus compounded by mutual lack of recognition of the other's tragic fate, which itself is tragic. For neither comes to understand the nature of the other's rejection, which could, potentially, complement his own. Instead the road to rejection is a solitary rut with its own impasse, and life in Costaguana goes on, cyclical, corrupt, disastrous.

Despite the spectacular success of *Nostromo* as a novel which fully justifies its immense complexity, there is in it an absence which characterises all of Conrad's political fiction. It is the absence of a political militant with whom the author himself senses an affinity, one whose fanaticism, faith and commitment is in some measure Conrad's own. This, the conservative absence, is filled only in a story which is not directly political by a character who barely appears there. It is of course Kurtz in *Heart of Darkness*. From the outset Kurtz is already a myth, the man whose reputation has reached Marlowe even before his quest has begun, whose voice is known before his presence is ever felt, whose existence at the heart of the darkness Marlowe has still to explore and overcome is absolutely taken for granted. Kurtz already is where Marlowe must go and has already become what Marlowe must discover. And what is there left to find out by the time that Marlowe actually reaches him but the circumstances of his death? And what then is there left to do but return to London and condone the lie of his life?

The political importance of Kurtz is made explicit in the text. A journalist who calls on Marlowe in London to enquire about the dead man remarks that 'Kurtz's proper sphere ought to have been politics on the popular side. . . . He would have been a splendid leader of an extreme party. . . . Any party.' Though the remark is vague, the point has been made. Kurtz's extremism had a madness and a force not possessed by the political fossils of landlocked Geneva or the sepulchral city of desolation, and unlike Nostromo he was not constricted by a holding action against barbaric revolt. One almost senses that he could have led that revolt with the ideological fanaticism that Montero lacked. And yet his goals would have remained obscure for, in Conrad's eyes, all that mattered was that they existed and were pursued with the utmost devotion. His final words 'The horror! The horror!' vibrate with a conviction, a 'strange commingling of desire and hate' which attracted Marlowe just as much as they repelled him. It is as if Conrad expressed, in this text alone, a strange ecstasy at finally discovering the destructive force which in his other works, distance and irony, aloofness and scepticism, had always prevented him from reaching. For what he has found is the fanatical anarchy at the core of his own being, and finally penetrated 'an impenetrable darkness'.

Conrad's fiction, at its best, presents us with a simultaneous image of the destructiveness and destruction of imperialism. Just as the beginning of *Heart of Darkness*, with its ironic account of the Roman conquest of the impenetrable British heartland, turns our conventional notion of imperialism on its head, so Conrad's whole work reveals the relativity of an enterprise which appears at the height of its triumph, as the essence of the natural order of things. The achievement, and the horror of Kurtz, is to push the imperial endeavour to its point of no return, that is the point where the promise of its completion can only presage its ultimate destruction. Kurtz is *conquistador* and *guerillero* rolled into one, a man who is already part of the darkness he is trying to penetrate. But if he is absent from Conrad's political fiction, that absence is a necessity. The political significance of his behaviour can only be inferred, as the journalist infers it, from the absence of any concrete political setting. The prototype for Kurtz cannot be transposed into the political novels, yet the impossibility of this transposition is genuinely felt within the novels themselves. It is not so much an inadequacy of Conrad's writing but a feature of the important differences in a tragic realism which is artistically politicised and one which is not. Kurtz could not be in *Nostromo* even though, at times, he might appear to be its missing element.

As a conservative anarchist whose anarchism was so deeply repressed, Conrad was a prophetic witness to the transformation of what we now call the Third World. His great fiction ends in creative exhaustion and even if he wanted it, which he did not, any rational utopia appended to it would have been meaningless. His work identifies and rejects, from a thoroughly humanitarian yet tragic viewpoint, the bourgeois ideology of progress. In a different way, Thomas Mann was to make the same rejection, with the same disdain of rational utopia and a similarly conservative response to a changing world.

9 Thomas Mann: Bourgeois Affirmation and Artistic Tragedy

I

It could be argued that Thomas Mann never wrote a political novel. Even in his short story, *Mario and the Magician*, an explicit attack upon fascism, there is not a political figure in sight. But if Mann shuns the overt workings of politics, his novels still exhibit the profound permeation of politics within modern society. He is barely concerned with the machinery of politics but much perturbed by its consequences. In particular his treatment of the complex and at times opaque relationship between ideology and politics raises the whole question of realism in the modern novel. Compared with Zola, Dostoevsky and Conrad, his novels after *Buddenbrooks* can hardly be called realist in the classic sense at all. The result has been a number of contradictory responses. While Lukács ignores much of Mann's stylistic innovation in order to label him a critical realist, Zéraffa sees him as one of the central figures in the 'revolution of the twenties' novel' whose heroes withdraw into authentic personal sensibility from an alien technocratic world. The truth of the matter lies somewhere between these extremes. Mann did help to transform the realist novel out of all recognition, a transformation balanced by serious losses and important gains. *The Magic Mountain* and *Doctor Faustus* are outstanding examples of a contemporary realism which had assimilated the revolutionary transformation of twentieth-century fiction. At the same time the detailed concern with the personal sensibility of the hero is always on the verge of degenerating into pure obsession. Yet, as most of his critics have noted, we can read in these novels the tragic history of modern Germany.

The significance of Mann's bourgeois upbringing for his later career lies in the authoritarian values of imperial Germany in which it was immersed. He was a prodigal son of the upper middle class who tried to remain loyal to the values of his disciplined childhood but failed. To his chagrin he found that he could not be normal in the sense prescribed, and within the deceptively stable environment in which he lived he had a vision of health challenged by sickness, vitality by decadence, and life by death. Yet though he rebelled, he never freed himself entirely from those values he rejected. Unlike the other bohemians of his day, Mann could not turn his back completely on bourgeois society.

His predicament is clearly expressed in his early story, *Tonio Kroeger*, which unconditionally asserts an irreconcilable relationship between artist and bourgeois. The letter Kroeger writes to his painter-friend Lisabeta in Munich clearly outlines Mann's own dilemma. Kroeger calls himself 'a bourgeois who has strayed off into art, a bohemian who feels nostalgic yearning for respectability, an artist with a bad conscience'. He continues:

> For surely it is my bourgeois conscience which makes me see in the artist life, in all irregularity and genius, something profoundly suspect, profoundly disreputable; that fills me with this lovelorn *faiblesse* for the simple and good, the comfortably normal, the average unendowed respectable human being. . . .
>
> I stand between two worlds. I am at home in neither, and I suffer in consequence. . . .
>
> I admire those proud, cold beings who adventure upon the paths of great and demonic beauty and despise 'mankind' but I do not envy them. For if anything is capable of making a poet of the literary man, it is my bourgeois love of the human, the living and usual.[1]

For Mann rather than Kroeger, it is the novel not poetry which salvages his love of the living and the usual. It is that art form whose representational nature is most conducive to the portrayal of bourgeois life where theatre, poetry, painting within the contemporary idiom increasingly come to desert it. In other words the novel was the most appropriate artistic vehicle for Mann's conservatism. Whereas his brother, Heinrich, satirised the authoritarian values of his society, Thomas Mann took their failings seriously. The serious and tragic elements of his fiction arise out of a situation where despite his repudiation of the values which had tyrannised him, the umbilical cord remains unbroken. While the subject of Mann's greatest fiction deals largely with everyday bourgeois life, it does so only to reveal what the author sees behind it, namely its sickness and damnation.

While *Buddenbrooks* is a family chronicle uncovering sickness in the midst of normality, *The Magic Mountain* is the opposite. Its Swiss sanatorium reveals the *Alltaglichkeit* of the diseased. The difference is significant. In the period between the appearance of *Buddenbrooks* and the completion of *The Magic Mountain* imperial Germany had collapsed. The context of everyday life itself was no longer normal in the conventional sense Mann had taken it to be. Though it actually ends with the beginning of the first World War, *The Magic Mountain* reflects the dissolution of normality which characterises that war's ignominious end for Germany. It was a situation in which Mann's studiously apolitical nature had to come to terms with the politics of defeat.

Mann had actually set about the task rather earlier in 1914. He accepted the myth of German superiority propagated by German professors—the so-called 'ideas of 1914'. It was a myth which saw the war as a spiritual crusade, a fight to establish the superiority of German *Kultur* over the commercial spirit of Western European civilisation. To start with, then, it was the politics of victory which enthralled him. But even then, his special concern was to show the necessity of a political victory which actually prevented culture from being politicised. It was a concern which reflected the degrading compromise made by a whole generation of bourgeois intellectuals in Imperial Germany; their acceptance of an authoritarian military tradition in return for recognition of learning and cultural tradition. If Germany was the land of Goethe and Beethoven, Hegel and Schopenhauer, it was also the land of Bismarck, as Nietzsche rightly remarked. The bourgeoisie, which dominates Mann's obsessions, and his realist fiction, still played a politically subordinate role in the Germany of his youth. But the dilemma he saw in its position was a matter of culture rather than politics. While he yearned for the security of bourgeois life, he detested its commercial spirit. During the war many of the ideas he developed as part of the spiritual crusade for Germany reflected this contradiction.

In his letters to Paul Amann in 1915 he talks of Germany's mission as 'the social reorganisation of Europe', which he saw as the only effective antidote to 'revolutionary sloganising' on the one hand and the 'commercial spirit' on the other. Mann expresses the view that German culture will become healthier and less inward-looking after a military victory:

> The German love of reality is ironically melancholic, rather gloomy and rather brutal. It does not have radicalism's gallantry of gesture. In the final analysis, it is not without contempt. For that reason the world refuses to grant it free play—the world which is filled with *cant* and defends the empty phrases and empty gestures of humanitarian optimism against this German realism . . . with the democratisation of Germany which will be an inevitable consequence of this war, Germany may be stripped of her gloom without being shallow; her relationship to reality may take a more intimate and happy form, so that she can lead the way to a democratic world-culture—for the leadership must not fall to America.[2]

The 'German love of reality' is the connecting link between Mann's sense of the political and his literary production. For the problem of reality is one both of politics and the novel. *The Magic Mountain* is an attempt to capture the relationship to reality in both its aspects. Arising out of the same obsessions which Mann expressed in his polemical *Reflections of an Unpolitical Man*, it goes further and transposes them into art. In his conservative polemic Mann actually wrote out of his system the purely analytical mode of thinking in order to leave his imagination free for the work of fiction which followed it. He viewed the process as a necessary stepping stone towards the completion of *The Magic Mountain*. Here his political obsessions leave their indelible trace. For his object was to express, through realistic artistic means, a healthy political relationship to reality.

Remarkable as it may seem for a novel with such a purpose, the dominating impression upon the reader is Mann's heightened sense of the *unreal*. The rarified atmosphere of the sanatorium where Hans Castorp goes to visit his cousin, its remoteness from the 'flatlands' below, signify an escape from the tribulations of normal life. Castorp stays on, not only to cure his 'illness', but to search for the truth about the world below which he has deserted. His fate is a perfectly realistic symbol of the Germanic retreat into inwardness, since the sanatorium has the same negative relationship to the world from which it is a refuge as pure introspection does to the world of public events. The problem for Hans Castorp is the same problem which Mann had earlier posed for German culture—to be stripped of melancholy without becoming shallow, to develop an affirmative relationship to reality. Yet, significantly Castorp fails. His seven years on the magic mountain provide him with encounters he would never have dreamed, but he does not return to the world below a changed man. The liberation from inwardness which Mann intended Castorp to undergo never takes place. His encounters with Clavdia Chauchat and Peeperkorn occur on the periphery of feeling. His encounters with Naptha, Settembrini and Doctor Krokowski take place on the periphery of consciousness. His inner life, replete with sophisticated ruminations on its diseased nature, is preserved intact.

The priority of spirit over matter, the guiding didactic theme of the novel, is mirrored in Castorp's own predicament. His introspective hypochondria leaves him vulnerable to the physical condition he eventually contracts. Obsessed by the symptoms which Hofrat Behrens diagnoses in him, his quest to know the source of his illness actually dissipates his strength to resist it. Castorp's search for self-knowledge is not the application of an enlightened rational philosophy but part of a more sinister attraction to death. His curiosity about his own illness leads him towards the melancholy contemplation that all life is disease:

> Disease was a perverse, a dissolute form of life. And life? Life itself? Was it perhaps only an infection, a sickening of matters? . . . Life was nothing but the next step on the reckless path of the spirit dishonoured; nothing but the automatic blush of matter roused to sensation and receptive to that which had awakened it.[3]

But matter itself is the imperfect materialisation of the spirit. Life, in Castorp's view, is the Fall which is identical with the Creation. Its public manifestations are the imperfect realisation of the Spirit it cannot faithfully reflect. In his own life the real world diminishes the images he creates of it. On *Walpurgisnacht* Castorp's consummation of his desire for Clavdia is a transient moment in the midst of a permanent obsession. To act is never to find genuine realisation. Castorp's sensibility is a locked treasure-house of the spirit opened to the temptations of the real world in a setting which would seem totally unreal were it not for the omnipresence of disease and death.

The main source of temptation comes from the ideological battle for his soul waged by Naphtha and Settembrini. Both hold to principles which are alternative modes of self-realisation for the introverted engineer. Settembrini, the confident nineteenth-century liberal repeatedly and monotonously celebrates the dawn of modern enlightenment over the darkness of medieval superstition. He is the disciple of the idea of progress *par excellence*, the 'windbag', the 'Hand-organ man' grinding out rhetoric in the lofty vacuum of Davos. The temptation of progress, to which Mann tokenly succumbed in his post-war years, makes no impact upon Castorp. The misconceived optimism which he rejected now reads like brutal satire. Here is Settembrini describing his scholastic endeavours:

. . . The League for the Organisation of Progress, mindful of its task of furthering human happiness—in other words of combating human suffering by the available social methods, to the end of finally eliminating it altogether: mindful also of the fact that this can be accomplished only by the aid of sociology, the end and aim of which is the perfect state, the League in session at Barcelona determined upon the publication of a series of volumes bearing the general title: *The Sociology of Suffering*. It should be the aim of the series to classify human suffering according to classes and categories, and treat it systematically and exhaustively. You ask what is the use of classification, arrangement, systematisation? I answer you order and simplification are the first steps towards the mastery of a subject—the actual enemy is the unknown. We must lead the human race out of the primitive stages of fear and patient stupidity, and set its feet on the path of conscious activity. We must enlighten it upon two points: first, that given effects become void when one recognises and removes their causes; and second, that all individual suffering is due to the disease of the social organism. Very well; this is the object of the *Sociological Pathology*. It will be issued in some twenty folio volumes, treating every species of human suffering, from the most personal and the most intimate to the great collective struggles arising from conflicting interests of classes and nations: . . . the publication will seek to take as its norm the dignity and happiness of mankind and seek to indicate the measure and remedies calculated to remove the cause of each deviation.[4]

This should not merely be seen as a prophetic parody of 'bourgeois sociology'. For it satirises the Panglossian optimism of all modern rationalist philosophy. Settembrini's vision of the intellectual mastery of a diseased world is pedantic and hollow. Mann felt that at a deeper level it was a movement away from life. Like Schopenhauer, he felt intellect to be secondary to the will, and Settembrini's grand design evokes intellect detached from the will, a detachment reinforced by the nature of the setting in which it is proclaimed. Settembrini's illness prevents him from ever finishing the project before his death, and his fate inverts Gramsci's famous formula: pessimism of the intellect, optimism of the will. For in the confined setting of a sanatorium, there are no truly healthy people to be stirred by the effort of will and none of the complexities of ordinary life to discredit the intellect. That he should spend so much time on the thankless task of trying to convince Castorp and the wooden Joachim is evidence, not of the persuasiveness of eloquence, but of its wastefulness when nothing underlines it.

While the doctrine the Italian humanist preaches fails to strike a chord of sympathy in Castorp's heart that of Leo Naphtha, the Jewish Jesuit, has a greater attraction. Naphtha is the literary heir to Dostoevsky's Grand Inquisitor yet his opponent is anything but silent. Consequently the Jesuit's casuistry is based on confrontation, not on admonition. He debates without observing the rules of debating, a mixture of fanatical belief and instant opportunism. With a sparse audience of patients at the sanatorium, sometimes Castorp alone, his aim is to tumble the whole edifice of Settembrini's liberal optimism. His world-view is fundamentally a counter-utopia, dependent upon the prior existence of the idea of progress but viciously biting the hand which feeds it. Naphtha is the master of scholastic terror, trying to wrench history out of the path which liberalism has ordained for it. Within his verbal strategy, everything is permitted. Yet he also rescues the Spirit from the prehistory to which Settembrini had banished it. His riposte to the idea of material progress takes the following form:

> Dualism, antithesis, is the moving, the passionate, the dialectic principle of all Spirit. To see the world as cleft into two opposing poles—that is Spirit. All monism is tedious.[5]

The origin of the character of Naphtha has been surrounded by notorious controversy. In one of his letters to Paul Amann during the war, Mann already had the idea of Naphtha as a 'witty reactionary'. But there is clear evidence that the final version of the character was crystallised by Mann's sole encounter with Georg Lukács. After the novel was published Mann never denied that Lukács was the model for Naphtha. But the proof actually lies in the text itself. The physical description of the Jesuit is almost an exact replica and the name of the tailor's shop in the village above which Naphtha lodged is called Lukaçek. That Lukács should denounce a fictional version of himself as a fascistic and reactionary mystic was an irony Mann probably foresaw, and perhaps even intended. For the critic, in applauding Mann's conception of such a sinister figure, seemed to be lunging at the bait which the writer had dangled in front of him.

Yet Naphtha is not Lukács. He is more and less. While Lukács was clearly wrong in seeing him as a reactionary mystic, equally wrong are those who see him as a militant Leninist. For Mann already had the image of the reactionary in front of him prior to meeting the Hungarian, and besides, at the time of writing he did not really know what a militant Leninist was. What Naphtha represents are not the dynamic and ruthless qualities of a professional revolutionary but the qualities of a militant apologist sheltering under the sacred canopy of a universal church. Mann's vision is prophetic rather than contemporary. It looks forward to the time when world-communism had become a universal church and Lukács himself was a militant but obedient apologist. Mann fails to find the Christian correlative for the Marxist revolutionary but out of his failure arises something very different—a feeling for the latent metaphysical underpinnings of a materialist doctrine which is perverted to deny the fulfilment of human needs and also a sense in which the institution is superior to the people it is meant to serve. Mann, through Naphtha, prophesies a future Communist Party whose claims to hegemony rival the medieval Catholic church in their totality. But Naphtha, as a Jesuit priest, does not 'symbolise' the orthodox Communist Party militant. He is first and foremost a Jesuit, belonging to an archaic order but sensing the possible successes of a secular movement, similar in organisational and psychological terms to his own. The speech in which he attempts to posit the relevance of his own order to the modern world indicates both the irrelevance of its other-worldly doctrine and the appropriateness of its this-worldly behaviour.

Naphtha advocates two spheres through which obedience can be inculcated—work and education. In doing so he discerns what they later became under backward communism—ascetic mortification of the spirit. Both are forms of collectivism in which the individual is eliminated by 'discipline, sacrifice', 'the renunciation of the ego, the curbing of the personality', or as Castorp describes it later in awe, man as 'anonymous and communal'. While the dynamics within which such political attitudes have flourished are those of social transformation, the attitudes themselves have an ideological origin. They contain a debased anthropological view of man as heroically obedient, self-sacrificial, and unquestioning. They originate, in Naphtha's view, from the triumph of Spirit over Matter. His vision of a revitalised Church rising to new heights as a result of proletarian revolution is historically laughable, but if we replace Church by Party, the prophecy is serious and forbidding. The proletariat is merely the vehicle of a metaphysical mission which affirms the triumph of Spirit:

The world-proletariat . . . is today asserting the ideals of the *Civitas Dei* in opposition to the discredited and decadent standards of the capitalistic bourgeoisie. The dictatorship of the proletariat, the politico-economic means of salvation demanded by our age, does not mean domination for its own sake in perpetuity; but rather in the sense of a temporary abrogation in the Sign of the Cross, of the contradiction between spirit and force; in the sense of overcoming the world by mastering it; in a transcendental transitional sense, in the sense of the Kingdom. The proletariat has taken up the task of Gregory the Great, his religious zeal burns within, and as little as he may it withholds its hand from the shedding of blood. Its task is to strike terror into the world for the healing of the world, that man may eventually achieve salvation and deliverance, and win back at length freedom from law and from class-distinction, and his original status as Child of God.[6]

The passage points to the metaphysical materialism of a communist movement which sanctifies the party's divine role in changing history according to its own premises. But it also highlights a specific dilemma of German idealism which actually limits its political impact. Many German intellectuals of Lukács' period were faced with the dilemma of forming some attachment in the new secular age to a predominantly materialist world. Conversion to the Communist Party was one such alternative. But in their new-found militancy writers such as Lukács, and Walter Benjamin who did not join the party, unconsciously embedded their idealist frame of mind within a new materialist philosophy. When Mann calls Naphtha 'a reactionary revolutionist' he has this particular dilemma in mind, which also drove many intellectuals towards fascism. Its relevance to Hans Castorp can now be brought out. Naphtha's course was a tempting one. It offered to the young German an externalisation of his spiritual inwardness, which Settembrini's monistic materialism could not. In the stable pre-war atmosphere of Davos, Naphtha might as well be an inhabitant from another planet. But writing retrospectively, Mann had inserted into the pre-war setting a post-war solution, a solution, that is, for Castorp once his stable world is in ruins.

This illustrates the strength and weakness of Mann's literary genius. It was prophetic, profoundly so. Yet Naphtha is not the revolutionary character that Mann sought to create. The result is a blessing for Mann's realist fiction. For the attempt to disguise a Marxist revolutionary as an unorthodox Jesuit is pure dissimulation. Naphtha works precisely because he is part of the unreal world of privileged illness and death which collapses in 1914. His own illness, and later his suicide, only make sense as signs of a conservative despair. Like the duel he demands with Settembrini, the Jesuit is archaic. His thinking, so to speak, has begun to move forward without him, suggesting the possibility of a new political order to which he is incapable of belonging. As the deadlock of his argument with

Settembrini grows, he relapses into a romantic worship of the Middle Ages which characterised the conservative revolutionaries of post-war Germany. The origins of this are to be sought in German romanticism, for neither Jesuit nor Marxist would praise the daughters of the medieval nobility who contracted mouthsores from sucking the wounds of lepers, and called them their roses.

The Jesuit remains a realistic, though exceptional, creation precisely because of the reactionary elements in his thinking. But this also conspires to destroy the momentum of the narrative. Mann said that he had written 'a dialectic novel'. But its dialectic remains at the level of argument and is never transformed into action. The outcome of the gargantuan debate between *homo humanus* and *princeps scholasticorum* is stalemate. Nothing happens. The pedantic dispute which devours so many pages of the novel finally grinds to a halt without resonance. Hans Castorp finds welcome relief in the effortless charisma of Mynheer Peeperkorn, who infuses the sick community with the illusion of well-being. On one occasion, when the two ideologues have argued themselves to a standstill he distracts their attention by pointing out the black speck of an eagle circling high in the sky. He imitates the bird of prey striking at its victim, its talons in their entrails, its beak dripping with blood. 'He had wrought himself to a pitch. All interest in Settembrini and Naphtha's antinomies was fled away. But the vision of the eagle remained. . . .' Locked in abstract combat, neither having anything as concrete as the vision of the eagle to offer. Hence nothing emerges from their dispute except its unlikely resolution in a duel, where Mann misguidedly plagiarises from Russian fiction. Nothing about Castorp has altered. Nothing at Davos has changed.

But what of the episode of the snowstorm? Is that not vitally significant in showing Castorp's rejection of death? And does not his rejection of death imply a rejection of all the temptations Naphtha had offered him? This undoubtedly is how Mann intended it. Castorp's dream, when he shelters from the storm against the wall of a locked mountain-hut, ends with the only italicised words in the whole novel: '*For the sake of goodness and love, man shall let death have no sovereignty over his thoughts.*' But the dilemma, and its resolution, remains locked in Castorp's consciousness, exclusive to his private world. No one comes to know of the incident in the snow, and it, in turn, has no impact upon other events in the novel. The dialectic conflicts within the novel are contained within Castorp's imagination and have no outlet. As a problematic hero, Castorp is a passive nonentity. His predicament, then, is neither heroic nor tragic. After his rejection of the sovereignty of death, it is several years more before he breaks the spell of 'the ocean of time' and finally leaves the sanatorium. To the extent that its hero is passive, the novel's realism is affirmative. But it is the involuntary affirmation of a sick world which Mann rejected. And the experience of the magic mountain has changed nothing for its survivor. In the last scene where Castorp is found at the front, his is the normal fate of war.

In *The Magic Mountain*, tragic realism is never attained. In the sanatorium, the privilege of dying expensively can never sound a tragic note. If Castorp had died in the storm, there would have been no sense of tragic loss because the possibility of self-fulfillment is never broached. Like Conrad's revolutionaries Castorp is in a place of exile. The very context in which he can question his previous existence gives him no opportunity for changing it. The sanatorium gives Castorp a freedom from the cares of everyday life but constricts that freedom to a series of stifling infatuations, infatuation with disease, infatuation with feminine mystique, infatuation with ideology, infatuation with death. Unlike Faust, he resists the temptations of the devil. But that is because he never generates a Faustian desire for mastery of the world. Most certainly, Mann changes the traditional form of figural realism by concentrating in such complex psychological detail upon the sensibility of his hero. But he eschews heroism and tragedy by making Castorp assimilate the world to his inner sensibility, rather than projecting himself into it body and soul. The true test of Castorp's impact upon his fellow-patients could only be achieved by a switching of the point of view which Mann never attempts. Instead we have to be content with the sardonic but truthful assessment of Clavdia Chauchat on Walpurgis night: '*petit-bourgeois d' une tache humide*'. Castorp's bloated dimensions are, by a remark such as this, drastically cut down to size. But this additional external perspective is never consistently followed through, and an important dimension of reality eludes us. The problematic hero lacks tragic stature, because there is in Mann's wish to cast an unfamiliar light upon the real a profound refusal of reality beyond a certain imaginative point. He cannot, after all, alter the constricting nature of 'the German love of reality'.

II

Disease in Davos is a metaphor for the sickness of Europe. Castorp's failure to extricate himself from it for seven long years expresses Mann's lingering attachment to a precious bourgeois world which was not only diseased but superfluous. The sanatorium presents one with a lingering image of superfluity. And this too is something which Castorp finds more attractive than repulsive. Only in post-war Germany does Mann find the true seeds of alienation from bourgeois life. For here he came to encounter it in its most abnormal form—fascism. The rise of fascism, first in Italy then in his own country, constituted the final break. It also produced his greatest fiction, in the shape of *Mario and the Magician* and *Doctor Faustus*. One cannot, however, derive such a literary achievement from political wisdom. Instead, it should be attributed to the creative tension caused by the absolute necessity of a break from a bourgeois Germany resorting to new forms of political barbarism. The strain of brutal romanticism in Naphtha's personality, which was most unjesuitlike, later found a political correlative in Nazism.

Mann's short story *Mario and the Magician* was written in 1929, when fascism was well entrenched in Italy and beginning to make its presence felt in Germany. Like *The Magic Mountain* it is a treatment of politics in a non-political setting. As a story about a sinister magician it could be seen as an allegory or a fable, something which could be read as much by a child who knew nothing of fascism as an adult who did. But the story is not a fable for its setting is realistic. It takes place in a northern seaside resort in fascist Italy and one is meant to assume that the town, the magician and his audience are real. The reality of the fascist ambience is heightened by the narrative preceding the entry of Cipolla. Italy is the living example for the German narrator of what his country could become. The nasty incident on the beach, where the narrator is reprimanded for allowing his children to play naked, foreshadows his growing distaste for the new patriotic Italy.

The encounter of the German family with Cipolla the magician takes place in circumstances where they are already disconcerted. But the way in which the outraged narrator assesses the disagreeable phenomenon of Cipolla baiting his audience is itself conservative in the extreme. Cipolla's behaviour is measured largely as a deviation from the respectable, honest and privatised values of the conventional bourgeois. He is an affront to conservative decency. But if the story hinges upon the relationship of the magician to the German family, it would undoubtedly be a failure. While a conservative narrator commandeers the point of view, the tragic victim of Cipolla's exploits is an ordinary working-class youth. This represents something of a radical departure for Mann. Ordinary people are noticeably lacking from most of his fiction. Yet it was fascism, paradoxically, which compelled Mann to consider the masses. Nazism deliberately intended itself as a mass movement. Financed by private enterprise, both large and small, it appealed to the lower-middle classes, the working-class and the unemployed. Its mass politics remained distasteful to some of the more respectable and prosperous sections of the German middle class.

Cipolla is not only an illusionist, a man with a top hat and a silver-handled whip. He is also Hitler, a man 'with a sharp, ravaged face, piercing eyes, small waxed moustache, and a so-called imperial in the curve between mouth and chin'. It is an exact resemblance right down to the 'side hair . . . brushed forward to the corners of the eyes'. The occupation of magician illustrates Mann's interest in the real political upstart he so despised. He was fascinated not by his charisma as such, but by the specific type of charismatic appeal he generated. It was a charisma, in Mann's eyes, based upon a contempt for his followers. Cipolla's act, or performance, does not concentrate like the conventional magician on formal skills of magic. It is a conscious attempt to degrade his audience yet bind them to his will in that very process of degradation. Strictly speaking, it is anti-charismatic since it corrodes the very sanctity of the bond between leader and follower on which it is based. Cipolla's amoral cynicism even leads him to simulate the blind compliance of his following. Making the audience pass an object around from hand to hand, he allows himself to be guided after it with eyes closed, in a groping attempt to find it:

> The suffering receptive performing part was now his, the will he had imposed on others was shut out, he acted in obedience to a voiceless common will which was in the air. But he made it perfectly clear that it all came to the same thing. The capacity for self-surrender, he said, for becoming a tool, for the most unconditional and utter self-abnegation, was but the reverse side of that other power to will and command. Commanding and obeying formed together one single principle, one indissoluble unity; he who knew how to obey knew also how to command, and conversely: the one idea was comprehended in the other, as people and leader were comprehended in one another. But that which was *done*, the highly exacting and exhausting performance, was in every case his, the leader's and the mover's, in whom the will became obedience, the obedience will, whose person was the cradle and womb of both, and who thus suffered enormous hardship.[7]

But Cipolla's 'enormous hardship' is a fraud. It is merely the effort of creating the illusion which deceives his audience. The triumph of the will, one might almost say, is an act of deception. Cipolla's act is sheer opportunism. The boy who writhes on the floor thinking he has colic, the hypnotised woman who trudges around the hall after Cipolla despite her husband's desperate pleas, are victims of improvised humiliation. Yet if the masses are deceived by the fascist demagogue, they nonetheless have a positive and frightening relationship with him. Mann clearly saw the emphasis on absolute domination and absolute surrender as a form of debased eroticism. He sees fascism artistically the way that Wilhelm Reich saw it analytically—as the political sublimation of repressed sexual impulses. But it is an impersonal sexuality, a point which is poignantly illustrated in the fate of Mario.

Mario, who belongs to a crowd of easygoing youths, is initially the most sceptical but potentially the most compliant of Cipolla's victims. By hypnotising Mario into believing that he, Cipolla, is Mario's fiancée, Silvestre, he contaminates the idea of the personal beloved. The place of the beloved is taken by the fraudulent intruder who extorts the kiss on the cheek which is meant for another. Mann meant this false rapture, not merely as a surrogate form of sexuality, but as a perversion of passion itself. The chance for self-fulfillment, through love or desire, is expropriated by Cipolla and transformed into a power for evil.

Yet the monstrous and tragic transaction, which is almost completely erotic, unfolds its political dimension in Mario's response to his own humiliation. He shoots Cipolla. The story ends in catastrophe and confusion, with the audience screaming and the German narrator hastily dragging his children from the hall. But the ending mingles tragic horror with a sense of justice and hope. It is tragic that Mario should allow himself to be so deeply wounded that violent retaliation is his instinctive response. But that response is also a revolt against deception and false promises, a revolt which Mann obviously hoped would prevent Germany from capitulating to Nazism. In 1929 the ending had a plausible political significance, even if, four years later, it was proved to be hopelessly optimistic. The tragedy lies in the prior capitulation of Mario which can only be expiated by violence and force. Here Mann saw prophetically that fascism would have to be fought by force of arms if its persuasiveness was successful. The real horror of Nazism was that the many German Marios deceived and cheated by Hitler did not turn on their master but stayed loyal to the bitter end. Mann, at the time, underestimated the solidity of a mass movement whose phenomenological features he grasped so well. Only when defeat was inevitable did it actually collapse. But the ending of the story retains a strong element of ambiguity. One can read into it both the hope that ordinary Germans would turn against their Nazi deceivers or the feeling that the destruction of Nazism would be bloody and violent.

An interesting comparison offers itself between Mann's short story and Brecht's *Arturo Ui*. Both use realistic symbols of Nazism, but it is Mann whose use of literary realism is superior. Cipolla, the disguise for Hitler, is hardly significant as a mere magician, whereas Chicago gangsters have a mythology—and a reality—all of their own. The significant feature of Mann's story is that the setting is already unmistakeably fascist, a fact which draws out from the start its political dimension. While Mann captures something of the flavour of a unique political phenomenon, Brecht reduces it to a type of organised crime which flourishes quite happily in any capitalist country.

Mann's story is also superior to the documentary novels of Ernst von Salomon or Ernst Juenger's allegory *On the Marble Cliffs*. It has a psychological realism which Salomon's journalistic fiction lacks and a feeling for social reality which Juenger's allegory, for obvious political reasons, distorted. In not dealing directly with the Nazi movement in Germany, Mann's writing is yet more realistic than scores of books which have done so. Far from transposing Hitler from reality into myth, it transposes him from one plane of reality to another. Mann's tragic vision is expressed through the personalisation of the impersonal power of the charismatic dictator, through hypothesising the direct effect of his power upon single individuals where, in political reality, that same power sways anonymous masses of people. His insight was unquestionable. The German tragedy was that fascism became a successful mass movement. In 1929, Mann saw the tragedy before it had fully materialised.

Mann's most tragic work, *Doctor Faustus*, approaches the trauma of fascism from a completely different perspective. Instead of the relationship of leader and masses, we find portrayed there the cultural ambience giving the movement its intellectual respectability. Mann, seriously ill in post-war America and on the brink of old age, returned to the problem of German culture to which *The Magic Mountain* had expressed no real answer, which in some ways it had postponed answering altogether. Nazism was a kind of answer to that problem, but one which Mann, in 1920, had not conceived of, because it was so horrifyingly brutal. *Doctor Faustus* is a tangential portrait of fascism. Its narrator, Serenus Zeitblom, is a conservative humanist, much as Mann himself was after his conversion to German republican and democratic ideals. In the main, however, the novel is about the life of Adrian Leverkuehn, the talented composer, and his tragic insanity. Its bearing on Nazism is consistently indirect; the Third Reich barely appears in the novel at all. In fact, it is the key absence at the centre of the text. The record of Leverkuehn's life is made by Zeitblom between 1943 and 1945, the last years of the Third Reich. But the story itself actually ends with Leverkuehn's madness in 1930, three years before Hitler's seizure of power. The gap between hero and narrator, between 1930 and 1943, is Nazism in its period of triumph.

The novel makes no concession to 'jackboots on the march' or other melodramas of the 'coming evil' after the stereotyped manner of retrospective documentaries. But the manner in which the story is told, the way in which it takes shape, works precisely because the reader responds to the political absence at the centre of the text. He knows what has happened in Germany. Mann's method is to illuminate the phenomenon by leaving it practically untouched. Instead the reader sees it refracted through the life and tragedy of one man who is as remote from it as it is possible for anyone to be. After his paralytic stroke, Leverkuehn lives on for a further ten years, dying finally when Germany is 'at the height of her dissolute triumphs'. But he knows nothing of the outside world during the course of those ten years, and in his madness remains oblivious to events which outraged mankind. The dialectical tension springs precisely from the complete alienation of the hero from the public world. Mann never made the mistake of trying to portray politics in the novel by politicising his characters. Instead he portrays the vast disparity between his hero's private world and the increasingly politicised life around him. The tragic realism of the novel arises through its artistic vision of a relationship which *does* exist, in spite of the condition of personal alienation which Leverkuehn willingly accepts as his natural artistic fate.

Leverkuehn is a composite portrait, combining his author's date of birth with explicit features of Frederic Nietzsche's life and Arnold Schoenberg's musical composition. In no sense, however, is he a representative figure of the German intelligentsia. A socially isolated figure, Adrian is intellectually isolated too. Rather than embodying a clichéd 'remoteness from life', Adrian is profoundly alienated from the very intellectual circles within which he moves. Among student friends, musical colleagues, academics or critics he possesses a distracted and distant air, often bordering on contempt. His twofold alienation, social and intellectual, makes him, like Nietzsche, a solitary figure. But it is more. It is the outward mark of artistic genius. It is this genius whose secret Zeitblom tries to reveal to his reader. The novel is conceived as an inward movement towards the secret hidden by Leverkuehn's aloofness and isolation. But it is, at the same time, a movement outwards towards a historical understanding of its relationship to the world it ignores.

Such a relationship to the world is far different from that of Hans Castorp. We are plunged into Castorp's inner sensibility from the very beginning, a morbid and delicate sensibility conventionally more associated with an artist than an engineer. Such a direct entry into the stream of consciousness is forbidden to us in the case of the real artist Adrian Leverkuehn. We glimpse him from the outside, much in the way that Marlowe glimpses Kurtz. The novel is a journey of discovery, in which Zeitblom is the medium for the unravelling of the artist's secret. Mann's method is the very opposite of romantic empathy. He withholds the composer's consciousness from the reader just as the composer withholds himself from the world. The novel disavows the traditional romantic and baroque conceptions of the artist. The revelation of Leverkuehn's suffering is objective and brutal, not empathic and self-indulgent. Technically Mann has to rely on Zeitblom to provide the sole and continuous point of view throughout the novel. Of Adrian's conversations with the devil, we are allowed to feel nothing, only to witness the horrifying but unequivocal document scribbled on music paper which has fallen into Zeitblom's hands after Adrian's death.

Sustaining the narrator's point of view through such a complex narrative as Mann gives us presents a major difficulty. This is Zeitblom's unrelieved pedantry. It contrasts beautifully with the medieval demonic of Adrian's own secret language and with the insane despairing speech which is the prelude to the composer's paralytic stroke. But Zeitblom provides no real point of contrast with Leverkuehn's politicised contemporaries. There are two political circles whose existence impinges upon Adrian's own—an idealistic student circle whose ideas would not be out of place in the pre-war *Wandervoegel*, and later the more ominous group of post-war conservative revolutionaries, the Kridwiss circle, whose eminent members meet significantly enough in Munich during the twenties. Zeitblom provides the critical commentary on the defects of both these groups, but at times his own pedantry is indistinguishable from theirs. Often Zeitblom plods his scholarly path towards total unreadability only to be rescued by the interest which the life of his main subject compels in the reader, almost in spite of him. But his heavy pedantic indignation seriously impairs the chapter on the Kridwiss circle.

Without adhering to a norm of biographical accuracy, the Kridwiss circle conjures up, among others, the sundry spirits of Georg Simmel, Ernst Haeckel, Walter Rathenau and Stefan Georg. It was 'an old – new world of revolutionary reaction, in which the values bound up with the idea of the individual—shall we say truth, freedom, law, reason—were entirely rejected and shorn of power'. In fact Mann saw it as an intellectual precursor of Nazism. But Zeitblom is powerless to ridicule the intellectual seriousness with which the group approaches all sorts of barbarism and crude authoritarianism. He is equally unable to portray it as demonic, for his pedantry is in fact incapable of evoking either the demonic or the ridiculous in a political context. The political significance of the group is consequently blurred. Yet Zeitblom cannot refrain from seeing, and this is his importance, a parallel between Leverkuehn's work and the political events of the day.

This parallel has two aspects: the response of the artist to the events of the moment and the objective relationship of the artist's work to the society in which it has been produced. The strength of Mann's novel lies more in the first aspect of the parallel. Here he has to show the importance of politics upon an artist who has disdained political commitment, who has turned his back on political ideology of any sort. Adrian's life is, in one aspect, a test of the complete separation of art and politics. It is a test which poignantly fails. Zeitblom describes his friend's condition in 1919, when, closeted in his rural retreat, Adrian displays indifference to a first-hand account of the Intellectual Workers' Councils in Munich:

> Leverkuehn, to whom I conveyed these impressions of mine was unusually ailing at this time, in a way that had something humiliating in its torments. It was as though he were pinched and plagued with hot pincers, without being in any immediate danger of his life. That, however, seemed to have arrived at its nadir, so that he was just prolonging it by dragging it from one day to the next. He had been attacked by a stomach ailment, not yielding to any dietary measures, beginning with violent headaches, lasting several days and recurring with a few more: with hours, yes, whole days of retching from an empty stomach, sheer misery, undignified, niggling, humiliating, ending in utter exhaustion and persistent sensitivity to light after the attack had passed. There was no thought that the condition might have been due to psychological causes, the tribulations of the time, the national defeat with its desolating consequences. In his rustic not to say cloistered retreat, far from the city, these things scarcely touched him. . . .
>
> And still! Little as it was possible to connect his worsening health in any temperamental way with the worsening misfortune, yet my tendency to see the one in the light of the other and find symbolic parallels in them, this inclination which might after all be due to the fact that they were happening at the same time, was not diminished by his remoteness from outward things, however much I might conceal the thought and refrain from bringing it up even indirectly.[8]

Leverkuehn does respond, however involuntarily, to the changing political fortunes of his day. They agitate him mentally and physically, challenge his very nervous system. But they do not politicise his art. The second aspect of the parallel indicates this. It is Zeitblom, not Adrian, who sees the parallel between the composer's aesthetic barbarism and the political barbarism of the Kridwiss circle. Yet the rest of the novel actually invalidates Zeitblom's provisional hypothesis, which Lukács, typically, takes to be the truth of the novel as a whole in spite of the ending. The paths of Adrian and the Kridwiss circle diverge and in the end become totally incompatible. The ideas of the Kridwiss circle find a distorted expression, and vulgarisation, in the policies of the Third Reich. That same regime suppressed music of the kind which Adrian produced and denounced it as cultural bolshevism. The parallel between composer and right-wing ideologues suggested by Zeitblom is actually only possible from the standpoint of a traditional bourgeois decency which shifts uneasily at the prospect of anything demonic. It is a tribute to Mann's literary talent that he goes beyond the conventional views of his intellectual upbringing.

Leverkuehn has no social relationship at all to the Kridwiss circle except through the mediation of Zeitblom. But in the end that mediation is crucial. Zeitblom invites members of the circle to a special recital Adrian intends to give of his new choral symphony. What they hear instead, along with prestigious members of the musical profession, is the horrifying secret of the composer's artistic inspiration. One by one they walk out at the ranting despair of a man who believes he has made a pact with the devil, and conspired to destroy all the goodness which life has shown him. Adrian's insanity is disowned by the very people who have paved the way for the collective insanity of the Third Reich. In 1930 they were not prepared to concede madness as the price of art, but three years later, with Adrian dead to the world, they ushered in the barbarians who were to destroy Germany and half of Europe in the process.

Leverkuehn's stroke reinforces the feeling of political absence at the centre of the novel. In the remaining ten years of his life, he knows nothing of the events which engulf the lives of those present at the fateful recital. Still alive, he is too much of a vegetable to be able to respond to Nazism at all. The fundamental test of the impact of politics on intellectual life, which Nazism was, passes him by because his art is already finished. His madness, however, cannot be explained by the political events of the time. There is a more profound absence in his life than the absence of politics. It is the absence of passion, or rather the failure to generate a mutual passion with other beings. It is to this, the more fundamental absence, that his music is a response. The trauma of his first and only prostitute, his ensuing illness, the shambles of his marriage proposal to Marie Godeau, the murder of his perfidious friend and go-between Rudi Schwerdtfeger, and finally the tragic death of his nephew, Nepomuk—these are the events which inspire his music and which finally prompt him in his final work *The Lamentation of*

Doktor Faustus 'to take back the good and the noble'. The Kridwiss circle respond to the catastrophe of German politics. But Adrian responds to the catastrophe of his own life. Their response results in capitulation to fascism, but his is the transcendence of suffering and even madness itself. The last dying note of the *Lamentation* 'abides as a light in the night'.

In one vital respect, however, the absence of politics is similar to the absence of passion. It is never permanently possible. Adrian rejects politics through scorn and passion through fear, but his life as an artist cannot be lived without them. At the same time, and this is his tragedy, they are held in abeyance at a terrible price. For Mann, the price of passion was greater than the price of politics, its relationship with art more incestuous, more vital. Literature, far from expressing the identity of art and passion, did the opposite. It expressed their necessary estrangement. As *Death in Venice* had already demonstrated, tragedy sprang from their ultimately irreconcilable natures. By comparison with passion, the political in Mann's fiction is scarcely tragic. Only in *Mario and the Magician* does the tragic element spring from the political. But in *Doctor Faustus* Mann achieves a remarkable fusion of the passionate and the political through the delineation of their absence. It is a remarkable and unique achievement, possible only because the hero possesses the one quality beyond both these absences—the quality of genius. Only thus can modern fiction have its tragic hero who is never committed and never loves.

10 The Severed Continuum: Soviet Realism and the Case of *The Silent Don*

The continuity of Russian realism has always been a controversial issue. After the Russian Revolution, the wholesale rejection of cultural tradition by many left-wing artists and critics also entailed a rejection of classic mimetic forms. Futurists, Constructivists and Suprematists rejected representational art as a relic of bourgeois individualism and committed themselves to new experimental techniques in poetry, film, drama and architecture. In the sphere of literature *LEF* and *On Guard*, the magazine of the *Na Postu* group, made violent attacks upon pre-revolutionary literature. Advocating a didactic, proselytising literature they rejected representational fiction as static and conservative and hence useless in the task of politicising the masses through art. Later, in 1928, the various anti-mimetic groups became absorbed into the new proletarian writers' organisation of Leopold Averbakh, RAPP. New forms of attack were made on representational art, less by rejecting the principle as such than by subjecting it to criteria which were severely constricting. Class background, active commitment to the party, and the choice of fictive themes relevant to the tasks of socialist construction were all weighed positively. Their absence provoked condemnation and often a refusal to publish. But the constrictions upon realist literature which increased rapidly during the period of the first Five-Year plan were nothing compared with the official dogma which ended RAPP's literary dictatorship. The period of socialist realism, which centralised all writers into one politically controlled organisation, was one in which literature was treated purely and simply as an asset of the state. The doctrine of socialist realism, purporting to rescue the representational principle from its previous attacks, actually went further and completely destroyed it. The period between 1934 and Stalin's death was the most barren literary period in modern Russian history. The novel, as a work of art, was defunct.

Within Soviet circles in the twenties, there were those sympathetic to an autonomous literary tradition which dated back to pre-revolutionary days. The tolerance of 'fellow-travellers', writers who were not rev-olutionary but whose writing nonetheless reflected the historical transition to a new revolutionary state, was proposed in his own rather arrogant manner by Trotsky. It was put into practice by Voronsky, the editor of *Red Virgin Soil*, the periodical officially charged by Lenin with the task of creating a new literary tradition. But despite official patronage, the fellow-travellers were the most vulnerable of all artists to attack under the Soviet regime. When their patrons became the first victims of party purges, their official independence ceased. Literature became increasingly subversive, largely because it was so labelled by its persecutors.

Remarkably enough, considering the persecution which has surrounded Soviet writers, much of the best literature of the twenties became acceptable to the new dogma of socialist realism. The early work of Fedin, Leonov, Babel, Alexei Tolstoy and the first volume of *The Silent Don* have been justified by a doctrine which accepted them simply because they were written before it came into force. For they could never have been written in the thirties, just as Mayakovsky, the official poet of socialist realism, could not have been enshrined if he had continued to live. But the doctrine went further than this. By officially endorsing the classic nineteenth-century realism of Balzac and Tolstoy, it set up a three-tier system. Firstly, realist literature of capitalist societies, which in some way reflects the nature and contradictions of capitalism; secondly, Soviet literature of the twenties which reflects the upheavals of the transition to a new revolutionary order; and thirdly, a utilitarian literature of the Stalinist period which is written largely to order, and marks an effective break with literary realism as such. The literature of social command which dominated this period provoked massive capitulation on the part of talented writers previously concerned with artistic self-expression. Sholokhov, Alexei Tolstoy, Ehrenberg, Fedin, Fadeyev, Leonov and many others wrote literature designed to satisfy their new political masters. Only the poetry of the time, the poetry of Mandelstam, Akhmatova, Pasternak and Tsvetayeva, was true to itself, a truth which exacted a terrible price.

The paradox of the Soviet novel is that its greatest fiction does not fulfil the requirements of its official doctrine. The demand for a *parteinost* fiction with a positive Soviet hero and a beneficial view of Soviet society is not to be found in *The Silent Don, Two Sisters, Cities and Years, The Thief* or Olesha's *Envy*. Instead one sees the struggle between the new and the old, a sense of loss and confusion side by side with revolutionary optimism, intellectual hesitation as well as political resolution. Indeed it is the dialectic facets of this representationalism which had provoked the earlier opposition from *LEF* and *On Guard*, an opposition which at times questioned the validity of the novel as an art-form. For if the novel reflects significant dimensions of contemporary reality, then it cannot concentrate narrowly upon the revolutionary forces of the future, which is what the Futurists demanded of art. It must also reveal those aspects of life endangered by the revolutionary process and which finally do not survive it. Bulgakov's nostalgia for a bustling Kiev under White domination or Alexei Tolstoy's nostalgia for the bohemian world of the pre-revolutionary symbolists illustrate, in a fiction which only condones the future very indirectly, a conservative longing for worlds which the revolution has destroyed. Boris Pasternak's novel *Doctor Zhivago*, written much later and never found acceptable by the Soviet regime, actually builds upon a literary tradition of nostalgia which is to be found in early Soviet Realism. In the most unlikely circumstances, the political novel had once again revealed the dialectic of conservatism and revolution.

The outstanding example of this is, without question, *The Silent Don*. But unlike other literature of the period, *The Silent Don* is enshrouded in the vexed question of authorship. A number of dissident Soviet intellectuals and many people in the Don area have regarded it as the work of a Cossack writer Fydor Krukov. Krukov was a war correspondent during the Great War and later fought with the Cossacks against the Bolsheviks during the civil war. He died of typhus in 1920. Recently Solzhenitsyn and Roy Medvedev have separately argued the case for Krukov's authorship of the novel.[1] According to Medvedev, the novel has two authors, Krukov who left an unfinished manuscript at the time of his death and Mikhail Sholokhov, a young Bolshevik into whose hands the manuscript passed. Medvedev has concluded that well over half the published text belongs to Krukov and the rest to Sholokhov, with the Soviet writer's contribution most in evidence during the later volumes.

The question of its authorship remains unresolved to this day. Sholokhov has never produced the original manuscript and a commission was convened by RAPP in 1929 to put an end to rumours about its origin. The commission exonerated Sholokhov but Medvedev claims that two of its members did not agree with its conclusions. If one accepts Medvedev's assertion that Sholokhov adapted a partially completed text, there are still enormous problems. The stylistic continuity, except for brief passages, makes it a philological impossibility, even for experts, to establish which sections belong to which writer. For if two men wrote it, the second is largely faithful to the style and the spirit of the first. On the other hand there are glaring anomalies within the novel which a dual authorship theory could explain. Moreover the difference between *The Silent Don* and Sholokhov's later work *Virgin Soil Upturned* is so vast that it defies a conventional 'capitulation' theory which could be applied, for example, to the difference between the first and third volumes of Alexei Tolstoy's *The Road to Calvary*.

There are two major types of anomaly in *The Silent Don*. A minor but irksome one is the imposition of a Soviet historical commentary upon a flowing fictional narrative, especially where large-scale events in the War or the Civil War have to be strictly interpreted from an official Soviet perspective. These sections read very much like interpolations. But the major defect is in the creation of the Bolshevik characters in the novel. Bunchuk, Stockmann, and the later Misha Koshevoi have a one-dimensional crudity and a brutality which compares very unfavourably with all the Cossacks despite their personal failings. Moreover the introduction of Stockmann and Bunchuk into the text is abrupt and unexplained, their appearance largely unrelated to the preceding events. But perhaps the most curious imbalance of all is created by the lack of contact between the Cossack hero Gregor Melekhov and his Bolshevik opponents. These are limited to one or two very brief scenes. The Cossack hero's life runs parallel with those of his enemies but they never intersect. Only in the original break-up of Gregor's friendship with Misha Koshevoi after the latter decides to join the Reds, do we encounter fully the Cossack dilemma of which political choice to make, that is as a dilemma which divides the Cossacks amongst themselves.

Like *Germinal*, *The Silent Don* has both an individual and a collective hero. It traces the tragic fate of one of the outstanding individuals of the Cossack community, but also the fate of the community itself. Unlike Étienne Lantier, Gregor Melekhov does not survive the tragic fate of the community he leads. He is not an outsider linked to the community, like Lantier, for temporary political purposes. He is born into the community and shares their fate through the entirety of his life. Unlike Lantier who can move on to pastures new, Gregor's fate is tragic because he must ultimately share the fate of the people to whom he belongs. The initial separation of Lantier from the community he leads diminishes his heroic stature and ultimately it is the community which becomes the collective tragic hero of the novel. But Melekhov's fate is tragic because it mirrors, through a series of turbulent and bewildering events, the tragic fate of the Cossacks as a whole. Both Lantier and Melekhov learn from experience, but Lantier has a previous life bequeathing him the political mould within which that experience can be cast. Melekhov starts from scratch and has little opportunity to distance himself from the tragic and terrible events which convulse his whole being and his whole life. His political education is forged through bitter experience, not through theories informing him *a priori* about experiences he has never known.

There is another reason why *The Silent Don* is superior to *Germinal* as a novel of collective *praxis*. It reinstates passion as the foundation of the political novel. Not deliberately so, for the events which politicise the life of the hero occur long after the predicament of his passion has been revealed. But Gregor's violent oscillation between red and white on the political battlefield has its parallel in his oscillation between marriage and passion, between the stability of family life and his unrestrained desire for Aksinia Astakhov. The earlier personal conflict is woven into the later political one, never superseded by the cruelties of the Civil War but made more poignant by the tragic predicament within which it is tragically resolved by the suicide of Natalia, Gregor's wife. It could be said that Natalia's death is symbolic of the fate which awaits them all. But in fact she takes her own life in spite of that fate, and by doing so actually intensifies the tragic element of the story. Passion is pitilessly constrained by the politics of war, but never supplanted by it.

Gregor possesses many of the romantic characteristics of the epic historical novel. He is brave, reckless and without fear, yet in the midst of battle is still moved by human suffering and repelled by atrocities which all sides—Cossacks, Reds and Whites—commit. But what makes him such a remarkable creation is the permanent indecisiveness of his commitment to one side or the other. Revolution and civil war propel him into a situation which never existed for the traditional romantic hero—scepticism and uncertainty about what and whom he is fighting for. It is not an uncertainty occasioned by an aversion to act, for Gregor is above all a man of action. It is uncertainty about the goals of action, though act he must. Gregor's indecision is thus completely different from that of the superfluous man of earlier fiction. The very situation in which he finds himself disallows superfluity. Exhausted by war, wounded, Gregor returns home only to face the reality of the revolution. He joins the Don Revolutionary Committee only to be wounded again, this time in the first stages of the civil war. Then, helpless, he witnesses the massacre of captured officers by fellow Red Cossacks. Both war and civil war have nearly taken his life and both have deprived him of his life on the Don:

> He was broken by the weariness engendered of war. He wanted to turn his back upon all the tempestuous, hate-filled, hostile and incomprehensible world. Behind him everything was entangled, contradictory. With difficulty he had found the right path; but as soon as he set foot upon it the ground had risen up beneath him, the path had dwindled to nothing, and he had lost all confidence that he was on the right course. He had been drawn towards the Bolsheviks, had led others after him, then had hesitated, his heart had turned cold. 'Is Izavarin right after all? Who are we to trust?' But when he thought that soon it would be time to get the harrows ready for spring, mangers would have to be woven of willows, and that when the earth was unclothed and dry he would be driving out into the steppe, his labour-yearning hands gripping the plough handles; when he remembered that he would be breathing in the sweet scent of the young grass and the damp smelling earth turned over by the ploughshare, his heart warmed within him. He longed to collect the cattle, to toss the hay, to smell the withered scent of the clover, the twitch, the pungent smell of dung. He wanted peace and quietness; and so his harsh eyes nursed a constrained gladness as they gazed at the steppe, at the horses at his father's back. Everything reminded him of his half-forgotten former life.[2]

His longing for the land of his youth is never fulfilled. During the war it is a definite absence, but in the civil war it is part of the very territory over which he is fighting. As the battle rages back and forth he endures a semi-fugitive semi-exiled existence, in which he sporadically returns to Tatarsk from his unit until it eventually falls into Bolshevik hands. In his absence the land is worked by the women and the old men, until, decimated by war, it becomes a lost world. Like many of the Cossacks, this longing for their land overrides all political affiliations. The latter indeed is merely a means of saving their land from their enemies. But politics fails them and Gregor's ties to nature are finally severed. The strongest impression one gains from the book is what war and revolution have tragically destroyed—the closeness of the Cossack peasant to his land.

It is this close tie, unknown to the landowner or the rich Kulak, which is the key to the tragic dimension of the novel. It is quite unlike anything to be found in Turgenev or other gentry literature of the previous century, for it is a natural relationship, the antithesis of social privilege. The Cossack Uprising of 1919, provoked by unnecessary Bolshevik atrocities and extortion, was not counter-revolutionary but a reassertion of peasant rights.[3] The Cossacks, once notorious for their repressive cruelty under the Tsar, had repudiated the monarchy and Mother Russia. Instead they were willing to fight only for their own land. Like other peasants who spontaneously expropriated landed estates, the February revolution had brought them undreamed of political opportunities. But after the Bolshevik revolution in October, it became clear that a centralised political order was to be forged once more. Neither among the Whites who supported the former landowners, nor the Bolsheviks who supported the urban working-classes, were the peasants the first priority. But the Cossacks with their own distinctive identity and cultural traditions were difficult recruits for either side. Unwilling to fight beyond their own territory, neither anti-bolshevism nor workers' revolution had much meaning for them.

The Bolsheviks in the novel, Bunchuk, Stockmann and later Misha Koshevoi, interpret their fight against the Cossack uprising as part of the class struggle of the poor against the privileged. But the real class animosity in the novel takes place elsewhere. It is the hatred that Gregor feels for the more privileged and more educated officers of the White Army. The key personal conflict here is between Gregor and Eugene Listnitsky, the young officer from a landowning family who exercises a *droit de seigneur* over Aksinia when she works as a serving-girl in the family household. Gregor's jealous passion for Aksinia is inseparable from his resentment of Listnitsky's social privilege, and the class prerogative with which it endows him. Returning home after an operation for a Front wound in a Moscow hospital, Gregor goes to reclaim his mistress:

On the steps Gregor opened his pack, and from the bottom drew out a hand-painted kerchief carefully wrapped in a clean shirt. He had bought it from a Jewish trader in Zhitomir for two roubles and had preserved it as the apple of his eye, occasionally pulling it out and enjoying its wealth of rainbow colours, foretasting the rapture with which Aksinia would be possessed when he should spread it open before her. A miserable gift! Could he compete in presents with the son of a rich landowner? Struggling with spasms of dry sobbing, he tore the kerchief into little pieces and pushed them under the step.[4]

As his grief transforms itself into rage, he finds Listnitsky and beats him brutally with a knout. The violent confrontation foreshadows the conflict between Gregor and White army officers when the Cossack insurgents join forces with the counter-revolutionaries.

This was the key to the tragedy of the Cossack peasantry. Their desire for self-determination was militarily impossible in 1919 and an agreement was reached to join forces with the White Army under Denikin operating in the Don province. In the uneasy alliance of White and Cossack, social antagonisms come straight to the fore. The Cossacks who fought at the front already hated the officer class and their own army was organised in a more egalitarian manner along the lines of the 1917 Soviets. Gregor finds himself in the situation where those of superior military rank among the White officers are nonetheless military equals in terms of the amount of men at their disposal. His refusal to disband the insurgent division he commands brings the following exchange with General Fitzhelaurov, his White counterpart:

Fitzhelaurov jumped up with unexpected agility and seizing the back of his chair shouted:

'It's not military forces you command but Red Guard rabble! They're not cossacks but the dregs of humanity! You, mister Melekhov, shouldn't be put in command of a division, you should be working as a batman. You ought to be cleaning boots! Do you hear? Why wasn't the order obeyed? You weren't holding a meeting, were you? You weren't discussing the order by any chance? Beware! We're not "comrades" here, and we won't allow the introduction of Bolshevik methods. We won't allow it!

'I must ask you not to shout at me!' Gregor said in a thick voice, and rose, pushing back the stool with his foot.

'What did you say?' Fitzhelaurov cried hoarsely, panting with agitation, leaning across the table.

'I must ask you not to shout at me!' Gregor repeated in a louder tone. 'You sent for us in order to decide. . . .' He was silent for a second, lowered his eyes and not removing his gaze from Fitzhelaurov's hands, dropped his voice almost to a whisper.

'If you, your Excellency, attempt to lay even your little finger on me, I shall sabre you on the spot!'[5]

The personal and social tension between Gregor and Listnitsky is transposed into a military and political conflict. Gregor and Fitzhelaurov, theoretically equal as divisional commanders, confront each other with a naked class hatred. Gregor's term of address 'your Excellency' is not so much ironic as contemptuous. It contains the traditional mark of deference which his subsequent threat completely shatters. Politics and war have destroyed the 'natural' superiority of the officer-class. One of the chief characteristics of Gregor, indeed a heroic characteristic, is his unrelenting hatred of any display of social privilege. Yet, at the same time, he is doomed to go to the wall, along with those whom he hates. Gregor's fate is tragic because the very process of revolution which stirs his hatred of privilege and injustice sweeps him away as one of its victims. Weary and exhausted, Gregor fights long and hard in vain for a just cause.

Despite the unevenness of the third and fourth volumes of the novel, Gregor's tragic fate is cumulative, a fight against growing odds which can never be won. This refers not only to the military battle but to his personal life. He suffers isolation from his village, Natalia's suicide, his army's flight to the sea, Aksinia's illness and then his own. The luxury of dying heroically in battle is denied him. Instead he sees his own life, and the Cossack way of life, gradually disintegrate until nothing but his children are left him. His tragedy is identical with that of his people and the novel does not alter the balance of sympathy by portraying the new beneficiaries of Soviet power. Brutal and vindictive, authoritarian and bureaucratic, they only serve to highlight the tragic integrity of Gregor, and to suggest that what replaces the old is inferior to it.

The idea that Sholokhov, as a Soviet author, portrays the fate of the Cossacks with admirable impartiality, is not merely questionable on grounds of authorship. The evidence of the finished text, whoever wrote it, testifies to the contrary. No sense of balance is achieved because the moral and heroic stature of the Bolsheviks is completely dwarfed by the Cossack hero. They simply do not measure up to him. As the four volumes of the novel were published from 1929 to 1940, Soviet critics of the period came to accept the Bolshevik figures—Bunchuk, Stockmann and Misha Koshevoi—as the positive heroes of the novel. But this testifies only to the degeneration of moral and literary sensibility under Stalinism. The positive evaluation of the Bolshevik characters is judged not by their personal qualities, but by their political success. From a Stalinist viewpoint the fact that Misha Koshevoi is a turncoat who betrays his people and destroys his own village can be safely ignored because he is one of the victors. Stockmann, the callous and cruel Bolshevik commissar can be praised for his bureaucratic talents of organisation, qualities he shared with Siemon Davidov, the organiser of collectivisation in *Virgin Soil Upturned*. His total insensivity towards the Cossack predicament can safely be ignored.

The case of Gregor, however, is a major stumbling block. After the appearance of the first two volumes, readers among the party faithful actually wrote to Sholokhov demanding that Gregor be converted to the communist cause. But to the very end, in the period after 1920, Sholokhov remains faithful to the original conception of the tragic hero. In the last, slim volume which appeared in 1939 and 1940, eight years after its predecessor, he opposes the communists to the bitter end, returning only to his village when all opposition is exhausted to give himself up to the Cheka. The only concession Sholokhov makes to the 'bolshevisation' of Melekhov is to state that he served with Budenny's Red cavalry in Poland before returning home. But this part of his life is only referred to, never described. Politically and emotionally it makes no sense, given Gregor's experience of the last tragic retreat of the Don Cossacks to the sea before the advancing Red forces. What does make sense is Gregor's growing isolation and grief as the Cossack life he knew and loved is gradually destroyed. This experience commands the reader's sympathy more and more as the book progresses, in spite of the more frequent presence of the 'victors'. The ending belongs not to the victors, but to the doomed Gregor Melekhov:

> And now the little thing of which Gregor had dreamed during so many sleepless nights had come to pass. He stood at the gate of his own home, holding his son by the hands.
> This was all life had left to him, all that for a little longer gave him kinship with the earth and with the spacious world which lay glittering under the chilly sun.[6]

The immense popularity of the book in the communist world, where sales have run into tens of millions, raises an interesting question about its vast appeal. Does its readership agree with the Soviet critics who praised Misha Koshevoi, the plunderer of Cossack villages, and denounced the unrepentant Gregor for his 'ideological errors'? Apart from the most inflexible party militants, this seems unlikely. Gregor's tragic fate strikes a chord among its readers because it reflects the suffering and doom of so many under a repressive system which managed to destroy all notions of humanity. The dilemma of Gregor, a man striving for justice amidst total political confusion and immense personal deprivation, only to be punished mercilessly for all his efforts, was the predicament of millions of people in the Soviet Union. The most famous and most widely read work of socialist realism actually subverts everything the doctrine stands for. It reflects a widespread tragedy which no veneer of revolutionary optimism could ever conceal, no positive literary hero ever eradicate.

The artistic consistency of Gregor's tragic fate vanquishes the serious flaws in the characterisation of the Bolsheviks. If the novel was written by two men, and not one, it is clear that the power of the initial vision is sustained by the writer who copies it, at least with regard to the fate of its hero.[7] Seen in this light Bunchuk, Stockmann and Misha are a series of half-hearted attempts to depose Gregor from his central heroic role. They all fail. Even the attempt to duplicate and rival his passion for Aksinia in the love affair of Bunchuk and Anna Pogoodko is a failure. It results in a sentimentalised imitation of Cossack passion. In another book, perhaps, its literary merits might stand out. But here they are easily surpassed. The original conception of Gregor Melekhov is so powerful that he cannot be diminished by the creation of political rivals or himself be converted to the political cause which is alien to him.

As it stands, *The Silent Don* is the one major novel of tragic realism to be condoned by the Soviet authorities. Its original value has outlasted the degrading revision forced on Sholokhov during the Zhdanov period. Bearing comparison with Tolstoy and Dostoevsky, it is the exception to the rule of the severed continuum—that is, the continuity of Russian realism claimed in principle by the Soviet critics and destroyed in practice by political intimidation and literary censorship. It is, above all, a novel of passion. The passion of Gregor and Aksinia is not a socially forbidden passion. Nor is it a passion within a privileged class which it subsequently undermines. Its unique feature is in compensating for the loss it causes, in healing the wound it opens. After Natalia's tragic suicide, Aksinia comes to care for Gregor's children just as she cares for him. Under the pressure of his constant absence and the privations of civil war, their affair draws together the remaining threads of love and compassion amidst impending disaster. As it does so, it goes from strength to strength, building upon itself, opening outwards towards the story's inevitable ending, enduring the terrible illnesses they both suffer. As the enemy closes in, it is the prevailing note of hope amidst desolation and despair. By the end, when Gregor finally returns to the village, his arrest almost certain, *The Silent Don* has already become a landmark of tragic realism. Never before, and never since, has a primitive peasantry been given such literary stature. In its treatment of the pride of the oppressed, only *Germinal*, among western literature, can rival it.

11 Malraux and Hemingway: The Myth of Tragic Humanism

The story goes that in Madrid in 1937, Ernest Hemingway and André Malraux agreed, half in jest, to write novels about different periods of the Spanish Civil War. This is in fact what happened. Malraux's novel *Days of Hope*, which he finished in the same year, ends with the defeat of the Italians at Guadalajara in March 1937. Hemingway's *For Whom the Bell Tolls*, however, is set only two months later in the last week of May.[1] While Malraux attempts to give a panoramic picture of the whole of that early part of the war from the first day of the military rebellion, Hemingway's novel covers only three days out of the whole of the war. Malraux had dashed back to Paris to write his novel in the hope that the war might be won. When Hemingway began his novel in March 1939, the cause was already lost. Difference in the time of writing and difference in the scale of writing are both crucial in evaluating their respective novels. Malraux's diffuse war-panorama and his glowing eulogy to human solidarity are indicative of his revolutionary optimism; Hemingway's intensive focus and his feeling for the heroic in the midst of betrayal are indicative of tragic realism.

It seems curious therefore that of the two, Malraux should be the one to define himself as a tragic humanist.[2] But it should be remembered that, unlike Hemingway, this was not Malraux's first attempt at a political novel. He already had a reputation as a master of political fiction based upon his novels of the Chinese revolution, *The Conquerors* and *Man's Estate*. Here there is undoubtedly a tragic vision of political action which contrasts very strongly with *Days of Hope*. But the reason for the change in Malraux's fiction must be sought in the earlier work and the subsequent change of political attitude in the thirties which brought him closer in sympathy to Soviet communism. Of these two factors it is the literary one to which we must give the most attention. Politically Malraux had moved in the thirties from a position of loose sympathy to Trotskyism to loose sympathy for Stalinism. But his novel of the Spanish Civil War, while revealing this change of sympathy, more importantly reveals an attempt to overcome the obsessions of the earlier novels. In order to understand the literary failure of *Days of Hope* we have to look at the inadequacies of his earlier, more talented fiction.

Goldmann has suggested that *Man's Estate* is the quintessential novel of the collective, problematic hero in the age of modern capitalism. Nothing could be further from the truth. Though it portrays a revolutionary uprising, it is not about a revolutionary proletariat. It is about a group of communist leaders and their links with the capitalist world. Malraux was more interested in the diversity of individual destinies within the common framework of a revolutionary event, than the collective destiny of the class involved in the uprising. It is also very conspicuous that his revolutionary leaders are either European or highly Europeanised. Trotsky's claim that the European revolutionaries in *The Conquerors* are merely practising an imperialism in reverse, comes close to the mark. In *Man's Estate* we find that Katow and Hemmelrich are Europeans while Kyo is Japanese like his father, and always regarded as a foreigner. Their main enemies, Ferral, Clappique and Koenig are also Europeans. The only important Chinese figure in the novel is Chen and he is the solitary terrorist, a figure so isolated that he feels no sense of community with the men he leads during the uprising. The Shanghai workers on whom the success of the uprising depends are like shadows in the night. The novel makes no attempt to reveal them to us.

Chen is the most compelling figure in the novel because of his individual sense of destiny, and his horrifying obsession with murder and death. This is clear from the opening scene of the novel—one of the best things Malraux has ever written—in which he murders for the first time. His victim is an arms dealer who possesses a chit for weapons in dock which are crucial for the forthcoming insurrection. Why is Chen so compelling, more compelling than his more orthodox comrades? It is because everything he does is a gamble on life itself. The fate of the revolution takes second place to the sensation of having killed a man in cold blood:

> It was not fear which possessed him, it was a frightful and at the same time solemn sensation of panic such as he had not known since childhood: he was alone with death, alone in a place where no man was, feebly overcome by horror and the taste of blood. . . .
>
> There were millions of lives in that world, and each one had cast him out: but what did their puny outlawry avail against the relief he felt now that death was leaving him, the feeling that it welled out of him in long gushes, like that man's blood? . . .
>
> Murder had absorbed him into a world of his own, and he found it as hard to escape from as the heat itself. There was no sign of life. Not the least movement, no noise anywhere near: not even the cries of hawkers, not even the barking of stray dogs. . . . In the room, face to face with the body, once full realisation had come to him, he had been quite certain: he had *felt* Death. . . .
>
> The memory of the hardness of that body haunted him: he felt an urge

to press his arm hard up against the first thing he came across. Speech would shatter the intimacy of his communion with death. . . .

Now that he had killed a man, he had the right to feel anything he wanted. The right.[3]

In these passages which follow the assasination Malraux manages to capture the primeval horror of murder felt by the murderer but also the sense of power which his murder brings to him. Their intensity recalls Raskolnikov in *Crime and Punishment*. Yet the context is totally different. Chen is surrounded, and supported, by the comrades of his movement. Soon afterwards he has to lead his workers' section into action. But his political loyalty provides neither true justification nor psychological compensation for the terrible loneliness which leads him to murder. The official reason that Malraux offers for his tragic humanism is that the political fighter must face the prospect of his own death in order to gain a necessary victory. But in the case of Chen, murder is the compensation for a terrible loneliness. As he surveys his section at the start of the uprising, he thinks to himself:

> He didn't belong with them. Despite the murder, despite the fact that he was there. If he died today, he would die alone. Their course was clear enough: they were fighting for bread to live and recognition as human beings. As for him . . . apart from the sufferings of the common cause, he was quite unable even to talk to them.[4]

Chen does not share in the fate of those who are communists 'for the sake of dignity'. More important for him is 'the communion with death' and that other special reason for which Malraux admired Marxism, 'a worship of the power of the will'. Death and the will-to-power form the undertow of that official debate on revolutionary strategy which occupies much of the novel. Malraux was one of the first writers to bring to light the betrayal of the Shanghai communists by their Soviet advisers who counselled a continued alliance with the Kuomintang. But despite the political tensions and betrayals which the novel explores so well, it is wrong to see this betrayal as the tragic element in the novel. Through the figure of Chen, whose obsession with death infects all the other communists, Malraux transforms potential tragedy to a final and horrifying acceptance of 'the human condtion'.

While Chen's terrorist methods are never accepted by the other leaders, his metaphysical example is too compelling to resist. In his previous novel *The Conquerors* the terrorism of Hong is primitive and brutal, based on a fanatical hatred of class privilege. But Chen's world is metaphysical. The world of other men exists in the shadows, secondary to the philosophy of the violent act which ends in death. The influences upon Chen are significantly Western ones; terrorism is less a rejection of traditional China than of the Christianity and its world of grace taught to him by American missionaries. There is a strong literary lineage between Chen and the anarchists of Dostoevsky, Conrad and Zola, with the important difference that Malraux is on the side of the possessed. He has transported the Nietzschean rejection of Christianity and the cult of the overman to the Orient, but the sensibility of his characters remains European. It is only in the distant colonial setting that they manage to accomplish the astonishing devaluation of values for which Chen ultimately stands.

Murder, for Malraux, is a debased erotic metaphor, passive death the humiliation of the raped victim. He regards the pleasure of passive sexuality—which for him means female sexuality—with a sense of horror. After May has been unfaithful to him, Kyo sees his wife's face as 'a death mask'. But the active role is a ritual act of triumph whether it is the stabbing of the victim or the penetration of the beloved. Either action brings in its wake a kind of death. Thus Kyo 'understood now that to be willing to lead the woman he loved to her death was perhaps love in its most complete form, the love beyond which nothing can go'.[5] This sadomasochistic relationship also governs Katow's reminiscence of his dead Russian wife: 'No sooner had she grown inured to the suffering which he inflicted on her, than the realisation of the amazing tenderness of the creature which suffers for the being by whom the suffering is imposed, had overwhelmed him'.[6] But it is Chen who provides the strongest link between murder, eros and death. The stabbing of the arms dealer was the act of the virgin deflowering himself. Now hardened to murder and its sensations, he plots the assassination of Chang Kai Shek. Asked why he dislikes the thought of other groups plotting Chang's murder, he replies: 'Because I dislike the idea of *my* woman receiving kisses from others.'

The full significance of Malraux's perversion of passion is only felt when the communists are captured by the Kuomintang and thrust into prison. Torture and death at the hands of others are the ultimate forms of passive humiliation. 'To die is passive,' Kyo thinks, 'but to kill oneself is to turn passivity into action.' Suicide is the only escape from the passive humiliation of murder by others. Kyo and Katow are more obsessed by their cyanide capsules than they are by the fate of Chinese communism. The common idea of most political militants, that it is a good thing to be martyred for the cause when death is unavoidable, scarcely occurs to them. Chen has already blown himself to pieces, falling ecstatically on his bomb in front of the car he mistakenly imagines to hold Chang-Kai-Shek. For Kyo and Katow, the prime imperative is to follow his example and take their own lives. Death is not tragic because it is a kind of mystical affirmation, in which the activist finds fulfilment when it is accomplished by his own hand.

The alternative to Kyo's suicide by poisoning is, for Katow, the altruistic act of donating one's cyanide to others whose need is greater. In the endeavour to avoid passive humiliation, the giving away of cyanide is the supreme act of self-sacrifice, the great act of human kindness:

> He, Katow, too, pressed his hand—he was beyond the meaning of tears, overcome by the sadness of this unseen and barely heard gratitude (all murmurings here were alike) that was being offered him, blindly, in the surrounding darkness, in return for the greatest gift he had ever made. . . .[7]

The cyanide is dropped on the floor, then found again. Katow's two comrades poison themselves, and as he is led out to be shot this provides him with a makeshift triumph.

The political ending to the book seems little more than a token postscript. With Ferral's explanation to his colleagues in Paris of the economic significance of the communist defeat, and Hemmelrich's eulogy to industrialisation in the Soviet Union, we have a mandatory Marxist ending superimposed upon the ecstatic acceptance of death. Like no other modern novel, Malraux's book combines elements from Marx, Nietzsche and De Sade. But while the Marxism is never superficial, it basically gives way to deeper concerns. Chen, Kyo and Katow all achieve a mystical fulfilment through suicide and violent death. Such a fulfilment, which is still realistic in the figural sense, is nonetheless a negation of the tragic. Deprived of victory the communist leaders save themselves from tragedy by trying to control the nature of the death which awaits them. The ecstatic experience of violence remains, nonetheless, the key to the human condition. Malraux shares with Ernst Juenger and other fascist writers an irrational obsession with the mystique of violent death which is neither humanist nor tragic. It was ominous, perhaps, that in the next decade, the Axis powers set the standards for sacrificial suicide during their own defeat. Japan provided its *kamikaze* pilots and the Nazi leadership a large number of deaths through cyanide capsules. And it was Goebbels after all who sang the glories of total destruction.

In our own age we know only too well how the mystique of terrorism which possessed Chen continues to exercise its attractions. In the case of Chen, it was only partly exonerated by its attachment to more positive goals. And it is he who provides the example for the fulfilment of a collective destiny—self-destructive, violent death. Looking back to this novel from a more orthodox, pro-Soviet point of view, it surely could not have escaped Malraux's attention that terror had triumphed over politics instead of politics over terror. *Days of Hope* seems at times to be a conscious atonement for his unpolitical excesses. But by rejecting the spirit of his earlier fiction, Malraux also abandons literary realism itself. In spite of his own claims, the realism of *Man's Estate* is affirmative rather than tragic. In *Days of Hope* the figural dimensions of realism escape him altogether. The book is the literary heir to Chernyshevsky, asking of the Spanish Civil War, the famous title of the Russian's novel—what is to be done? A documentary, almost journalistic account of the war at times, the novel super-imposes upon its descriptive technique a didactic debate about re-volutionary strategy. Malraux does convey quite vividly the courage of many Republicans in defeating the initial military rebellion. But the book does little more, and indeed spoils even this by its crude didacticism. The misleading judgment on *Man's Estate*, that the revolution alone is the hero, is almost true of *Days of Hope*. But the revolution of which Malraux speaks is incredibly narrow. It is the maximisation of military efficiency, in other words the means by which the war is to be won.

For this reason the novel revolves around a philosophically crude distinction between 'doing' (*faire*) and 'being' (*être*), which is translated politically into the difference between the communists and the anarchists. The distinction is unconvincing. Malraux overlooks the fact that different political ideologies imply different ways of acting. Indeed in the novel most of the Republicans act with courage, not only the communists like Manuel, but the uncommitted like Magnin, anarchists like the Negus, and Republican army officers like Hernandez. The difference lies in the military effectiveness of their courage. The problem for Malraux is to convey, in literary terms, the difference between spontaneous heroism and disciplined success. To do this, he uses the literary device of a *commandante* Garcia, who is scarcely involved in actual combat at all. Garcia is the sagacious commentator on the meaning of the events which take place before the reader's eyes, but is himself inert.

The difficulty with this device is that it causes Malraux's distinction between *être* and *faire* to backfire on him. Garcia is the repository of the author's political wisdom, his reflective mouthpiece. But this is only possible because he is not involved in the action himself. He strikes the pose of the neutral commentator rather than the militant officer. The very person in the novel who advocates the priority of *faire* over *être* is himself a living example of the 'being' he despises. This is unintentional on Malraux's part, but is the necessary consequence of a narrative which eliminates the subject from the actions in which he participates. Garcia is a didactic device to mediate between ill-formed character and frenetic event. His contrived omniscience, his placid pipe-smoking style, are totally inappropriate for desperate events such as the defence of Madrid or the fall of the Alcazar. Malraux's dilemma is that he can only argue the necessity for disciplined action through the medium of the very person who seems to possess no responsibility for events going on around him.

This point is most fully illustrated during the fight for the Alcazar. Garcia criticises strategy without apparently being responsible for it and without trying to alter it. He also points out his colleagues' personal failings in between their desperate attempts to force the rebels to surrender. During a 'brief lull in the truce' he tells Hernandez, the republican officer later to be captured and shot:

It's quite likely, Hernandez, that you're on the way to meet your destiny. It's never easy to give up what one has loved, all the things one's lived for. I'd like to help you; but the cause you're staking your life on is doomed from the outset. Because you have to live politically, you have to act in terms of politics; and your duties as an officer bring you every moment into touch with politics. Whereas the cause you have in mind is not political. It is based on the contrast between the world in which you live and the world of your dreams. But action can only be envisaged in terms of action. . . . The habit of thinking about what ought to be instead of what can actually be done is a mental poison. For which, as Goya says, there is no known antidote. The man who stakes his life on such a cause is bound to lose. It's a fool's game, my dear fellow. Moral 'uplift' and magnanimity are matters for the individual, with which the revolution has no direct concern. . . .[8]

The context in which this advice is delivered is clearly ludicrous. No-one pontificates so pretentiously at the front-line and gets away with it. But there is more to the unreal tone of Garcia's address than this. It is at once scolding and patronising, the advice of someone who is a cross between a wise uncle and an angry father. But what is the formal relationship of the two men? Is Garcia the military superior of Hernandez? Or is he the equal of the men whose tactical shortcomings he is always criticising? The novel is too vague to really tell us. We know Garcia is a major, Hernandez a captain, but the whole question of authority is blurred, not merely because the situation at the time was confused, but because Malraux never really portrays relationships of power. As an intelligence officer, Garcia is a kind of political commissar for fellow-travellers, extolling the communist virtues of organisation and discipline without actually advocating membership of the party. But logically, the choice suggested by his advice, is to join the party or go under. 'Our humble task is to *organise* the Apocalypse', he tells Magnin.

The advice which Garcia gives Hernandez actually contains the central malaise of the novel as a whole. He must destroy 'the habit of thinking about what ought to be instead of what can actually be done'. The text itself abandons any concern with moral values as such. The question of why the war needs to be fought, what the fascists stand for, what the republicans are socially and politically capable of achieving, all these questions are eliminated. One is left with a worship of efficiency, but no sense of the moral dilemmas which the quest for military efficiency creates in the life of the Popular Front or the Spanish people as a whole. The only value of the novel, as it were, is the shelving of the life-by-value.

A plea for efficiency is not, in itself, enough to sustain the tone of revolutionary optimism Malraux sought to create. Aside from this he had to create a mood of solidarity, of the 'virile fraternity' which stemmed from the combat of the good cause. Ironically, this also makes nonsense of the crude distinction between 'doing' and 'being'. Fraternity is a form of *être* born out of common action. Solidarity is a ritual, too, as the meeting of the air force pilots with the peasants of Linares demonstrates. But such solidarity is conditioned by the course of the war itself. The novel reaches a climactic note of affirmation with the battle of Guadalajara, because that represented the peak of Republican success in the war as a whole. Hope has its special conditions, and Malraux does not go beyond them.

Malraux's abandonment of figural realism has to do with the generality of mood, tendency and event. Like Zola at his worst, Malraux makes them indiscriminately the property of anyone and everyone. Characters do not work out their individual destinies so much as contribute to the general mood, the general political tendency, and the general war effort. The ending of the novel is realistic enough in the journalistic sense. Malraux took account of what had happened up to the very point at which he was writing. But from a literary point of view, this has much the same disastrous consequences as *Virgin Soil Upturned*. It stems the flow of experience, which has already been generated, in an artificial manner. Not only that, it is powerless to portray the historical *volte-face* which subsequently took place. Lacking any prophetic element, it appears deliberately myopic, almost as if the transient half-truth it presents is intended to conceal the whole truth which outlives it.

Malraux's commitment to immediacy, to writing the instant novel as if circumstances were so pressing there was no justifiable alternative, conspires to dig its own grave. For this sort of fiction merely hires itself out to events beyond its control. In fact it celebrates the events themselves as if they heralded final victory, and at this point the novel is a continuation of politics by other means. The novel wills a Republican victory in the same sense as the slogans of *La Pasionaria*. But unlike the slogan which can be produced instantaneously the novel must wait until it is published and read. The fate of Malraux's book was to be read when defeat was certain or had already happened. It was disastrous for a book stressing no positive values other than those of winning the victory.

If we turn to Hemingway we find his political views of the war very similar to those of the Frenchman. He had no time for the anarchists whom he regarded, as did Malraux, as being reckless and counter-productive. He admired the efforts made by communist military leaders to weld together a disciplined army which had to face superior forces and superior firepower. Yet despite this similarity, which included an intense commitment to winning whatever the cost, Hemingway's novel is different from Malraux's in practically all respects. He forsakes Malraux's panoramic view of the battlefront to focus more clearly on the moral dilemmas of the war hidden beneath Malraux's hollow rhetoric about military efficiency. *For Whom the Bell Tolls* is a fictional test of Republican values, of whether they can lead to a better way of life for the Spanish people. But it is a test which works itself out in the fate of its individual and collective hero. An isolated incident of the war is seen and lived through their eyes. But this microcosm of the war is an exact one. The meaning of the war emanates from the experience and interpersonal relationships of the characters Hemingway creates. It is very different from *Days of Hope* where characterisation is a function of fighting in the major strategic battles and engaging in ideological debates about them.

The clarity of Hemingway's perspective is a good example of the use of literary space. Robert Jordan is both insider and outsider in the fight against fascism, the international volunteer with a strong understanding of the life of the Spanish people. The band of peasant guerillas, isolated in nomadic life behind enemy lines, nonetheless embodies the fate of Spain itself. Jordan is the key link between the leadership in Madrid and the partisans in isolation in the mountains. There are differences of power, of role, of culture, of class in the Republican movement here to which Malraux, typically, paid little attention. For Malraux, with his one-dimensional literary frame, differences must be political differences or they are not differences at all. *For Whom the Bell Tolls* explodes this myth. It portrays the lives which politics alters, and it does so without illusions.

The synthesis of individual and collective hero is reminiscent of *Germinal*. But Robert Jordan already carries the seal of authority of the General Staff. He does not seek conversion like Étienne Lantier, but merely demands loyalty. While the relationship of the individual and collective hero is less problematic than in Zola, this very fact allows Hemingway greater depth of characterisation. There are lulls in the tension created by Jordan's assignment; almost leisurely interludes during which Pilar relates the atrocities of Pablo and the anarchists at the start of war, and Maria her own humiliation at the hands of the fascists. By flashback, Hemingway expands the stream of experience beyond the limits of its temporal compression. The novel lasts only three days but by expanding backwards through time, it lends the necessary perspective to the narrative movement of the story towards its ending. Flashback is a necessary feature of its figural dimension. It is a device which Malraux never used, or could use, because of the contrived sense of urgency in *Days of Hope*, as if, by deflecting his glance, he would miss the loss or capture of an important military position. But temporal compression actually aids Hemingway in his quest to portray the variety of human experience in the midst of civil war. In that fateful period between Saturday and Tuesday in the last week of May, on the forest covered slopes of the Sierra de Guadaramas, it seems that everything happens which could happen. The range of sensibility he captures is extraordinary. But this range of feeling and the compression of time, complementary opposites in every way, are derived precisely from Hemingway's tragic vision of the war. They mark the point at which politics and tragic realism intersect.

The dominant value of the International Brigades helping the Republican cause was, as the novel puts it, 'ascetic idealism'. No passion rivals that of the cause, for as Robert Jordan thinks at one point, 'continence is the foe of heresy'. But passion is of profound importance in the novel since it is the one unpredictable factor in those three final days of Robert Jordan's life. He could predict Pablo's treachery, predict the loss of the surprise element in Golz's offensive, even predict his own death. But his affair with Maria is the one element he could not have foreseen. Like the other foreign volunteers, he puts the passions of politics above the passions of flesh and blood. But he betrays the artificial puritanism he brings with him on his mission. Among Malraux's characters such a 'betrayal' is unthinkable. His early revolutionaries possess an erotic passion but it is a passion for murder and death, not for women. And in *Days of Hope*, where all the characters are remarkably passionless, there are no women at all. In the immediacy of revolution, women are superfluous.

For Whom the Bell Tolls completely undermines Malraux's passionless convention. The essence of Hemingway's temporal compression is expressed through passion. In Jordan's affair with Maria, the urgency of revolution and the urgency of passion complement one another. Jordan, to his utmost surprise, discovers the seriousness of the truth about which Golz had jokingly teased him. Guerilla war, its isolation, danger and threat of death produce the social context for a love affair which in a normal civilian life would take months or years to develop. But Hemingway avoids the sentimentality into which this use of passion could easily degenerate. Robert Jordan's consciousness is two-dimensional, forever contrasting the miraculous fortune of his affair with the reality of his position as a saboteur and a foreigner in the mountains. But the contrast is not merely within his own mind. It is a contrast between his personal relationships with Maria, Pilar, Anselmo and El Sordo and his inward scepticism about the mission, its organisers and their own political schemes for the future of Spain. The contrast is sustained, stylistically speaking, by the profound difference of speech and consciousness.

Hemingway's dialogue, with its use of the archaic second person familiar, its formal dignity, and its flowery oaths, has sometimes been criticised as contrived. But this amazing synthesis of Shakespearian English and Spanish idiom is the positive antidote to the lacerating scepticism of Robert Jordan's mind. The balance between them is very fine and needs to be. Were one to dominate, the result would be disastrous. At every opportunity, Jordan indulges his favourite iconoclasm, namely to deflate (*dégonfler*) political myth. But the rough poetry of the partisans' speech is something which cannot be deflated. It attains the authentic voice of the people which *Realpolitik* constantly endangers. Consider the following extracts which exemplify this remarkable contrast between what is said and what Robert Jordan thinks, between what is done in those three days and what shibboleths of the war the sceptical spirit demolishes. This is Jordan's reaction to Joachim's account of his family's murder:

How many times had he heard this? How many times had he watched people say it with difficulty? How many times had he seen their eyes fill and their throats harden with the difficulty of saying my father, or my brother, or my mother, or my sister? He could not remember how many times he had heard them mention their dead in this way. Nearly always they spoke as this boy did now: suddenly and apropos of the mention of the town and always you said 'What barbarians'.

You only heard the statement of the loss. You did not see the father fall as Pilar made him see the Fascists die in that story she had told by the stream. You knew the father died in some courtyard or against some wall, or in some field or orchard, or at night, in the lights of a truck beside some road. You had seen the lights of the car from the hills and heard the shooting and afterwards you had come down to the road and found the bodies. You did not see the mother shot, nor the sister, nor the brother. You heard about it: you heard the shots and you saw the bodies.

. . . The *partizans* did their damage and pulled out. The peasants stayed on and took the punishment.[9]

Jordan's scepticism, his bitterness, is based upon a perception of a general truth. His perceptiveness goes far beyond that of the guerilla bands in the mountains who must fight, unaware of the consequences of their actions. For he sees more clearly than anyone else the moral dilemma of the form of warfare in which he is engaged. Yet his awareness does not harden into cynicism, or petrify him into paralysis. The significance of his love-affair is that Maria is one of the many victims to which he had been referring, her parents killed by fascists, herself the victim of brutal rape. The sense of *now* heals, exonerates and transcends:

Then they were walking along the stream together and he said 'Maria, I love thee and thou art so lovely and so wonderful and so beautiful and it does such things to me to be with thee that I feel as though I wanted to die when I am loving thee.'

'Oh', she said. 'I die each time. Do you not die?'

'No. Almost. But did thee feel the earth move?'

'Yes. As I have died. Put thy arm around me, please.'

'No. I have thy hand. Thy hand is enough.'

He looked at her and across the meadows where a hawk was hunting and the big afternoon clouds were coming now over the mountains.

'And it is not thus for thee with others?' Maria asked him, they now walking hand in hand.

'No. Truly.'

'Thou hast loved many others.'

'Some. But not as thee.'

'And it was not thus? Truly?'

'It was a pleasure but it was not thus.'

'And then the earth moved. The earth never moved before?'
'Nay. Truly never.'
'Ay', she said, 'And this we have for one day'.
He said nothing.[10]

Here there is no possible division between doing and being, for passion has been created in the face of death. It is not the passion of someone who merely reflects on the war, like a hard-bitten journalist, but of someone who knows that action brings death. The distance created by Jordan between himself and the peasantry in the way he reflects on their fate is overcome by his passion for a woman whose fate is theirs, the fate of a victim whose passion destroys the stigma of her past. Maria, in loving Jordan, leaves her past behind her. She also unites him with the people for whom he is fighting.

Passion is at the core of Jordan's unity with the guerilla band, reflecting its short-lived intensity. Emotions develop quickly through propinquity, the friendship with Pilar and Anselmo, the distrust of and contempt for Pablo. Nothing could be further removed from the abstract collective solidarity at the end of *Days of Hope*, which, though stirring, never descends to the level of the individual person. Interpersonal relationships are of immense importance to Jordan in his work, because in his mind solidarity is already *unmasked*, an abstract quality open to treachery and deceit. 'The closer to the front', Jordan tells Karkov, the cynical Russian journalist, 'the better the people.' The journey to the front is an escape from cynicism into dignity, even though it means coming face to face with the cowardice of someone like Pablo.

The difference is again set out in the contrast of speech and consciousness. Jordan's mind unmasks the reality behind the leadership of the war, but later on Anselmo and Agustin debate with feeling their hopes when the war has ended. The two realities are politically incompatible, but it is through the second that Jordan's optimism can override his gloom about the shady world of Soviet influence at Gaylord's hotel in Madrid:

> He had not liked Gaylord's, the hotel in Madrid which the Russians had taken over, when he first went there because it seemed too luxurious and the food was too good for a besieged city and the talk too cynical for a war. But I corrupted easily, he thought. . . .
>
> It was at Gaylord's that you learned that Valentin Gonzalez, called El Campesino or The Peasant, had never been a peasant but was an ex-sergeant in the Spanish foreign legion who had deserted and fought with Abd el Krim. That was all right, too. You had to have peasant leaders quickly in that sort of war and a real peasant leader might be a little too much like Pablo. You couldn't wait for the real peasant leader to arrive and he might have too many peasant characteristics when he did. . . .
>
> At Gaylord's too, you met the simple stonemason, Enrique Lister

from Galicia who now commanded a division and talked Russian too. And you met the cabinet maker Juan Modesto from Andalucia who had just been given an Army Corps. He never learned Russian in Perto de Santa Maria although he might have if they had a Berlitz school there that cabinet makers went to. . . .

Sure Gaylord's was the place you needed to complete your education. It was there you learned how it was all really done instead of how it was supposed to be done.[11]

In contrast to this, in contrast to the stories Karkov tells him about Soviet manipulation, the arguments of the peasants are simple and clear. They resemble a kind of ideological innocence, untainted by the odour of corruption running through the corridors of Gaylord's in Madrid. Jordan cannot find it among his own kind, in 'the puritanical religious communism' of the International Brigades because they were already tainted by complicity with directives beyond their control, by the very fact of ideological compliance. The conversation of Agustin and Anselmo, simple and direct, with its clear signal that they wish to be masters of their own destiny, is not one which the international idealists could ever indulge in:

'So say I,' Anselmo said. 'That we should win the war.'
'And afterwards shoot the anarchists and the Communists and all this *canalla* except the good Republicans,' Agustin said.
'That we should win the war and shoot nobody,' Anselmo said. 'That we should govern justly and that all should participate in the benefits according as they have striven for them. And that those who have fought against us should be educated to see their error.'
'We will have to shoot many', Agustin said. 'Many. Many. Many.'
He thumped his closed right fist against the palm of his left hand.
'That we should shoot none. Not even the leaders. That they should be reformed by work.'
'I know the work I'd put them at', Agustin said, and he picked up some snow and put it in his mouth.
'What bad one?' Robert Jordan asked.
'Two trades of the utmost brilliance'.
. . . What trades?' Robert Jordan asked him. 'Speak, bad mouth.'
'Jumping from planes without parachutes.' Agustin said, and his eyes shone. 'That for those we care for. And being nailed to the tops of fence posts to be pushed over backwards for the others.'
'That way of speaking is ignoble', Anselmo said. 'Thus will we never have a Republic.'[12]

It was clear to Hemingway that whoever won the civil war would take a terrible revenge, and that even among the Republicans there could have been a settling of accounts. But such actions, in all cases, would have been promoted under the banner of justice. The dialogue here, simple and non-ideological, portrays revenge and justice as totally incompatible. Hemingway's portrait of the simple courageous peasant, vicious as well as virtuous, is a fictional portrait. But it is more real than the Soviet trained protégés of the communist party such as Lister, Modesto, El Campesino, and La Pasionaria. For the political indoctrination they have undergone has effectively removed them from the authentic simplicity they are supposed to represent. The communist party projects a fictitious public image of them as the people they might once have been but no longer are. The concealed fact, as Robert Jordan realises, is their Soviet in-doctrination. The notion that they have arisen spontaneously from the ranks of the Spanish people is a controlled and cynical lie.

At every stage of the novel, the action invalidates the party myth. Pablo, the real peasant leader, is fickle and treacherous, 'flaccid' and 'afraid to die'. He has had his share in the terrible atrocities at the start of the war in which the anarchists had taken a major part. But even El Sordo, the other guerilla leader, who is the very opposite of Pablo, does not fit the communist stereotype. During his last stand against the fascists on a hill 'the shape of a chancre', the doom which awaits the band surrounded by superior forces and helpless against enemy aircraft is contrasted with the euphemistic slogans of the Party. When Joaquin, the youngest of the party, repeats the slogan 'Hold out and fortify, and you will win', he has to face abuse from his comrades who know they are going to die, who think as Sordo does, that they are the 'very pus' of the chancre. As the planes close in on them, Joaquin changes from the slogans of Pasionaria back to the Hail Marys of his childhood. The band is massacred. But if the band rejects La Pasionaria in their hour of death, La Pasionaria turns their death into a myth. Back at Gaylord's the incident, miles behind enemy lines, is completely distorted. La Pasionaria claims that the fascists are fighting amongst themselves. The isolated act of heroism remains grist to the ideological mill. What is real is transformed into what can be used.

Malraux had acclaimed the need for organisation amidst fraternity. Hemingway's novel sees the dream turn into nightmare. As the job of organisation progresses, what replaces it is the need for propaganda amidst liquidation. Karkov comments in his cynical deadpan fashion upon the disappearance of Andrés Nin, leader of the P.O.U.M. But as far as the novel is concerned the test of Party trust and fraternity comes with Andrés' attempt to relay Jordan's message back to Golz. Stretching the literary imagination a bit, Hemingway has him come face to face with the biggest monster in the whole system of political commissars, thinly disguised by the name André Massart. Massart is the internal liquidator, the chief commissar who purifies Stalinism by murdering all its political deviants. Thus when Andrés and Gomez hapfully fall into his hands, his first thought is not to have them executed as spies but find evidence to condemn Golz for being in contact with the enemy.

Massart shook his head again. He was looking at Andrés but he was not seeing him.

Golz, he thought in a mixture of horror and exultation as a man might feel hearing that a business enemy had been killed in a particularly nasty motor accident or that someone you hated but whose probity you had never doubted had been guilty of defalcation. That Golz should have been one of them too.[13]

Massart's paranoia merely confirms what Golz has told Jordan before he sets out on his mission, that there existed a priority of political rather than military control over the fate of the war:

'They are never my attacks' Golz said. 'I make them. But they are not mine. The artillery is not mine. I must put in for it. I have never been given what I ask for even when they have to give. That is the least of it. There are other things. You know how these people are. It is not necessary to go into all of it. Always there is something. Always someone will interfere . . . I am General Soviétique. I never think. Do not try to trap me into thinking.[14]

The naïvety of Malraux's idea of organising the apocalypse is brutally exposed. While the communist military leaders perform wonders in creating a disciplined army, the political dynamics of the situation are a poison which threatens not only the war but also the possible victory. The direct attack on André Marty was more than enough to make the communists denounce Hemingway's novel. Yet interestingly enough some American critics regarded him as a Stalinist, regarding the favourable portraits of Golz and Karkov as proof that Hemingway condoned the communist role in the war. By condoning its military discipline, and condemning its political deceit, not only is he exposed to attack from both flanks, but he also presents the dilemma which faces Robert Jordan—to maintain his own values despite personal friendship and the acceptance of communist discipline. The life of moral values must transcend political expediency.

The major flaw in the novel, a flaw which prevents it from attaining the same high level of tragic realism as Tolstoy or Dostoevsky, lies in the character of Robert Jordan himself. In any major novel, one expects to read into the life of the hero some idea of the passage from innocence to experience. In the those three fateful days of Robert Jordan, there is none at all. Or if there is, it is only with regard to his love affair. That alone surprises him, confounds him. That it could happen in three days is something he would never have previously believed. But all the political events, those he could well have believed, even the misfortunes of his messenger Andrés about whom he was never to find out anything. The massacre by Pablo at the beginning of the war, the brutal rape of Maria, can horrify him but not substantially change his outlook on life. What Hemingway cannot consistently convey is how experience forms sensibility. Jordan's political sensibility is preformed, revealed to us in flashback. So that while it is true that Karkov's revelations do surprise him, do change him gradually from a green volunteer into a hardened sceptic, that change has been accomplished before the mission of his final three days on earth. This is not a failure on Hemingway's part so much as an excessive reliance upon the preformed, upon the frame of meaning which Robert Jordan brings with him to the mountains.

This feature of the hero constrains the tragedy in a certain direction. Jordan is doomed by the nature of his mission, not by the nature of himself. What he discovers in those three days are not so much aspects of himself but of the group with whom he fights. He comes to realise how much their potential death constitutes a tragic loss, and yet at the end of the novel there remains the hope that, if the wounded Jordan delays the fascist detachment long enough, they may yet be saved. The ending of the novel is open so that although we know that the individual hero will die attempting to save the novel's collective hero, we have no knowledge of whether he succeeds. The portrait of the individual hero, supremely egotistic in the tradition of modern American fiction, nonetheless leaves room for the selflessness of his final actions.

The tragic sense of loss relates less to Jordan himself than to the Spanish people whom he meets for the first time during his final three days. It is them, what they stand for, and his relationship to them, which is to be destroyed. Jordan consoles Maria at the end by telling her that she will take a part of him with her back to Madrid, even though he must stay behind. But what he does not say is that she of necessity will leave a part of herself behind with him to die as he does. In helping or hindering Jordan's mission to blow the bridge, Pilar, Pablo, Anselmo, Maria, El Sordo and the others share a collective fate in which their individual natures find separate fulfilment. It is this collective individuality which is endangered by Soviet propaganda and harassment and finally destroyed by fascist brutality. Hemingway's unshakeable humanism proceeds from a literary vision of imminent loss, of what the ordinary Spanish people might be, but are not to be. The artistic vision of human promise comes in the hour of defeat.

There is a final comparison between Malraux and Hemingway which can be made in respect of tragic realism. Coming from two of the most advanced capitalist countries of the modern age, they wrote predominantly about countries other than their own. Hemingway changed, indeed reversed, the whole meaning which Henry James had given to the American experience of Europe. His heroes are not trapped by the illusions of European sophistication, except, perhaps, for *The Sun Also Rises*, nor are they attracted by the glittering life of the European aristocracy. Spain is interesting and vital to Hemingway because it is both European and backward, primitive yet steeped in tradition. He achieved with Spain what

Malraux failed to achieve with both Spain and China; his fiction reaches its hinterland. Malraux's transient immediacy prevents him from portraying the life which lies beyond Great Events, but Hemingway can evoke the momentous and the humble in the same breath. Like *The Silent Don*, *For Whom the Bell Tolls* ushers the primitive peasants of Europe on to the stage of tragic realism.

Unlike most tragic realists, Hemingway was not a conservative writer. But his novel preserves the dialectic of conservatism and revolution in a different, and perhaps more substantial way. It lies in the difference between the urban and the rural setting. Williams has remarked that in the second half of the nineteenth century most English experience was urban and most English fiction rural. If we take Europe as a whole from 1848 onwards we can say the same of tragic realism. It is mostly rural or regional in its setting, despite the great increase towards the end of the nineteenth century in urban fiction. The major exception to this is Dostoevsky. But Dostoevsky wrote of city life in one of the most rural countries of all, and the relationship is reversed. Most of Dostoevsky's fiction is urban, most of Russian experience rural. And Russia was still a predominantly pre-bourgeois society. In the increasingly urbanised bourgeois societies of the twentieth century, the major works of tragic realism take place outside of an urban, and bourgeois, context. With the exception of a handful of novels, including *The Secret Agent*, tragic realism finds its literary space in a predominantly rural or maritime setting. *For Whom the Bell Tolls* exemplifies this perfectly, without ever losing sight of the relationship between city and country, between Madrid and the Sierra de Guadaramas. Hemingway's attainment of the tragic can be contrasted with the failure of the tragic in Malraux's urban Shanghai. The tragic element of modern realism has largely expressed itself in the clash of the conservative and the revolutionary. Urban life, more appropriate than ever to the real in fiction, is too dynamic, too frenetic, too atomised to suggest this tragic clash of opposed elements.

The problem can be put in perspective in a different way—by looking at an urban, tragic fiction which abandons literary realism altogether. In contrast to the affirmative realism of Joyce, Doeblin and Dos Passos, the portrait of the city in Kafka and Orwell evokes tragic nightmare. Kafka was never a realist in any sense of the word. *The Trial* is tragic fiction held together by the logic of dream. But Orwell had been a realist writer, and in writing *Nineteen Eighty-four*, he departed from realism without totally abandoning it. On this decision, as we shall see, there hung one of the great dilemmas of contemporary fiction.

12 George Orwell: The Nightmare of the Real

English writing has never been the same since George Orwell. The very clarity of his style is a model of its kind, to be contrasted with the general deterioration of contemporary language. Yet Orwell's literary talent has forced the English novel into a predicament from which it has yet to recover. Though unintentionally so, Orwell's talent always raised the question 'Why the novel?' His remarkable gift for writing was dispersed equally amongst social commentary, memoir, cultural criticism, political journalism and fiction. Raymond Williams has gone so far to suggest it pointless, even impossible, to separate Orwellian documentary and Orwellian fiction. But such an assertion by a major critic merely shows the damage done by Orwell's legacy to the very idea of fiction. More than anyone he has undermined conventional notions of the fictional preserve of the novel. The tragedy is that his own fiction has suffered in the process. For paradoxically the combination of Orwell's social awareness and his gift for writing in a wide range of genres, has had an adverse effect upon his literary legacy.

To state the problem in a different way, we can note the immense success of his satirical fable, *Animal Farm*. Written in the tradition of Swift and Voltaire, it was his most effective work of fiction precisely because it posed no problems about representationalism. His realist fiction on the other hand is problematic because of its closeness to the documentary style of writing he created in *Down and Out in London and Paris*. As a writer, he found it remarkably easy to transfer back and forth from one medium to the other, and to express similar themes in both. It is true that at times, as in *A Clergyman's Daughter*, his fiction was more experimental. Yet even in this novel, scenes such as the hop-picking scene are derived from earlier journalism. Orwell's problem was one he shared with quite different writers altogether, with Sartre, Camus and Malraux, for example. And later the same problem destroyed altogether the literary talent of Norman Mailer. All these post-war writers found that what can be accomplished by fiction becomes problematic. After the war, Sartre turned from the realist novel to the allegorical drama, while Camus wrote allegorical novels. Similarly, Orwell turned away from realism. *Animal Farm* is a fable and *Nineteen Eighty-Four* is a dystopia in the tradition of Wells, Zamyatin and Huxley, a form of writing Orwell had previously never attempted. Why, then, did he choose it at all?

This literary question cannot be separated from Orwell's attitude to the politics of his day. After the Great Depression, the rise of fascism, and the triumph of Stalin, the question of political commitment became more pressing for all writers. The demand for all artistic forms to be politically relevant was more strident than ever. Yet Orwell was extremely suspicious of the politicisation of art. He identified it with artistic compromise and political control. Whether didactic writing was subject to external pressures or self-imposed, he saw it as having a debilitating effect upon the creative powers of the writer. In England, as opposed to Europe, Orwell regarded the vast mass of ordinary people as immune to the ideological blandishments of fascism and Stalinism. Only among a section of middle-class intellectuals did he claim to see any ideological fervour comparable to that sweeping the continent. This discrepancy, under English conditions at least, between political ideology and everyday life had some influence on his literary tastes. It led him to admire the work of the relatively unknown Henry Miller. In his famous essay, *Inside the Whale*, he acclaims Miller for lacking a guilty conscience about politics. Here was a writer who concentrated on the minutiae of everyday life despite the increasing politicisation of culture. It was an authentic but 'shrinking' life where politics could not penetrate. Miller had come closer than any contemporary writer to portraying 'average sensual man' because he was 'passive to experience'. Besides, he had no fear of politics. 'Good novels,' Orwell concluded, trying to explain the lack of them, 'are written by people who are not frightened.'

But Orwell himself was frightened. His political allegiance to democratic socialism did little to allay his fear. For this unique form of political fear, different from the conservative forms it took in previous writers, was a constant emotion which spurred him to literary eloquence. Orwell himself realised the dilemma. 'Where I lacked a *political* purpose,' he wrote after the war, 'I wrote lifeless books.' Despite his polemical demands for a complete separation of politics and literature, he found politics indispensable for his own purposes. His best writing came from a political hatred of totalitarianism. In this respect he and Henry Miller were about as alike as chalk and cheese. The remark about 'lifeless books' seems to indicate at best a feeling of disappointment with his earlier non-political fiction. But it also points to something else. Politics was a key element in his abandonment of the realist tradition.

Indeed it is possible to argue that Orwell's politics had a more profound effect on his fiction than on his social commentary. *Homage to Catalonia* is not a marked literary departure from *Down and Out in London and Paris* or *The Road to Wigan Pier*. But *Animal Farm* and *Nineteen Eighty-Four* do mark a significant break with his earlier fiction. Before we look at this more closely, it is important to remember the key point of division between Orwell's fiction and his documentary work during the thirties. The documentary writing is concerned mainly with the poverty of the working-classes, the vagrant and the unemployed. But the fiction has as its theme *respectable* poverty. George Bowling in *Coming Up for Air*, Dorothy Warburton in *A Clergyman's Daughter*, Gordon Comstock in *Keep the Aspidistra Flying* all share common characteristics; a lower-middle class background and a neurotic fear of poverty. Fear of poverty is the predominant social fear of Orwell's early heroes. Comstock's assessment of his parents, of their petit-bourgeois attitude to money, applies also to him:

> It was not merely the *lack* of money. It was rather that having no money, they still lived in the money-world—the world in which money is virtue and poverty is crime. It was not poverty but the downdragging of *respectable* poverty that had done for them. They had accepted the money-code and by that code they were failures. They never had the sense to lash out and just *live*, money or no money as the lower classes do.[1]

This portrayal of lower-middle class life in London and the Home Counties, where many people were on the brink of poverty without actually descending into it, is one in which Orwell displays his many naturalistic talents. With Gordon Comstock, however, he has a hero who actually goes over the brink and experiences poverty as a form of humiliation. Comstock learns at first hand the incompatibility between the reality of being poor and the lower-middle class ethic that poverty does not exist for the morally blameless. Try as he might, he cannot escape the moral stigma of poverty even through his writing. In fact the opposite happens. The stigma fatally destroys his capacity to write:

> He learned what it means to live for weeks on end on bread and margarine, to try to 'write' when you are half starved, to pawn your clothes, to sneak trembling upstairs when you owe three months rent and your landlady is waiting for you. Moreover in those seven months he wrote practically nothing. The first effect of poverty is that it kills thought . . . you are the hopeless slave of money until you have enough to live on—a 'competence' as the beastly middle-class phrase goes.[2]

Comstock attributes all his troubles to material deprivation. But this attitude merely reveals his psychological failure to endure such deprivation. The nagging, moralistic constraint of respectable poverty he cannot shed, also explains the *Schadenfreude* he shows towards the bourgeois socialism of Ravelston, his prosperous publishing friend. The money-world even advances the security of the politically *engagé*. Lack of money is a fatal constraint on Comstock's sexual and intellectual freedom, because it atrophies his will to act. He cannot believe in himself either as a writer or a lover.

But this sense of social constraint Orwell's heroes feel never has tragic consequences. Invariably they compromise with the world which constrains them. The eccentric Dorothy Warburton returns to her local village as if nothing scandalous had ever happened to her. After his strange pilgrimage to Lower Binfield, George Bowling slinks sullenly home to his nagging wife. And Comstock, the most defiant of the early heroes, ends up married to Rosemary with the symbolic aspidistra in his front window. Like Flory in *Burmese Days*, their disaffection is rhetorical, their rebellion half-hearted. A point of genuine breakdown, of irreconcilability between the Orwellian hero and his social world, is never reached.

When Orwell came to write *Nineteen Eighty-four*, much had changed from the England of the previous decade. A war against fascism, a post-war victory for the Labour Party, a widespread fear of Soviet communism in the process of taking over Eastern Europe; all these factors reflected a greater public awareness of politics. Yet often it was awareness of something regarded as foreign to British life. The British had not suffered Nazi occupation; neither had they experienced the growth of a mass communist movement. Both these factors separated Britain from the European mainland. They also prompted Orwell to retain his image of the English people as decent, law-abiding, stoical and immune to ideology. At the same time he must have realised, instinctively, that he had an audience for a political novel about totalitarianism. Already he had some evidence in the success of *Animal Farm*, totally reversing his unhappy experience with the production of *Homage to Catalonia*. The key element of the public consciousness to which Orwell could, and did, effectively appeal was the fear of an unknown tyranny, a tyranny whose true nature was not fully known and, in the popular imagination, still shrouded in sinister mystery.

The widespread success of *Nineteen Eighty-Four* is due to the fact that it sustains that mystery rather than attempting to disperse it. Orwell correlated the fear, even phobia, of the totalitarian unknown with the futurism of the dystopian novel. He grasped the connection, as Wells had before him, between the fictive world of the future and the dream world of nightmare. But his success also lay in retaining some of the naturalistic gifts he had displayed in his earlier fiction. The reader had to identify the country under the yoke of Oceania as the country in which they themselves lived. There had to be recognisable attitudes and recognisable landmarks. Unlike the science fiction which Orwell undoubtedly inspired, there had to be within the text, a contrast betweeen the old and the new. The London of 1948 had to be present in the Oceania of 1984.

Orwell's vision of the old is barely changed from his previous fiction, except that he now had in front of his eyes the crumbling masonry of a blitzed London. Yet the rotting Victorian slums are there, Winston Smith's abode in Victory Mansions right out of the boarding houses of the thirties in which 'the hallway smelt of boiled cabbage and old rag mats', and the 'proles' of 1984 remarkably similar to the cockney Londoners Orwell had known and recorded in his pre-war writing. The political nightmare, as it were, is superimposed upon this naturalistic painting. The Constructivist paradise of Oceania, which Orwell largely derived from Zamyatin, overlays the decaying blitzed London of the 1940s. The extraordinary and often overlooked feature of *Nineteen Eighty-four* is that the proles, eighty-five per cent of the population, are outside the reign of totalitarian terror, free of telescreens and Newspeak and largely left to their own devices. The image of a semi-criminal working-class subculture, immune to ideology and public life, which permeates Orwell's earlier work, is faithfully preserved.

This enables us to pinpoint more accurately the social transformations from the earlier to the later Orwellian novel. The constraints of lower-middle class life give way to the more rigorous political surveillance of the intelligentsia. Gordon Comstock suffers from prying landladies, lack of money, and lack of sexual opportunity. But he does not suffer, like Winston Smith, from the full-scale political surveillance of every aspect of his life. Comstock is a writer who can earn neither money nor recognition, but Smith is a subordinate bureaucrat in the Ministry of Truth whose occupation consists in destroying the meaning of writing altogether. In a liberal-capitalist society the writer's petit-bourgeois status guarantees him a modicum of freedom and a vast quantity of indifference to what he produces. His expropriation by the totalitarian state of the future turns him into an obedient bureaucrat whose every movement is watched.

The values of the Party against which Smith rebels are essentially those of the Ministry of Truth—the control of the human personality by regimentation of knowledge, information, culture and the creative imagination. As many critics have realised this broadens the scope of the novel beyond the explicit condemnation of Nazi- and Soviet totalitarianism. It raises broader questions about the independence of the intelligentsia in a highly rationalised, bureaucratic world. But hidden in this concern is a specific obsession of which Orwell was not fully conscious—the possibility of the realist novel as the most effective antidote to the Ministry of Truth. Orwell concentrates at great length on the destruction of those cultural qualities which are vital to the preservation of the realist novel—the idea of the person, of interpersonal relationships, of individual destiny, of a past and different world, of an authentic language, and finally of human passion. These are the things whose destruction the Ministry of Truth perfects and in which Smith himself complies.

This enables us to understand Smith's affair with Julia as a major defiance of the Party in addition to his Goldsteinian heresy. Loyalty to Julia endures after his political rebellion is crushed. It is the last autonomous element of his personality to be destroyed. At the end of the novel this final surrender is important because Orwell has to present us with some active measure of the positive human values which the Party destroys. This can only come from the love-affair since, by 1984, the destruction of political freewill has already been accomplished. Orwell creates a very vivid image of political repression, but since the people of Oceania are already so compliant, there is no real political alternative to threaten the Party. Even Goldstein's theories, a strange amalgam of Trotsky and James Burnham giving an uncensored view of Oceania's historical origin, do not provide one. While Smith pledges himself to the destruction of the Party, he has little idea of what he wants to put in its place.

Apart from the proles, the affair of Winston and Julia is the only indication of a quality of life different from that ordained by the Party. Their relationship is sacrosanct. When asked by O'Brien what they are prepared to do to destroy the Party, they pledge themselves to any action, except separation from one another. Since Orwell stresses the integrity of their relationship so greatly, we are entitled to ask of what it consists. The immediately striking thing about Winston and Julia is not their difference in background, like Robert Jordan and Maria, but their sameness. Julia too works in the Ministry of Truth, significantly enough in the Fiction Department.

The passion of Jordan and Maria is generated very rapidly by the exceptional circumstances in which they find themselves, but the context of Winston and Julia's meeting is ordinary and mundane, a chance encounter of everyday routine. That such a meeting should engender instant passion, that Winston's aid to the girl after her fall should induce the immediate response of the scrap of paper saying 'I love you' goes beyond the bounds of realist fiction. It is a fantasy. We do not know who or what the girl is, any more than Smith does. She has no preformed character, but appears suddenly like a figure in a dream.

This encounter is only credible in the context of futuristic fantasy, very similar to the first meeting of D-503 and E-330 in Zamyatin's *We*. Winston's passion has no social context because it is generated, like hers, for a person without a past, who is not known. The absence of the past is an important reflexive element in the novel. The Party of Oceania has liquidated cultural tradition, and literally abolished the past, creating a state of collective amnesia amongst the people. But Orwell too had difficulty with the past, especially when dealing with relationships of passion, of evoking the loved one's past, their personal identity as independent of the desire of the lover. Amnesia is a recurrent element in his fiction. One recalls the black dreamless sleep of Dorothy Warburton finding herself in the New Kent Road without any knowledge of her past, or George Bowling returning to the Lower Binfield of his childhood and being unable to recognise it. In *Nineteen Eighty-Four* Smith's failure to know the past is a result of political indoctrination, but in both the earlier and later fiction, also of the hero's rootlessness. His lack of a sense of the past is a feature of his sensibility. The reader *feels* the rootlessness in Winston Smith, the permanent blank which Goldstein's heresy inadequately fills. It is not merely a political artefact. When Smith pumps an old man in a prole pub for knowledge of the pre-revolutionary era, the anecdotes related to him only increase his irritation. 'The old man's memory was nothing but a rubbish-heap of details. One could question him all day without getting any real information.' Yet, ironically, the old man, his mind untouched by Newspeak, does have his own sense of the past. And this, Smith still lacks.

For the reader of 1976 approaching the ominous date whose significance has already passed into the English language, the novel actually conveys more about the time when it was written than about the future it was intended to describe. Paradoxically, therefore, it contains that very sense of the past which its characters know nothing of. For in their future world, they are ideologically cut off from the past. Yet when the novel is read in retrospect, the brief glimpses of the past which Winston Smith gains from observing the proles—the washerwoman singing a sentimental ballad in the yard—are not as disconsonant with the wider world of the novel as Orwell would wish them. For Orwell has to fill in his futuristic world of Oceania with his contemporary world of London in 1948. And his use of contemporary and naturalistic detail is far greater, for example, than that of Zamyatin. Smith's ideological amnesia does not, therefore, make sense. At least, it does not make sense in the context of what Orwell portrays. It only makes sense as an ideological element in the writing itself. Smith's amnesia refracts his author's unconscious wish to deny the fictive portrayal of the past. The choice of the future world as the dream or nightmare in which the past has no place, is one which abandons the vital element of the real, and at the same time symbolises the abandonment of a realist fiction. The hero's ignorance of the past is reflexive. It reflects the process involved in the writing of the novel of which he is the hero.

Within the novel itself, it is the Party of course which has annihilated the past, though this is hardly a realistic feature of totalitarianism. And it is the Party which eventually destroys the love-affair of Winston and Julia—though why this should be high on its list of priorities also lacks political credibility. On the question of Winston and Julia's affair, which is the key to the novel, Orwell is ambivalent. Officially, the party abolishes the orgasm, not the love-affair. But the couple's relationship is written, and read, as a forbidden passion carried out in defiance of the Party. It is this very defiance which defines the lovers' destiny. But in the first love-making scene, we find the 'passion' Orwell equates with defiance to be chimerical. Winston and Julia explicitly deny passion. The extraordinary sleight-of-hand needed to insinuate its presence throughout the rest of the novel is beyond Orwell's creative power. The fact that he tries shows not only a contradiction, but also a marked insincerity in the writing of it.

Smith's seduction of Julia in 'the Golden country' is reminiscent of Comstock's visit with Rosemary to the Thames countryside. The difference is that Smith succeeds where Comstock fails. The attitude of Orwell's two heroes to women is chauvinistically similar; selfish pleasure rather than involvement, lust rather than passion. But the different outcomes result directly from the different themes of the two novels. First, Rosemary and Comstock in *Keep the Aspidistra Flying*:

> He pulled her to the ground beside him, kissed her, pulled off the flat felt hat, lay upon her breast to breast kissed her face all over. She lay under him yielding rather than responding. She did not resist when his hand sought her breasts. But in her heart she was still frightened. . . . And at heart too he was half reluctant. It dismayed him to find how little, at this moment he really wanted her. The money-business still unnerved him. How can you make love when you have only eightpence in your pocket and are thinking about it all the time?[3]

Comstock's obsession with money ruins his desire to make love to her. In *Nineteen Eighty-Four*, the constraints on sex are no longer purely, and absurdly, economic but directly political. Copulation is regulated by the Party. But for that very reason, the effect on Smith is the opposite. The priggish Rosemary has been replaced by the promiscuous Julia:

> He knelt down before her and took her hands in his.
> 'Have you done this before?'
> 'Of course. Hundreds of times—well scores of time anyway.'
> 'With Party members?'
> 'Yes, always with Party members.'
> 'With members of the Inner Party?'
> 'Not with those swine, no. But there's plenty *would* if they got half a chance. They're not so holy as they make out.'
> His heart leapt. Scores of times she had done it: he wished it had been hundreds—thousands. Anything that hinted at corruption always filled him with a wild hope. Who knew, perhaps the Party was rotten under the surface, its cult of strenuousness and self-denial simply a sham—concealing iniquity. If he could have infected the whole lot of them with leprosy and syphilis, how gladly he would have done so! Anything to rot, to weaken, to undermine! He pulled her down so that they were kneeling face to face.
> 'Listen. The more men you've had, the more I love you. Do you understand that?'
> 'Yes. Perfectly.'
> 'I hate purity, I hate goodness! I don't want any virtue to exist anywhere. I want everyone to be corrupt to the bones.'
> 'Well then, I ought to suit you dear. I'm corrupt to the bones.'
> 'You like doing this? I don't mean simply me: I mean the thing in itself?'
> 'I adore it.'
> That was above all what he wanted to hear. Not merely the love of one person but the animal instinct, the simple undifferentiated desire:

that was the force that would tear the Party to pieces. He pressed her down upon the grass among the fallen bluebells. This time there was no difficulty.

On awaking he thinks to himself:

> You could not have pure love or pure lust nowadays. No emotion was pure, because everything was mixed up with fear and hatred. Their embrace had been a battle, the climax a victory. It was a blow struck against the Party. It was a political act.[4]

At any level, the idea of promiscuity as a political weapon against totalitarianism cannot be taken seriously. The whole scenario is a fantasy, a pornographic fantasy in the author's mind which the hero acts out. If Smith thinks that sex is a weapon in politics, then Orwell is clearly attracted by the direct intervention of politics in sex. The mere thought of Julia's party-minded promiscuity is sufficient to give Winston Smith the erection which Comstock, the non-political, could not attain. The scene negates the whole idea of passion and resorts instead to the old pornographic standby of the contagions of lust. One thing should be made clear. It is not the idea of the totalitarian which destroys passion, but the idea of the political. Politics is the shibboleth which severs the connection between sexual relationships and moral values. Such is the confusion of emotions in the hero that he identifies his struggle against the Party as a struggle against 'purity' and 'goodness'. In rejecting totalitarianism he rejects all moral values. Yet Orwell is obliged to foster the illusion that Winston and Julia's affair is the last repository of moral values in an amoral society. Their defiance depends upon the juxtaposition of passion and totalitarianism. But from the very outset, passion does not exist. As a result, they have nothing of value to protect from the Party and when they betray each other after torture, nothing of value to betray. Faced with the army of rats in Room 101, Smith renounces Julia to save himself. But in spite of what Orwell intended, he saves his life by an empty gesture. There is no life-by-value which he can meaningfully betray. The last refuge of the human heart in the hopeless fight against Big Brother is nothing more than pornographic sentimentality.

There are thus two levels of meaning in the novel which contradict one another. The Party ostensibly destroys the 'passion' which defies it: but the author also destroys the passion characteristic of the realist novel. By doing so, he removes the very pillar of the tragic story he hopes to write, and casts it ceremoniously aside, along with the past, as the relic of an ancient genre. But Orwell would not have recognised his dubious achievement in this way. The Party's attack on humanity as a mirror of his own attack on realism is the very opposite of what he intended. Yet in reading the hopelessness of the couple to withstand the Party we are reading the slow death of a kind of writing which by 1984 is already dead.

In Orwell's fantasy world, the flight from realism arises out of a distinct failure to grasp the significance of the political. Amnesiac, aphrodisiac, the political world of Big Brother performs a service Orwell never intended. The corollary is the absence of politics from the centres of power. Despite his position in the Ministry of Truth, Smith has no inkling of how power operates in the Inner Party. It is significant that apart from Goldstein's pamphlet, Julia is the other main source of information—but only about Party members' moral laxity. Orwell does pinpoint an essential truth of the modern bureaucratic world, the absence of information even for the individual, like Smith, at the very centre of information. But the total lack of rumour, of gossip, of hearsay, is not the feature of a future world. It is the feature of a dream world, the familiar void one encounters in a nightmare. And O'Brien, the only representative of the Inner Party to appear in the story, is at times like a shadow, a figment of Smith's imagination. Orwell gives his hero the best of both worlds. He is alien to the Party yet subject, unlike the proles, to their discipline. Watched day and night like someone of importance, he feels himself ignorant of the forces which oppress him. This ignorance of the nucleus of power inclines most readers to see him as Everyman subject to mysterious forces beyond his control. Yet Smith is an insider. He professionally distorts information. He is an intellectual whose curiosity leads him to Goldstein's heresy. But in his quest for knowledge, there is a crucial defect. He deflects his gaze from the cruel Party Gods and from the ubiquitous face of Big Brother looking down on him from every direction.

The relationship between politics and fiction is also reflexive with regard to the question of language. The Party has no ideology. Of course, it has slogans, exhortations, Hate weeks and so on. But it lacks any conception of its historical mission in the world. O'Brien makes the point when he tells Smith that behind the Party's propaganda, there lies only ruthlessness, cruelty and power. 'The object of persecution is persecution. The object of torture is torture. The object of power is power.'[5] What then of Newspeak? Officially, it is the language of Ingsoc, the ideology which underlies it. But the nature of Ingsoc is never made clear. Despite what Orwell claims in his appendix, Newspeak is a kind of ingenious and self-sufficient language game. Not only does it confuse and distort, it severs language from experience. Orwell puts his finger on a dilemma of all modern culture, which is increasingly invaded by rationalised vocabularies impoverishing the meaning of human experience. But in other ways, Newspeak is curiously limited in its effects. No one in the novel, not even O'Brien, uses it in conversational speech. Only in the slogans of stage-managed demonstrations and the newsprint emanating from the Ministry of Truth does it make itself felt.

It could be said that despite Orwell's immense vision of the deterioration of modern language, the novel does not adequately put it to the test.

Language as speech is not a problem for Orwell as it was for Joyce or Hemingway. He continues to use the naturalistic dialogue of his earlier novels, and the talk of his characters is seemingly unaffected by Newspeak. We are given no examples of how a debased language debases experience. Even in the torture chamber, O'Brien, the interrogator uses the clear succinct prose of Orwell the writer. He never clouds his motives with the cunning gibberish of Newspeak even when torturing Smith into recognising its rightful existence. Despite Newspeak the figural dimension of authentic speech is never a problem for Orwell's characters.

As Smith nears the end of his torture, much of which is genuinely horrifying, O'Brien remarks that he is 'the last man' of civilisation, 'the guardian of the human spirit'. But Orwell's hero has done little to justify such high praise. Scared and masochistic, he behaves like a born victim, or like a person in a nightmare who feels complete and utter helplessness. His abiding emotion is one of humiliation. He does not possess that rare quality of resilience shown by the historical survivors of labour camps and concentration camps which might have justified O'Brien's assessment. And the political heresy curiously gets lost in the process of torture. O'Brien never demands a detailed repudiation of the theories of Goldstein. The novel shirks ideological heresy and returns to the fictional one—the memory of the past. The Party's control over reality, frightening though it is, is purely negative. Truth is never subverted for any purpose except the continuation of its own power, and certainly not for any ideological principle which legitimates its existence. Totalitarian parties rewrite the past; they do not abolish it like the *nouveau roman*. Orwell overlooks this elementary political fact because he is unconsciously charting the future of fiction.

In *Nineteen Eighty-Four* we find something which is quite unique: a novel about the destruction of human freedom which is also a parable about the destruction of the novel. It is no coincidence that Winston and Julia are technicians of Rewriting in the Ministry of Truth. For in writing about a future world where there is no novel, Orwell is actually writing by means of a novel the end of the novel itself. With similar pessimism, but less involvement, Claude Lévi-Strauss has made the same message explicit. The historical function of the novel, he claims, was to tell a story which ended unhappily. But now we can see that the novel is a genre which is ending unhappily itself. The publication of *Nineteen Eighty-Four* fits into this historical scheme of things. It appeared in 1949, two years after *Doctor Faustus* and *Under the Volcano*, the last major novels of tragic realism to appear in the West. The subsequent disappearance of tragic realism is a phenomenon which, quite uncannily, it appeared to underwrite by putting its symptoms into political disguises. For have we not witnessed in the literary criticism we have already discussed the acceptance of circumstances Orwell regarded as tragic?

This explains the attempt he made in his last book, at the end of his life, to write tragic fiction for the first time. Not only was it a tragic vision about the future of civilisation; it was also a tragic vision of the future of the novel and the future of tragedy. It was something which eluded both documentary and satire, beyond the pinnacles of achievement he had reached with *Homage to Catalonia* and *Animal Farm*. But when the time came, Orwell could not write it. The tragic element of the novel is destroyed by the very absence of the realism to which it referred and the recurrent presence of the political where it matters least. One cannot be tragic about the end of tragedy for the elements of tragedy have already departed. Orwell is admired by posterity much in the way he would have wished; as 'a writer' with all the eclectic virtues the word entails. The failure of the tragic was missing from the image of him that has been handed down to us. It is now part of our literary heritage.

13 Solzhenitsyn: The Permanence of Tragedy

Many faults, moral and political, can be detected in the early days of Soviet communism. What could not be denied was its vast reservoir of moral idealism. Only when this is recognised does it make sense to regard the last fifty years of Soviet communism as unique. For never before have so many intense human aspirations been destroyed in such a short period of time. Only during the limitless rule of Stalin was the process perfected. But its legacy remains. In literature, as in Soviet culture generally, the so-called process of de-Stalinisation was merely a breathing space before the reimposition of a less cruel and more faceless tyranny. The doctrine of socialist realism has had its cumulative effect, for sooner or later those who have opposed it have become its victims. The dilemma for any talented Russian writer since Stalin's death is that of risking his own life in order to breathe life into a corpse. Only an exceptional few have succeeded.

In 1925, Trotsky had optimistically, and perhaps myopically, forecast that tragic realism would be the dominant literary genre of a socialist society. By 1934 Socialist realism had killed tragic fiction stone dead. After Stalin's death, it became a leading question as to whether there were any writers talented and courageous enough to pick up the pieces. It was a question particularly relevant to the fate of the Soviet novel. During the Stalinist period, a tragic vision of life had been sustained largely through poetry, where the immediacy of personal experience was less politically vulnerable than the *Ideenroman* which critically portrays the life and values of the wider society. But as the cases of Mandelstam and Akhmatova testify, even poetry was subject to the most horrendous persecution. Yet somehow it survived, which is more than can be said for the tragic novel, now officially regarded as a species of prehistory.

Nadezhda Mandelstam has pointed out the great difficulty of resurrecting a tragic fiction under such vitiating circumstances, quoting from a unpublished manuscript of her husband the following significant remark: 'The tragic, however small the scene of enactment, inevitably amounts to a general picture of the world.'[1] It was precisely this that Soviet culture had destroyed. The one great writer of her own generation who tried to resurrect it was Boris Pasternak. But Pasternak was a poet, not a novelist, and the effort of writing *Doctor Zhivago* involved coming to terms with something which was both stylistically and historically unfamiliar. The poetic gifts of Pasternak are preserved in the novel—the lyrical passages of description, especially of nature, and the immense subtlety of conveying the personal impressions of his hero at any given moment in time. But Pasternak finds great difficulty in adding to these talents a wider vision of life which he clearly sought in the novel form. In one sense his literary instinct was right. Since the twenties the novel had failed to live up to the subject matter of Soviet life. Unfortunately his great belief in *Doctor Zhivago* as the culmination of his own literary work is misconceived. He certainly took advantage of circumstance in order to attempt it. As a favoured poet who did not overtly oppose the regime, he had avoided the persecution of many of his contemporaries. And he survived through to the period of Stalin's death where the hope of a new era gave him sufficient impetus to complete the novel.

Yet the novel form presented him with insuperable difficulties. The story of Zhivago is his own alternative autobiography, of a poet who, unlike himself, was critical of the Soviet regime from the outset. But the problem of fictionalising his alter ego was one that he could not solve. The genuine novelist would have created a doctor who writes poetry, but instead Pasternak invents a poet who happens to be a doctor largely, one suspects, because of the conventions of the novel. Thus Zhivago possesses nothing of the practicality which his profession demands. He thinks and acts like a poet upon whom the revolution is an unwanted imposition, a dreamer with an air of injured innocence who is essentially passive to life. His survival of the civil war is unconvincing, because he lacks the tenacity required of a doctor forced to work for revolutionary partisans under the most gruelling of circumstances. Zhivago's sensibility is nearer to Hans Castorp than to Gregor Melekhov, or further back to the heroes of Turgenev. Even in the midst of combat, he has the unrelieved *angst* of the superfluous man where resolution, of some sort, is needed. Pasternak's poet-doctor amidst revolution is a failed attempt to alter the portrayed reality of the pre-revolutionary novel, yet retain its sensibility. The hero merely proves that one cannot be altered without the other.

More generally speaking, Pasternak fails to capture the figural dimensions of the realist novel. Zhivago, like Melekhov, yearns for a past world which revolution is in the process of destroying. During his service with the red partisans, this merges into a pining for Lara from whom the civil war has divided him. But when he finally escapes to find her again, the reunion suffers from a crucial defect typical of the novel as a whole. Pasternak evades the moment when their eyes meet and when they speak to each other for the first time. He evades the question of whether they can recapture passion after involuntary separation. Instead, delirious with typhus, Lara appears to him as if in a dream; and continues to exist in the same light:

Suddenly he realised that he was neither dreaming nor delirious but that, in sober truth, he was lying, washed and in a clean shirt, not on the sofa but on a freshly made bed and that the person who was crying with him, sitting beside him, leaning over him, her hair mingling with his and her tears falling with his own, was Lara: he fainted with joy.

. . . All his life he had been active, doing things about the house, looking after patients, thinking studying writing!—to leave it all for a time to nature, to become her thing, her concern, the work of her merciful, wonderful, beauty-lavishing hands.

He soon recovered. Lara fed him, nursed him, built him up by her care, her snow-white loveliness, the warm living breath of her whispering conversation.

Their low-voiced talk, however unimportant, was as full of meaning as the Dialogues of Plato.

Even more than by what they had in common, they were united by what separated them from the rest of the world. They were both equally repelled by what was tragically typical of modern man, his shrill textbook admirations, his forced enthusiasm, and the deadly dullness conscientiously preached and practised by countless workers in the field of art and science in order that genius should remain extremely rare.

They loved each other greatly. Most people experience love, without noticing that there is anything remarkable about it.

To them—and this made them unusual—the moments when passion visited their doomed human existence like a breath of timelessness were moments of revelation, of ever greater understanding of life and of themselves.[2]

Pasternak wants to present his lovers as unique and defiant. But the passage degenerates into the worst sort of melodrama typical of romantic fiction. They appear, especially Zhivago, as spoilt and precious, and this in a context where we know that both of them have endured the most terrible deprivations. What is missing from Pasternak's account of their reunion? It is the clash of personalities which exists even at the height of passion, the human sexual differences which spring out of long separation and which must be demonstrated in the very process of reuniting. Pasternak avoids this dialectic element of passion. He cannot wait to tell the reader of the wonderful effect of reunion, to interpret it without portraying the important moment of contact. After the joy of being nursed, which borders on swooning rapture, there is a portentous statement on the philosophical meaning of passion. Human response is lost, and the consequent dialogue between Zhivago and Lara excludes either's point of view by which, fictionally speaking that response could be registered. Their conversation excludes indirect narrative, all indication of what they *feel*. And their speech itself does not incorporate it either. Pasternak, lacking the Tolstoyan gift for the switching of the point of view, also lacks Dostoevsky's gift for giving his characters a unique and authentic speech which marks them out and identifies them. His dialogues float in the ether.

Zhivago is passive to experience. And Pasternak tries to justify that passivity by the monstrous nature of the experience to which he is subject. But the passive is not tragic, for it generates no genuine opposition to the forces of injustice which Pasternak laments. His hero drifts through a wasted life and, like the heroes of Turgenev, the point at which that wastefulness is challenged is never reached. But the difficulty of writing tragic fiction cannot be overemphasised. Soviet experience had made tragedy a feature of everyday life yet Soviet ideology had tried to completely exorcise it from fiction. Mrs Mandelstam's memoir of her poet-husband is more tragic than Pasternak's fiction of a poet-doctor. Atrocity during the Stalinist period was so great, and so anonymous, that it almost defies the creative imagination just as the Nazi concentration camps did at the end of the war. At the same time the fate of Osip Mandelstam is all the more tragic for being the fate of a poet. The Party leaders had literally taken the place of the Gods of Greek tragedy, and Stalin's notorious phone conversation with Pasternak over the fate of the defiant Acmeist was like a cruel parody of divine intervention. When there were real poets like Mandelstam who perished in the way that they did, the fictional act of disguising a poet as a doctor seemed superfluous. Unlike Zhivago who wearily survives, Mandelstam was nursed all the way to a murderous death. The period of each is different so there are limits to the comparison. But it was Pasternak who choose not to write a novel about the period when writers like Mandelstam were sent to their death. And that choice resulted in a fatal dilution of Pasternak's tragic vision.

The thirties is a period with which genuine Soviet fiction has been unable to cope. Just as the best literature of the Nazi camps comes from the memoirs of Bruno Bettelheim and Primo Levi, so too in Russia the memoirs of Nadezda Mandelstam and Yevgenia Ginsberg are unsurpassed literary masterpieces. The experience of suffering is so intense that memoir outdoes fiction. And where fiction prevails it is in poetry and not the novel—the poetry of Osip Mandelstam and of Anna Akhmatova's *Requiem*. This living through a period where literature is decimated means, too, that there can only be a handful of survivors left to try and tell the tale. Pasternak survived because he was compliant, Mrs Mandelstam because she was not a poet. Alexander Solzhentisyn belonged to a different generation, a younger generation which escaped the purges of the thirties. And although his work is based equally upon the extremes of suffering and survival, this generational difference was crucial to the development of his literary vision. His early adult life was bounded by the patriotism of the war, the relapse into post-war repression, and finally the thaw after Stalin's death. He discovered anew the meaning of Stalinist terror, but during a period which saw more survivors, survivors that is who not only remained alive but were still alive after Stalin's death. As a writer he had an audience of survivors who had not compromised and were different therefore from most survivors of the previous generation.

Solzhenitsyn is the greatest novelist, perhaps the only major one, of the *univers concentrationnaire*. He is significant as a writer not only in the Soviet context, but in the development of modern literature as a whole. In his novels, the continuity of the tragic is inseparable from the continuity of the real. He revitalised Soviet realism by incorporating the intensity of personal experience that his epoch had given him. His work is highly autobiographical. Plot, characterisation and setting conform closely to the experience of his own life. Yet what he mainly writes about from his life is deliberately selective. It is his experience in total institutions. Solzhenitsyn's major fiction is the imprisoned survival of tragic realism. The limit of its setting is the condition of its tragedy. For some, the vastness of the tragic vision is too constricted by the closed environment of Solzhenitsyn's heroes. But since that closed vision is typical of the society about which he writes, the real acts as a necessary condition of the tragic. The vastness of the tragic is premissed on the vastness of the Gulag Archipelago.

In his first important work *One Day In the Life of Ivan Denisovitch*, Solzhenitsyn's vision is limited, and does not strive for that totality characteristic of the major novel. His peasant hero is limited by the lack of a life-by-value, imposed partly of course by extreme circumstances, but also by Shukhov's ignorance of politics, and consequently of the cause of his own suffering. The more one reads it, the more one senses that only here could Solzhenitsyn create a peasant hero. For Shukhov actually achieves what his author failed to do during his stay in the forced labour camps. That is, he develops a positive attitude to work which enables him to fulfil his impossible quotas, and also to derive a personal identity from his physical achievement. His practical success contrasts with Solzhenitsyn's personal difficulties. The author saw in the peasant inmate he created a physical resilience it took him so long to build up personally during his years in labour camps after the war.

Yet, lack of awareness of politics in a totally politicised society limits the tragic predicament of Solzhenitsyn's peasant hero. It may have made it easier for Krushchev to admire and Tvardovsky to publish but it also evades the problem of values crucial to the major work of fiction. As a result the fate of the hero is not developmental but cyclical, like that of Sisyphus. The novel gives us tragedy without catharsis, a feat of literary originality, but nonetheless a diminished tragedy. Solzhenitsyn clearly thought the fate of those who did not comprehend more poignant than those who did during his experience of life in the camps. But in his fiction the reverse is actually true. The tragic has more impact, the greater its range of vision. Its heroes are more fully developed the less they have to focus all the time purely, as Shukhov did, on strategies for survival. But Solzhenitsyn would have approved of Edgar in *Lear* saying 'the worst is not, so long as we can say this is the worst'. For the experience of the camps has given the thought a contemporary meaning beyond anything Shakespeare ever envisaged. It is why Solzhenitsyn thought the fate of Ivan Denisovitch to be the greatest tragedy of modern Russia.

In *The First Circle*, Solzhenitsyn goes beyond the limitations of his earlier work. Here is a political novel which attempts to give a boldly panoramic picture of Soviet society while still resorting to the concentrated time-span and the closed environment. The action lasts three days, and only rarely does it leave the prison environment. But this concentration in space and time is beneficial to the novel's development. It enables the author to develop first intensively, and then extensively, an image of the falsely organic totality of Stalin's Russia. The fate of its political rulers, Stalin and Abakumov, its political prisoners, Rubin and Nerzhin, and its political victim Innokenty Volodin, are interconnected. Its boldest step, un-doubtedly, is to portray the direct relationship of Stalin to his victims. It is precisely because of the political usefulness of its inmates that the special prison at Mavrino is a microcosm of the prison of Soviet Russia. The experience at Mavrino is not self-contained as it is for Ivan Denisovitch, nor can it be isolated from a wider experience of which it is not a part. Like *The Devils* it is primarily about the intelligentsia. But equally it is universal, since the implications of what happens at Mavrino are, like the incidents at Tver, fateful in the widest sense.

What are the special privileges of the First Circle of Soviet hell which Nerzhin eventually forfeits for a more terrifying fate? The first is that minimal degree of intellectual freedom which Stalin had destroyed in the outside world. The arguments which rage day and night between the inmates are not culturally typical, but an extraordinary release from the restraints of civilian and military life where silence is the greatest security against arrest. Only under conditions of imprisonment do the intelligentsia experience the freedoms which have been removed from everyday life. Prison is no protection against surveillance or informers like Doronin, but at Mavrino, in a closed environment, knowledge of these threats is much easier to come by than it is in the wider more anonymous circle of civilian life. Because of the free circulation and communication necessary to their specialist jobs, the inmates can form relationships based on a genuine comradeship impossible in the atomised world of suspicion outside. In 1949, the country-house just outside Moscow in which Solzhenitsyn was incarcerated must have been one of the few places in Soviet Russia where genuine debate about its fate was possible. Yet that same debate had no impact on the outside world. It certainly did not alter the task demanded of the inmates, most of which were related to a perpetuation of the very system the inmates so despised.

The intellectual dilemma at Mavrino, which actually existed, refracts the dilemma of the Soviet intelligentsia as a whole. The inmates are freer by virtue of being more dependent. The fate of those who reject, or even question, the terms of the dependency is the lower circles of hell, the labour camps from which there is no escape and often no return. The price extorted by the regime for the informal privilege possessed by Nerzhin and Rubin to shout and yell at each other is high. Their research on voice-prints is intended to improve the kind of electronic surveillance which can be used to produce more political prisoners. Nerzhin recognises the moral dilemma of his position and defies the authorities, thus sealing his fate. In prison as in civilian life the intelligentsia is privileged, but the threat hanging over its head is also the greatest. The first circle is equally a vicious circle which cannot be broken, except by those prepared for death.

Like *Nostromo*, *The First Circle* has two heroes, of whom only one is intended. The intended hero is Gleb Nerzhin, the most autobiographical of all Solzhenitsyn's characters, sceptic, historian, stoic and defiant opponent of Stalinism. The second hero, who eventually betrays his heroic potential, is Lev Rubin, philologist, Jewish intellectual, and a convinced communist who accepts Stalin's leadership of the Party. The villain is Stalin, who appears only once during an extended passage near the beginning of the book. Stalin's relationship to Rubin and Nerzhin is more oblique than that of Charles Gould to Decoud and Nostromo. But in a similar way his snap decision charts the route along which the two inmates are destined to travel, only to diverge at the most crucial point in the book. As in *Nostromo* divided heroism is a question of the dominant values of the novel. Rubin articulates and attempts to abide by the communist values the reality of Mavrino destroys. Nerzhin, who from the outset does not accept them, defies the worst effects of their perversion when Rubin finally capitulates to them. The personal relationship of the two men, who part close friends, is that of a dialectical interplay of ideological apology and sceptical disavowal. But the point must be made clear. While the values which come to grief are those of Soviet communism, there is no coherent set of values to oppose them. The ethical socialism of Oleg Kostoglotov, hero of *Cancer Ward*, is nowhere to be found. Again, the comparison with *Nostromo* is suggested, where opposition to the dominant ethos of liberal imperialism has no ideological foundation, but arises out of disillusionment and betrayal.

Yet the difference from *Nostromo* is also important. Gould's idealism is a model of liberal imperialism whereas Stalin's extreme paranoia is a perversion of communism. Solzhenitsyn's direct entry into Stalin's mind contrasts with the sinister veil of ignorance which Orwell casts over the personality of Big Brother. Big Brother is a mystified and falsely demonic caricature and Orwell's portrait seems constrained by the mystique of the personality cult which Stalin perpetrated. Solzhenitsyn's portrait is a supreme act of demystification. Not only does it give Stalin a human dimension but at the same time it restores the literary realism Orwell had forsaken. It is an achievement which could only have been accomplished inside Russia itself. Orwell had a fairly clear idea of the *univers concentrationnaire* which Sartre and many other socialist intellectuals were busy denying in 1948. But as a Western writer who knew nothing of Russia he could only translate that vision into nightmare. Having experienced it at first hand, Solzhenitsyn reveals its reality. The nearest approximation to his novel in Western political fiction is probably *For Whom the Bell Tolls*. The extended portrait of Stalin is reminiscent in its execution of Hemingway's cameo of André Marty. But the dimensions of characterisation are necessarily larger and bolder. In Spain, Marty's authority could be questioned, some of his excesses prevented. But in Russia there was no limit to the power of Stalin.

Unlike that of Winston Smith, the fate of Nerzhin is not predetermined by totalitarian omniscience. Such ideas belong to science fiction. Instead, Solzhenitsyn gives a comic portrait of the fallibility of his tyrant. As his memory begins to betray him in old age, Stalin forgets about the scrambler he wished to bring up in his interview with Abakumov. But upon the fading power of his memory hinges the insecure fate of Minister, bureaucrat and prison inmate alike. Solzhenitsyn manages to convey the absolute terror and panic Stalin causes in subordinates like Abakumov along with the intellectual mediocrity which makes his quest for absolute knowledge so ludicrous. A second-rate mind, with all earthly power at his disposal, Stalin is still saddled with an intellectual doctrine to which he can make no original contribution. His desire to know the world invariably degenerates into the wish to distrust it. Here Solzhenitsyn's gifts are comparable to Swift, to Voltaire or to *Animal Farm*—but in a realist context. He rejects the temptation to resort to fantasy. Consider the following unforgettable passage:

> Distrust of the people was the dominating characteristic of Joseph Djugashivili; it was his only philosophy of life. He had not trusted his own mother; neither had he trusted God, before whom as a young man he had bowed down in His temple. He had not trusted his fellow Party members, especially those with the gift of eloquence. He had not trusted his comrades in exile. He did not trust the peasants to sow the grain and harvest the wheat unless he forced them to do it and watched over them. He did not trust the workers to work unless he laid down the production targets. He did not trust the intellectuals to help the cause rather than harm it. He did not trust the soldiers and generals to fight without penal battalions and field security squads. He had never trusted his relatives, his wives or his mistresses. He had not trusted his children and how right he had been!
>
> In all his long suspicion-ridden life he had only trusted one man. That man had shown the whole world that he knew his own mind, knew whom it was expedient to like and whom to hate; and he had always known when to turn round and offer the hand of friendship to those who had been his enemies.

This man, whom Stalin had trusted, was Adolf Hitler.[3]

The dramatic effectiveness of this passage rests upon its element of surprise. As each sector of Soviet society rhetorically receives the kiss of death, the reader expects Stalin's trusted friend to be his most faithful henchman and executioner, Lavrenty Beria, or someone very similar. But instead it turns out to be the man who was Russia's most vicious and dangerous enemy. The passage works because it shows distrust exhausted upon Stalin's own people, and none left for their real enemies. Solzhenitsyn then goes on to point out the historical factors surrounding Stalin's failure to oppose Hitler before 1941. But these merely validate the imprint the initial image has made. Politically the message is clear: socialism in one country means external blindness and internal colonialism. But the literary originality of the passage lies in linking the perverted logic of Stalin's thought to the perversions of his political rule. The passage is a triumph in political fiction for the classic Tolstoyan point of view.

The portrait of Stalin, and his monthly interview with Abakumov, is the major departure that Solzhenitsyn makes from a setting which is largely autobiographical. But it is interesting to note how little Solzhenitsyn's departures from prison life open up the closed environment he portrays. He portrays Stalin as a prisoner of his own making, obsessed by security, retreating to the special villa built for him near Moscow where he is out of danger from his enemies. The Stalin we see here, in his small, windowless air-conditioned room, saving his most important work for the hours of darkness, lives in an extremely claustrophobic world. It is a world to which Solzhenitsyn's literary gifts are most perfectly suited. Once he departs from the closed environment into the social world of the *Nomenklatura*, the easy privileged life of Innokenty Volodin, his writing becomes diluted and diffuse. The party at the flat of Makarygin, the State prosecutor, provides a necessary contrast with Mavrino in more ways than one. Not only is it privilege which separates the *Nomenklatura* from the rest of Soviet society but also their role in the repression of the innocent. At the same time Solzhenitsyn loses the dialectic tension in his writing which derives from the closed environment and from the portrayal of relationships of power. The scene where Nadya, Nerzhin's wife, confronts her student flatmates is similarly unfocussed. When creating characters outside the closed environment, Solzhenitsyn seems at a loss as to what to do with them. The moment he is arrested, Innokenty Volodin somehow starts to become more real. The humiliating process of arrest, imprisonment and interrogation is also a figural *rite de passage* which turns him into an authentic Solzhenitsyn character. Solzhenitsyn transcribes his personal feeling of authenticity into his fiction. The only real person is the imprisoned Russian. The stigma which destroys his future life as a civilian becomes a literary sign of grace.

Yet Solzhenitsyn does not idolise or glorify the inmates of his novels. In *The First Circle* one of the key elements of tragic realism is the separation of Nerzhin and Nadya for which prison life, as a lawless punishment, is actually responsible. Prison destroys Nerzhin's marriage. The relationship of Gleb and Nadya is a remarkable departure with respect to the literary tradition of passion. Passion is usually juxtaposed to the security and convention of married love. But in the Stalinist context, married love takes on the attributes of a doomed passion. The social stigma of the political prisoner is felt as much by the spouse as by the prisoner himself. Nadya's life, like that of Solzhenitsyn's own wife at the time, was marked by the stigma of being married to a political prisoner, a fact she tries to keep secret at all costs. As a student studying for a postgraduate degree her career could be destroyed by revelation of the fact. She has to pretend she is not married. As a result the couple cannot exchange letters. In order to have his letters forwarded to her, Nerzhin must give the authorities her address, but this he refuses to do, knowing the danger it will bring her. They in turn refuse to forward his letters, which are written to her poste-restante. Consequently her visits to the prison are rare. And her position is in some ways worse than his. Solzhenitsyn captures her despair in a scene where she witnesses a column of prisoners being led to work on the wharf by the Moscow river. She intuitively follows, desperately hoping she might capture a glimpse of her husband:

> Nadya ran alongside the column shouting her husband's name, but her voice was drowned by what the old man was saying and by the furious barking of the guard dogs. Gasping for breath, she ran on just to feast her eyes on his face. How sorry she felt for him, rotting away all those months in a dark stinking cell. What bliss to see him here beside her. How proud she was that he still held his head up. And how hurt she was that he still seemed so cheerful—he must have forgotten her. And for the first time she felt sorry for herself, that he had done her an injury, that *she* was the victim, not he.[4]

Enforced separation first turns their married love into a defiant passion, the passion of prisoner and wife who are not even allowed to kiss. But in time it erodes the passion it has kindled. In Mavrino Gleb has a desultory surrogate affair with Simochka in which there is little feeling. At the same time he encourages Nadya to divorce him to further her career. The long separation fosters mutual misunderstanding. Secretly he wishes that she refuse to take up his offer, while she in turn hopes that he will stop insisting that her attempt to obtain a divorce is perfectly justifiable. But the misunderstanding is fostered by the political context of separation. The conflict between passion and society is more brutal in a police state than it is in an aristocratic Russia where Anna Karenin's fate is sealed by reactionary laws. And the result is more conclusive. The Stalinist state destroys the mutual feeling which symbolically opposes it. For Nerzhin, the passion which could preserve his marriage *in absentia* is finally eroded by the uncertainty of separation. As he is being driven in the prison bus to the assigned meeting-place for visits, the driver swerves to avoid a child in the road. The full significance of the future denied him comes to Nerzhin in a flash:

> Nerzhin had not given a thought to children for years, but now he suddenly realised that Stalin had robbed him and Nadya of their children. . . .
> In one of her letters Nadya had said: 'When you come back. . . .' But the horror was that there was no going back. To *return* was impossible. After four years in the army and a ten-year prison sentence there would probably not be a single cell in his body which would be the same. Although the man who came back would have the same surname as her husband, he would be a different person and she would realise that her one and only, for whom she had waited fourteen years, was not this man at all—he no longer existed.[5]

Gleb and Nadya's misunderstanding is tragic. But the form of mutual betrayal it represents and the political pressures which create that betrayal are fundamentally realistic. In *Nineteen Eighty-Four*, the Party intentionally masterminds the destruction of a passion it has kept under total surveillance. But Solzhenitsyn shows that in reality it needs neither the paraphernalia nor the omniscience of Oceania to achieve such an effect. Nor does it need torture, for it simply places the loved ones in an impossible situation where they torture themselves. The reunion of Nadya and Gleb for that brief half-hour is one of the most memorable passages in Russian literature. It poses agonisingly all the questions which Pasternak glosses over in his description of Zhivago's affair with Lara, and provides the tragic sense of the whole novel—the tragedy of a marriage unable to transform itself into passion in defiance of the separation threatening to destroy it. This is the greatest sense of loss the novel conveys, and Nerzhin's transfer to a forced labour camp at the end merely compounds it. The loss of intellectual freedom complements the loss of personal passion.

Yet the loss of freedom, though not as emotionally intense, is as indispensable to the author's tragic realism as the loss of passion. It is the double blow, felt consecutively which shakes Nerzhin's powers for survival to their very core. But as each blow falls in turn, his opposition hardens into an ascetic determination to resist. His fate is tragic in both the emotional and the intellectual sense but his experience over the years flows with him into the lower regions of hell. We sense that for Nerzhin there can be no cathartic ending, and that should death come, it would do so unspectacularly after a long cruel process of attrition. The sense of life exceeding the novel's ending comes from the threat of a worse fate constantly hanging over him, the damnation of a this-worldly hell. Dante's metaphor is given a supreme reality in an ending whose finality sheds all trace of the apocalypse.

A measure of the remarkable freedom Nerzhin is doomed to forfeit by his transfer is his constant clash with Rubin over their political fate. Rubin is as severely tested by prison life as his friend, but in a totally different way. He remains a convinced communist who justifies the objective necessity of his own imprisonment. On the outside his opinions were necessary for political survival. But in prison they are under attack from all sides. Rubin becomes the outsider, regarded as an apologist for the regime. In the prison environment his ideas are severely put to the test. For he has to defend himself against equals. His Marxist orthodoxy lacks the support of political legitimacy and coercion which it has on the outside, and consequently has no means of intimidation. Rubin is the ideologue without his robes, assailed on all sides by the victims of the system he supported. The real test of his heroism is whether he can maintain the integrity of ideological principles in a setting, and at a given historical moment when they are so abused. Rubin is not the virus of a poisoned creed, as some critics have seen him, but the potential antidote to that poison. In the political plot of the novel, he is the antidote which fails.

Rubin is a convinced Marxist-Leninist who believes with an overwhelming confidence in the doctrine of historical materialism. At the same time he is not prepared to see Stalin's rule, as the Trotskyists were, in terms of a historical deviation from history's predetermined path. The Party remains the bedrock of historical necessity. 'Why', he demands of Nerzhin, 'should we change our views just because we personally have come to grief?' That same day he has tried to forget the embarrassing failure of Traicho Kostov's show trial by plotting the victorious advance of the Chinese communists on a map specially made for the purpose. Yet during the course of those three days, his attitude does change, swayed by the hostile and hysterical arguments of Sologdin who seems determined to drive him to insanity. But the significant feature of Rubin's change of heart is that it is not translated into deeds. His increasing sense of the Party's inadequacy does not alter his personal loyalty, nor change his attitude to the demands made of him at Mavrino.

Hounded mercilessly by the other inmates, he finally conceives a scheme which is undoubted ideological heresy. Suffering from insomnia he dreams up a grandiose 'proposal for the Establishment of Civic Temples'. It is a gesture towards the humanisation of Party rule, by creating a group of ministrants within the Party whose humanity and moral example will contrast with past excesses and make the Party genuinely popular again. But Rubin dreams up his scheme under the spell of an opiate which life at Mavrino has given him—the opiate of freedom. His plan to smuggle it out of the prison to the Central Committee is pure fantasy, and practically tantamount to suicide. Though Rubin's proposal demonstrates a genuine change of heart he continues to comply with actions of which he disapproves. It is his expert knowledge which enables the Secret Police to arrest Innokenty Volodin for his warning telephone call to Professor Doubromov. As he listens to the tape of Volodin's voice, his contempt for the State Security officials demanding his co-operation fails to outweigh his misplaced sense of duty:

> The tape came to an end again. As Rubin took his hands away from his face and looked at the sullen Smolosidov and at Bulbanyuk's empty, pompous features, he found them both so repulsive he had to turn away; yet in this very minor juncture in history it was these two who were objectively the embodiment of progress.
>
> He must rise above his personal feelings. It had been thugs like these two, only from the army's political section who had put Rubin into prison because he was too clever and too honest for them. And again it had been thugs like this, only from the army legal department, who for four years had rejected appeal after appeal in which Rubin had pleaded his innocence.
>
> But he must rise above his personal misfortune, and although these two deserved to have a hand-grenade thrown at them right here in this room, it was not them to whom Rubin owed allegiance but to his country, to its principles, its flag.[6]

Rubin is unable to break the vicious circle of complicity which has dogged him ever since he informed on his cousin during the thirties. There lies a permanent question-mark over his heroism. He never compromises his intellectual qualities, and his personal integrity has not been destroyed by his actions. If Soviet society were as just as he wished it to be, then his contribution could be positive and fruitful. But since it is not, he has no alternative strategy, nor is he capable of developing one. Rubin's desire to act, but failure to do so, makes him something of a modern Hamlet. But he is actually closer to Nicholas Stavrogin, whose dilemma is the reverse of his own. Dostoevsky's aristocrat fails to act through lack of commitment. Rubin fails to rebel through an excess of commitment. But whereas Stavrogin follows his failure through to a tragic conclusion by killing himself, Rubin compromises. His ideology cushions his fatalism, by neatly allowing him to attribute his failure to historical necessity. Stavrogin faces the abyss of nothingness, but Rubin retreats into the womb of falsehood and lies.

The difference between Rubin and Nerzhin now becomes clearer. Nerzhin's refusal takes place while Stalin is alive: Rubin's can only take place after his death when it is no longer a refusal. The novel implies that Rubin could change after Stalin's death, but only after Stalin's death. During those three days which end with Nerzhin's transfer, there is no chance of such a change. At the end, the embrace between the two men is genuine and moving, but only one of them is being punished. Nerzhin's tragic refusal is impossible for the positive Lukácsian hero who clings to the system despite its abuses in the hope that one day the abuses will be rectified.

Nerzhin's own attitude towards politics has been widely misunderstood. Many critics have seen him as a populist endowed with the opinions of his author. Yet as we now know, Solzhenitsyn was, at the time of writing, still a Marxist but also a Christian who secretly held the beliefs he later dogmatised quite openly in his attacks on Marxism. In the tradition of Tolstoy and Dostoevsky, Solzhenitsyn has sought out total belief. Yet Nerzhin's admiration for Spiridon, the ordinary peasant prison caretaker, is not like this at all. Spiridon's life, it is true, mirrors the sufferings of the Russian people since the time of the Revolution. During his life, he has been in both the White army and the Red army, a Kulak and a commissar of collective farms, a labour camp prisoner and a German sympathiser, a Soviet Partisan and a political prisoner. Nerzhin admires his qualities of tenacity and endurance. But something else appeals to his sceptical spirit. Spiridon's life is an affront to all idealism and materialism. And Nerzhin's liking for him is a perverse idealisation of that which cannot be idealised. It is the epitome of a realist scepticism which denies the total belief Nerzhin's author constantly sought. Here Nerzhin is certaintly *not* Solzhenitsyn. He interprets Spiridon's life to defy all interpretation. No ideology can truthfully account for it. It is the key element in his tragic refusal of ideology as such.

This refusal is also linked to the degeneration of official language. The similarities between Mavrino and Orwell's Ministry of Truth are always evident. But Solzhenitsyn provides a more penetrating account of the relationship between language and ideology, or at least the ideological foundation upon which language rests. The 'clipped speech' laboratory is a concrete and realistic symbol of the practical degradation of language for political reasons. While complying with the demands made on them, the inmates invent their own counter-culture as a means of resisting the technological tasks they are forced to do. There are two centrepieces of the resistance to official language and ideology in the novel. The first is the mock trial of Prince Igor conducted by Rubin and the second is the story 'The Smile of the Buddha' invented by Nerzhin and Popatokov. Not only are they symbolic rituals of defiance, they also show Solzhenitsyn's superb satirical gift for exposing the means by which ideology can debase language. In Prince Igor's trial, 'evidence' is used from the first great work of Russian literature to condemn his hero—Soviet-style as a counter-revolutionary. Quotations from the poem are used in evidence but then 'translated' into the aggressive bureaucratic gibberish of the Soviet legal system as evidence of Igor's guilt. As the prosecutor, Rubin's speech is masterly. Igor's punishment, expulsion to the West, seems now like a prophetic foresight into Solzhenitsyn's own fate. For it is literature itself which is on trial.

Nerzhin's equally amusing tale about the visit of Eleanor Roosevelt to a Soviet prison throws into relief another important aspect of ideology—the control of information. Here reality is reorganised temporarily by the

Soviet authorities to validate the lie they have perpetrated about their exemplary prison conditions. The prisoners' lives are briefly changed to suit the lie. And when the wrong information has been accepted, their lives return to normal again. Narrative satire shows up the human dimension of the debasement of language and the acceptance of untruth. The Mavrino inmates are privileged captives to this process, but repudiate it by turning the weapon of language against its perpetrators. The freedom to laugh at bureaucratic gibberish, and to mock false information through the subversive tale is possible neither in civilian life nor the labour camps. Its true milieu is the privileged incarceration at Mavrino. Rubin and Nerzhin's freedom to discuss literature contrasts with the restrictions on Clara Makarygin, who cannot study fiction of relevance to her own life, and on Galakhov, the eminent socialist realist, who tailors his novels in advance to win official critical approval. The inmates have an artistic freedom of a sort denied to the civilian world. They can share their mock trials and tales and be their own audience. But the writer who has an audience has no freedom to write how or what he wishes and the student of literature can only read what is strictly assigned to her. Solzhenitsyn is reflexive here in the Dostoevskyan tradition. The perverted relationship in Soviet Russia of writer to critic, of art to ideology, of novel to society, is reproduced within the novel itself. *The First Circle* not only reflects upon the restrictions placed upon its own production, but also on its transcendence of them.

The most vital condition enabling Solzhenitsyn to write his major fiction was his personal escape from the closed environment about which he wrote. The bulk of his work on *Ivan Denisovitch*, *Cancer Ward* and *The First Circle* came from two places of residence. The first was his stay at Talnovo, the small village in Vladimir province he describes in 'Matryona's Place', and the second was the ten years or so he spent living in Ryazan.[7] As far as the impetus to write so prolifically was concerned, there seemed to be an elective affinity between the years of the 'thaw' and the relative freedom of living in rural Russia. While an open environment helped his writing, its fate as literary content in his work was rather different. *August 1914*, his major attempt to write a panoramic historical novel, does not capture the Tolstoyan dimensions he strove for, and often degenerates into laborious discussions of military strategy. But one thing must not be overlooked. His writing deteriorates as his persecution increases. After the fall of Krushchev, the vice of party control on literature was tightened considerably. Solzhenitsyn's hopes of publishing either *Cancer Ward* or *The First Circle* in Russia began to fade. How much increasing harassment affected his ability to write is unclear. But soon he attached himself to the very literary tradition he had earlier so strongly opposed. He started to think of literature purely as a political weapon, trying to rewrite history in *The Gulag Archipelago* and trying, in *Lenin in Zurich*, to turn the crude weapon of didactic fiction against its chief proponents. Isolated in his own country, explicitly persecuted on the orders of Brezhnev and with the collusion of Konstantin Fedin, Solzhenitsyn lost both his tragic sense of life and his talent for realism. His Nobel Prize lecture was the last moving testimony to those literary qualities fast deserting him. Expulsion from Russia was the kiss of death, exile to the West a banishment to a literary desert where his own kind of fiction had already voluntarily died.

Perhaps, from the point of view of the novel, Solzhenitsyn is Nietzsche's 'last man' of European civilisation. By comparison with the other art forms, with poetry or drama, art or music, the contemporary novel is in a sorry state, a state sustained by the effete expectations held of it by the Western intelligentsia. A source of cultural embarrassment, it continues to function as the myth of a certain kind of freedom—that of the private imagination. And the notion of privacy here, as what is present in the human psyche but absent from rational public discourse, is itself a kind of prison. In the fragmented networks of private writing which have spread throughout Western fiction, the novel has its own Gulag Archipelago. By being forcibly expelled, Solzhenitsyn has been plunged into a different kind of prison system of which, for once, he is totally ignorant.

Conclusion: Tragic Realism and Modern Society

The year 1848 has been acclaimed as the most significant date in modern fiction. But 1948, one hundred years later exactly, is of equal significance. The year previously, *Doctor Faustus* and *Under the Volcano* had been published. The year after saw the appearance of *Nineteen Eighty-Four*. In the last month of that year, December 1949, is the three days' duration of *The First Circle*. Between 1848 and 1948 lies the period of tragic realism in the modern novel. Before it is Stendhal, and after it Solzhenitsyn. In between is the work of Emily Brontë, Melville, Flaubert, Tolstoy, Dostoevsky, Conrad, Zola, Hardy, Mann, Faulkner and Hemingway. The transformation of tragic realism in the modern theatre is delayed and less prolific. But it actually outlasts its appearance in the novel. After Ibsen and Chekhov, there is O'Casey and O'Neill and, in post-war America, Tenessee Williams, Arthur Miller and the early Edward Albee.

Discussing the social context of tragic realism is a monumental task. But various strands have appeared and reappeared throughout the course of this book. They suggest a more general framework within which we can tentatively place its literary evolution. In the first instance tragic realism expresses the aristocratic resistance to bourgeois society. In tragic drama, in Marlowe, Shakespeare and Racine, it had appeared at the very beginnings of bourgeois life. But in Stendhal it occurs after the French revolution when the hegemonic elements of a bourgeois-capitalist society had firmly asserted themselves. That is to say, tragic realism reappears during the period of political liberalism. But as liberalism progresses, the aristocratic element in tragic fiction is preserved in Russian fiction in a society where liberalism had yet to make any mark.

What happens to tragic realism in a liberal-capitalist society? A major clue can be found in the theme of *Wuthering Heights*. Here we witness the introduction of a proletarian outcast into provincial landed society, an outcast who eventually takes control. In Brontë's novel, the bourgeois spirit is represented, if at all, by the temperament and stupidity of its narrator. In the story he tells, it is conspicuous by its absence. The struggle for power between Heathcliff and Linton is no more a reflection of the Marxian class struggle than Heathcliff's passion for Cathy is a sign of proletarian triumph. The conflict is there, certainly. But the writing is also reflexive. The landed Yorkshire gentleman and the urchin from the streets of Liverpool vie for heroic stature within the novel itself. The push and pull of tragic realism is largely between the aristocratic resistance to bourgeois society and the entry of the lower-classes into fiction. In the following century, Heathcliff's literary descendant, different in so many respects, is Joe Christmas, the illegitimate half-caste in a Deep South shedding its aristocratic heritage.

To demand typicality from tragic realism with respect to the portrayal of class situation is actually pointless. The very complex relationship of the tragic hero, or heroes, to bourgeois society, must be seen in terms of varieties of alienation. The alienated hero is marginal, not merely by virtue of attitude but also by virtue of experience. We can point out once again the recurrent social indices of this marginality—rural, aristocratic, peasant, proletarian, artistic. Of course, they have no organic connection to each other. But they do display the negative unity of opposition to dominant bourgeois, and industrialist, values. The point we have to grasp is that tragic realism strives to be universal within such a negative unity of opposition. Elizabethan tragedy attained universality through the noble. Tragic realism must attain universality in an age where the noble, both in its material and its ideal sense, has ceased to exist. The focal point of its universality is not therefore positive in the sense of tragic nobility, but negative in the sense of a defiance of the social world which has destroyed the noble. That is the crux, the fundament of its artistic defiance of bourgeois society.

It would be too presumptuous to suggest that tragic realism has its own social geography. But the pre-eminence of the rural or maritime setting, and the relationship between city and country, throws light upon the urban culture which is largely ignored in this type of novel. The question of the city is a crucial one. The sole occasion of a major Western city being used in a tragic realist novel is London in *The Secret Agent*. This is remarkable considering how much realist literature there is of the modern city—in Balzac, Dickens, Gissing, Zola, Wells, Joyce, Dos Passos and Doeblin. But just as Balzac and Flaubert, Mann and Musil generally lack a tragic vision of bourgeois life, so the city itself eludes tragic realism. The absences from tragic realism are crucial and explicit—urban and bourgeois and, in the twentieth century, suburban and bohemian. Zola leaves Paris to write *Germinal* and Thomas Mann, who had assembled a cross-section of the European bourgeoisie at Davos, finds tragedy elsewhere in the lone figure of the doomed composer. Significantly he provides the only other Western city of tragedy—Venice—in the short story which was the prelude to his tragic novel. But unlike Gustav Aschenbach, who comes to Venice to die, Adrian Leverkuehn spends most of his life in rural Germany, closeted in retreat. And while Stevie Verloc blows himself up within sight of the Meridian, Kurtz and Nostromo die at the very periphery of Empire.

The city is usually the setting of an affirmative realism. By this I do not mean that urban fiction fails to reveal the miseries of city life, for this it obviously does. But seldom is much misery the basis for conveying the irreparable loss we call tragic. It is ironic that the vast, immensely detailed urban vision of Dickens is transformed into tragedy by the two most important writers to come under his influence. For of these two, Dostoevsky did not live in an urbanised society and Kafka dispensed with realism in writing tragic fiction. The life portrayed in tragic realism is always marginal to the dominant social experiences of its time. But it is tragic for that very reason, and by being tragic, it is thereby central to social experience. The apparent circularity in this reasoning in fact turns out to be something else. It is a recognition of a fundamental paradox. In order to portray irreparable loss at the very centre of our modern social experience, tragic realism absents itself, is relegated to the periphery of characteristic ways of living. Only in the space it finds there does the element of universality emerge, does the tragic experience of its characters arise to reunite with the real experience of us all.

Significantly, in the recent political novel, attempts to convey a typical political experience have come unstuck. Orwell's *Nineteen Eighty-Four*, Malraux's *Days of Hope*, Camus's *The Plague* search for a general experience but find it only by abdicating both the tragic and the real. All are a response, in different ways, to fascism and totalitarianism, but the tragic experience of these evils is lost. Indeed, one might say that it is never attempted. The failure to come to terms with the experience of fascism in post-war literature—in the work of Sartre, Böll and Grass as well as Orwell and Camus—reveals the decline of tragic realism in political fiction. The defeat of Nazism has become a popular legend through memoirs, autobiographical novels and spy stories, all of them grist to the Hollywood mill. There are no novels to rival *For Whom the Bell Tolls* and the disaster of attempted tragedy which fails is nowhere shown more clearly than in *Across the River and Into the Trees*. We enter an age when nothing is easier for the best European writers than to proclaim the virtues of tragic humanism yet fail to write any tragic literature at all.

In looking more closely at this apparent deterioration, some of the salient sociological factors have already been hinted at. With the post-war stabilisation of the Western liberal-democracies, we have seen the growth of urban and suburban life, the growth of bureaucracy and the growth of an intelligentsia, a term now recognised as not being, after all, a relic of nineteenth-century Russia. We have also seen the growth, in-stitutionalisation perhaps, of a widespread bohemian counter-culture. But the co-existence of all these factors, their increasing cultural importance, have undermined the social context of tragic realism as well as its artistic production. Often the bohemian counter-culture is a negative revolt against the dominant values of a rationalised culture and lacks a tragic sense of life, in fact would polemically disown it. Despite publicist trumpetings of a democratisation of culture, the working-classes remain largely passive or indifferent towards art. And significantly enough, the vast dimension of tragic experience which working-class life is, is either ignored or polemically idealised into something which it is not.

It would be wrong, however, to attribute the contemporary absence of tragic realism to a decline in individualism and a growth of cultural uniformities. As new uniformities have sprung up, so have new types of individualism. The varieties of cultural consumption now available to us create a kind of diversity, a set of alternatives and even the possibility of protest and rejection. If anything, individualism in Western societies is increasing. In some ways, people are more different than ever before, but different because of the transience, fragmentation and atomisation of modern culture. And these factors invariably undermine the totalising artistic vision which sees the irreparable struggle of man against society and man against his fellow-men. In state-socialist societies, things are rather different. Artistic expression is more severely restricted, the element of political uniformity and bureaucratic dominance more crucial. There cultural individualism has its political price, fiction its official opponents. But in the West, indifference is more the order of the day. The tragic sense of life is in a competitive market situation like any other cultural product. And mass consumer culture breeds its new philistine oligopolies.

These factors refer not only to the production of art but its consumption. Any artistic form thrives not only through people wanting to create it, but even more people willing to experience it. In mass consumer culture the idea of an audience degenerates into the idea of a market for a product. In apparent contrast, the expansion of the media and the universities, concomitant with the growth of the intelligentsia, has had the effect of producing people dedicated to their own versions of the democratisation of culture. This involves abolishing traditional distinctions between high-brow and lowbrow, elitist art and popular culture, even 'art' and 'life'. But though this has given rise to new forms of cultural information in great quantities, it actually vitiates the tragic sense of life. The medium becomes the message, and the content of art is reduced to a series of marketable cultural styles which, though increasing in variety, package it as a product for mass consumption in the process. The professional missionary zeal of the cultural intelligentsia becomes unintentionally utilitarian. By propagating and institutionalising its enthusiasm for culture it contributes to the radical disenchantment of the world.

What are lost here are not the mystic and the non-rational, which still thrive in a limited way, but the vital artistic links between the imaginative and the real. We can recognise passively this blow to our cultural sensibility by enjoying Shakespeare or reading nineteenth-century novels and sensing that they have no contemporary equivalents. Or we can hope that the eclipse of tragic realism is a *trompe l'oeil*, and that great writers will emerge to make such fears appear hysterical and unfounded. But the renaissance of tragedy in a modern secular world could well come from outside the West altogether, in those countries still emerging from a colonial or traditional past. But this too is an unknown factor, which time alone will confirm or gainsay. Sooner or later in history, all great periods of culture have been succeeded by decay, their legacy rescued from oblivion by future civilisations which completely transform them. Despite the continuity of cultural information in our own age, this too could be the fate of tragic realism. A great, as yet not fully recognised period of modern literature may have now passed. But who is to say what future culture will resurrect and transform it, or when, or what form such a resurrection might take?

Notes

PART I

Chapter 1

1. See René Wellek, 'Realism in literary scholarship' in *Concepts of Criticism* (London 1963), p. 222ff; Raymond Williams, *Keywords* (London 1976), p. 216ff; George J. Becker, *Documents of Modern Literary Realism* (Princeton 1963).
2. *Theory of the Novel* (trans. Anna Bostock) (Cambridge, Mass. 1970), pp. 112–3.
3. *Ibid.*, p. 172.
4. *The Historical Novel* (trans. Hannah and Stanley Mitchell) (London 1969). Cited in T. Burns and E. Burns (ed.), *Sociology of Literature and Drama* (London 1973), p. 287.
5. Lukács writes: 'Obviously one cannot call Gregor's fate tragic in spite of certain tragic features.' *Der russische Realismus in der Weltliteratur* (Berlin 1952) (3rd ed.), p. 363.
6. *Studies in European Realism* (trans. Edith Bone) (London 1950), p. 63.
7. See *The Meaning of Contemporary Realism* (trans. Hannah and Stanley Mitchell) (London 1963), p. 17ff.
8. See his autobiographical record, *The Genesis of a Novel* (Princeton 1953).
9. *Modern Tragedy* (London 1966), p. 64.
10. *Ibid.*, p. 77.
11. Williams, on the other hand, feels that despite Lawrence's explicit rejection of the social as the basis of tragic necessity, *Women in Love* is a tragic work—a form of personal tragedy, in effect, which goes beyond society. Williams, *op. cit.*, p. 121ff.
12. *Mimesis* (trans. Willard B. Trask) (Princeton 1953), p. 328.
13. *Ibid.*, pp. 464–6.
14. *Ibid.*, pp. 482.
15. Williams, *op. cit.*, p. 55.

Chapter 2

1. See Frederick Jameson, *Marxism and Form* (Princeton 1971), chapter 1.
2. See 'The Author as Producer', *New Left Review* 62 (1970).
3. *Illuminations* (London 1972), p. 101.
4. *Ibid.*, p. 146.
5. Significantly, Benjamin moves away from the novel in his discussion of literary technique and concentrates his attention on theatre, journalism and film. While his discussion of the practical possibilities of these media is engrossing, there is still a basic element of theoretical mystification. His use of the term *Technik* has remarkable similarities with the usage of Ernst Juenger and Martin Heidegger in their proto-fascist writings. See Benjamin 'The Author as

Producer' *New Left Review*, 62, 1970; Ernst Juenger *Der Arbeiter* (Berlin 1932); J. Orr 'German Social Theory and the Hidden Face of Technology', *Archives européenes de sociologie*, XV, 1974, pp. 312–336.
6. *Noten zur Literatur*, vol. I. (Frankfurt 1965), p. 64.
7. See *The Dialectic of Enlightenment* (New York 1972); also Martin Jay *The Dialectical Imagination* (London 1973), p. 216ff.
8. *One-Dimensional Man* (Boston 1964), p. 77.
9. *Ibid.*, p. 229ff. Marcuse takes the term from Maurice Blanchot, whose influence on structuralism is discussed in the following chapter.

Chapter 3

1. For the classic study of Russian formalism see Victor Erlich *Russian Formalism*, The Hague 1955
2. 'On realism', in L. Matejka and K. Pomorska (ed.), *Readings in Russian Poetics* (Cambridge, Mass. 1971) pp. 40–1.
3. 'On literary evolution', *Readings in Russian Poetics*, p. 67.
4. *Ibid.*, p. 72
5. 'The Concept of the Dominant', *Readings in Russian Poetics*, pp. 82–91.
6. 'Art as technique', in Lee Lemon and Marion Reis (ed.), *Russian Formalist Criticism: Four Essays*, (Lincoln, Nebraska 1965), p. 12.
7. *Ibid.*, p. 13.
8. Matejka and Pomorska, *op. cit.*, p. 61.
9. 'Thematics', in Lemon and Reis, *op. cit.*, p. 65.
10. *Ibid.*, p. 81.
11. *Ibid.*, p. 71.
12. For the influence of Heidegger upon structuralism, see Frederic Jameson, *The Prison-house of Language* (Princeton 1972), p. 168ff.
13. *The Order of Things* (London 1970), p. 385ff.
14. The essence of Blanchot's theory is contained in 'La littérature et le droit à la mort', first published in 1947 and 1948, then republished as the last chapter of *La Part du Feu* (Paris 1949). The theory is elaborated at greater length in *L'Espace littéraire* (paris 1955) and *Le livre à venir* (paris 1959). There is a good critical study of Blanchot by Sarah Lawall, *Critics of Consciousness* (Cambridge, Mass. 1968). A translated extract from 'la littérature et le droit à la mort' can be found in Maurice Nadeau *The French Novel since the War* (trans. A. M. Sheridan Smith) London 1967.
15. *La Part du Feu* p. 325.
16. *Writing Degree Zero* (trans. Annette Lavers and Colin Smith) (Boston 1968), p. 33.
17. *Ibid.*, p. 77.
18. For a rather different interpretation of the murder, see Conor Cruise O'Brien, *Camus* (London 1970), p. 23ff.
19. See Susan Sontag's preface to *Writing Degree Zero*, p. viiff.
20. ' "Genetic Structuralism" in the sociology of literature', in Burns and Burns, *op. cit.*, p. 115.
21. *Towards a Sociology of the Novel* (trans. Alan Sheridan) (London 1975), pp. 123–4.
22. *Ibid.*, p. 134.
23. *Ibid.*, p. 135.

24. *Aspects of the Novel* (London 1963) p. 36.
25. *Fictions: The Novel and Social Reality* (trans. Tom and Catherine Burns) (London 1976), pp. 43–4.
26. For the argument postulating 'production' as the key element of fiction see Pierre Macherey, *Pour une Théorie de la Production littéraire* (Paris 1971), p. 83ff.
27. Zéraffa, *op. cit.*, p. 37.
28. *La Revolution romanesque* (Paris 1969), p. 18.
29. *Ibid.*, p. 55ff; *Fictions*, chapter 1, p. 7ff.
30. *Fictions*, p. 125.

Chapter 4

1. *Politics and the Novel* (New York 1957), p. 16.
2. 'Figura', in *Scenes from the Drama of European Literature*, p. 11ff.
3. *Ibid.*, p. 70.
4. *The English Novel from Dickens to Lawrence* (London 1974), p. 81.
5. Frank Kermode, *The Sense of the Ending* (New York 1967); Alan Friedman, *The Turn of the Novel* (New York 1967).
6. 'Henry James, An Appreciation', in *Notes on Life and Letters* (London 1924) pp. 18–19.

PART II

Chapter 5

1. For a study of the radical Russian intelligentsia of this period see Franco Venturi *The Roots of Revolution* (London 1960)
2. *Passion and Society* (trans. Montgomery Belgion) (London 1956), p. 233ff.
3. *Anna Karenin* (trans. Rosemary Edmunds) (London 1962), pp. 117–18.
4. *Ibid.*, p. 579.
5. *The Idiot* (trans. David Magarshak) (London 1958), p. 133.
6. *Ibid.*, p. 611.
7. *Ibid.*, pp. 592–6.
8. *The Brothers Karamazov* (trans. David Magarshak) (London 1964), vol. 1, p. 305.

Chapter 6

1. 'Dostoevsky', in R. Wellek (ed.), *Dostoevsky* (New Jersey 1962).
2. *The Notebooks for the Possessed* (ed. E. Wasiolek) (Chicago 1968).
3. For a portrait of Nikolai Speshnev and his role in the Petrashevsky circle see Leonid Grossman, *Dostoevsky: a Biography* (London 1974), p. 112ff.
4. *The Devils* (trans. David Magarshak) (London 1962), p. 420.

Chapter 7

1. Preface to the second edition of *Thérése Raquin* (trans. Leonard Tancock) (London 1975), p. 22.
2. An excellent account of how Zola collected his material is given by Richard

Zakarian, *Zola's Germinal: a Critical Study of the Primary Sources* (Droz 1972).
3. *Germinal* (trans. Leonard Tancock) (London 1976), pp. 273–4.
4. *Ibid.*, p. 424.

Chapter 8

1. *Under Western Eyes* (London 1964), p. 21.
2. *Ibid.*, p. 291.
3. *The Secret Agent* (London 1963), p. 215.
4. For an account of the Greenwich bombing incident and Conrad's reaction to it see Ian Watt, *Conrad, the Secret Agent: a Casebook* (London 1973).
5. *Nostromo* (London 1963), p. 75.
6. *Ibid.*, p. 81.
7. *Ibid.*, p. 458.

Chapter 9

1. *Tonio Kroeger* (trans. H. T. Lowe-Porter) (London 1962), p. 190.
2. *Letters to Paul Amann* (London 1961) p. 39.
3. *The Magic Mountain* (trans. H. T. Lowe-Porter) (London 1962), pp. 285–6.
4. *Ibid.*, pp. 245–6.
5. *Ibid.*, p. 374.
6. *Ibid.*, p. 404.
7. *Mario and the Magician* (London 1975), p. 141.
8. *Doctor Faustus* (trans. H. T. Lowe-Porter) (London 1971), pp. 329–30.

Chapter 10

1. See Roy A. Medvedev, *Problems in the Literary Biography of Mikhail Sholokhov* (London 1977); Alexander Solzhenitsyn, 'Sholokhov and the Riddle of "The Quiet Don"', *Times Literary Supplement*, 4 October 1974, p. 1056; Vladimir Molozherenko 'About a certain undeservedly forgotten name', *ibid.*, p. 1057; and the article on Medvedev's study by Peter Osnos in the *Guardian*, 19 April 1975. Molozherenko, a Soviet critic, re-affirms Kurkov's literary importance as a Cossack writer. In the opening paragraphs he explicitly compares the fate of Krukov with that of the novel's hero Gregor Melekhov. Both were forced to flee the Red advance on the Don in 1920 and both contracted typhus during the retreat. In the novel, Gregor survives the fever, but in real life Krukov died from it. Molozherenko has since claimed, as a result of the controversy arising from his article in the Soviet Union, that Sholokhov is the sole author of *The Silent Don*.
2. *And Quiet Flows the Don* (trans. Stephen Garry) (London 1967), pp. 510–11.
3. From a Bolshevik point of view, Trotsky criticised his party's military strategy on the Southern Front, and claimed that it lacked social and political understanding. The Red army had driven the Cossacks into the hands of Denikin's Volunteer army by invading Cossack land and committing unnecessary atrocities. Instead, Trotsky suggests, they should have bypassed the Cossacks to confront Denikin's army directly, so depriving the Whites of the chance to use Cossack help or Cossack territory. See *My Life* (New York 1960), pp. 453–5.
4. *And Quiet Flows the Don*, p. 311.
5. *The Don Flows Home to the Sea* (trans. Stephen Garry) (London 1972), p. 420.

6. *Ibid.*, pp. 827–8.
7. It is impossible to make any definitive judgment about the authorship on the basis of the abridged English translation in two volumes (London 1967 and 1972). More than a hundred pages have been cut out from the original Russian text. Apart from general historical commentary on the civil war, the two most vital elements missing are the story of Liza Mokhova, which is taken from the diary of a dead Cossack, and a fuller portrait of Eugene Listnitsky. Sections covering Listnitsky's relationship with Aksinia have been omitted, as have his letters to his father. The English edition, translated at the end of the thirties, does have the virtue of excluding the postwar Soviet revisions of the novel forced on Sholokhov by the Zhdanov cultural regime. For a discussion of the English omissions see David Stewart, '*The Silent Don* in English', *American Slavic and East European Review*, vol. xv, 1956, pp. 265–75.

Chapter 11

1. Both novels are of direct historical interest for their recognisable portraits of leading Republican figures in the war. But one must not overlook the fictional dimensions of such portraits. To use Forster's famous distinction, Malraux's characterisations tend to be 'flat', while Hemingway's, on the whole, are 'round'. In *Days of Hope* Colonel Escobar of the Civil Guard in Barcelona was the model for Colonel Ximenez, while Enrico Lister was the model for Manuel. Hemingway, more intrigued by the personalities of the communists he met, provided the more controversial fictionalisation. André Massart is modelled on André Marty. General Golz is modelled on the military adviser to the International Brigades, Karol Swierczewski, code-named General Walter. It was Walter who, commanding the XIVth International Brigade, mounted the counter-offensive on the Segovia front described in the novel. Karkov, the Russian journalist, was modelled on Michael Koltsov, the *Pravda* correspondent who later perished in the Great Purge. There is some evidence to suggest that Koltsov was Stalin's personal agent in Spain. See Hugh Thomas, *The Spanish Civil War* (London 1965), p. 336. Mitchell, the British economist whom Karkov and Robert Jordan jointly ridicule as a self-important fellow-traveller with a '*gueule de conspirateur*', could well be a malicious portrait of Malraux himself. See *For Whom the Bell Tolls* (London 1964), pp. 230–4.
2. Malraux's claim to tragic humanism is scattered through numerous written articles and interviews. See C. D. Bland *André Malraux: Tragic Humanist* (Ohio 1963), p. 49ff.
3. *Man's Estate* (trans. Alistair Macdonald) (London 1972), pp. 8–15.
4. *Ibid.*, p. 84.
5. *Ibid.*, p. 191.
6. *Ibid.*, p. 196.
7. *Ibid.*, p. 290.
8. *Days of Hope* (trans. Stuart Gilbert and Alistair Macdonald) (London 1970), p. 196.
9. *For Whom the Bell Tolls* (London 1964), pp. 130–1.
10. *Ibid.*, p. 155.
11. *Ibid.*, pp. 219–21.
12. *Ibid.*, p. 272.
13. *Ibid.*, p. 395.

14. *Ibid.*, pp. 9, 12.

Chapter 12

1. *Keep the Aspidistra Flying* (London 1975), p. 49.
2. *Ibid.*, p. 55.
3. *Ibid.*, p. 149.
4. *Nineteen Eighty-Four* (London 1973), pp. 103–4.
5. *ibid.*, pp. 211–12.

Chapter 13

1. *Hope Abandoned* (trans. Max Hayward) (London 1974), p. 347ff.
2. *Doctor Zhivago* (trans. Max Hayward and Manya Harari) (London 1975), pp. 434–5.
3. *The First Circle* (trans. Michael Guybon) (London 1970), pp. 132–3.
4. *Ibid.*, p. 251.
5. *Ibid.*, pp. 241–2.
6. *Ibid.*, p. 237.
7. For an account of Solzhenitsyn's years in Vladimir province and Ryazan see David Burg and George Feifer, *Solzhenitsyn* (London 1972), pp. 137–55.

Index

ACKNOWLEDGEMENTS

The author and publishers wish to thank the following who have kindly given permission for the use of copyright material:

The Bodley Head (published by Putnam & Co. Ltd.) and Alfred A. Knopf Inc. for extracts from *And Quiet Flows The Don* and *The Don Flows Home To The Sea*, by Mikhail Sholokhov, translated by Stephen Garry

Jonathan Cape Limited and Charles Scribner's Sons, on behalf of the Executors of the Ernest Hemingway Estate, for extracts from *For Whom The Bell Tolls*, by Ernest Hemingway, © 1940 Ernest Hemingway

Jonathan Cape Limited and Harcourt Brace Jovanovich Inc., for extracts from *Illuminations: Essays and Reflections*, by Walter Benjamin, translated by Harry Zohn, (1969)

Jonathan Cape Limited and Farrar, Straus & Giroux Inc., for extracts from *Writing Degree Zero*, by Roland Barthes, translated by Annette Lavers and Colin Smith, from the French edition *Le Degré Zéro de L'Ecriture*, © 1953 by Editions du Seuil. Translation Copyright © 1967 by Jonathan Cape Limited. Extracts from *Elements of Semiology*, by Roland Barthes, translated by Annette Lavers and Colin Smith from the French *Eléments de Sémiologie* © 1964 by Editions du Seuil, Paris. Translation Copyright © 1967 by Jonathan Cape Limited

Chatto and Windus Limited and Stanford University Press for extracts from *Modern Tragedy* by Raymond Williams

William Collins Sons & Co. Limited and Pantheon Books, a Division of Random House Inc., for extract from *Dr. Zhivago*, by Boris Pasternak, translated by Max Hayward and Manya Harari

William Collins Sons & Co. Limited and Harper & Row, Publishers Inc., for extract from *The First Circle*, by Alexander Solzhenitsyn, translated by Michael Guybon

Doubleday & Co. Inc., and Withers, Solicitors, on behalf of the Trustees of the Joseph Conrad Estate, for extracts from *Nostromo, The Nigger of the 'Narcissus'* and *Under Western Eyes*

Hamish Hamilton Limited, for extracts from *Man's Estate*, by Andre Malraux, translated by A. Macdonald, and *Days of Hope* by Andre Malraux, translated by S. Gilbert and A. Macdonald. Copyright © 1968 by Andre Malraux

A.M. Heath & Co. Limited on behalf of the George Orwell Estate, for extracts from *Keep the Aspidistra Flying* (1954) and *Nineteen Eight-Four* (1949), published by Martin Secker & Warburg Limited

The Merlin Press Limited and Humanities Press Inc., for extracts from *The Historical Novel* by G. Lukács, translated by Hannah and Stanley Mitchell. Copyright © 1962

MIT Press, Cambridge, Massachusetts for extracts from 'On Realism' by R. Jacobsen in *Readings in Russian Poetics: Formalist and Structuralist Views*, edited by Ladislav Matejka and Krystyna Pomorska (1971)

Martin Secker & Warburg Limited and Alfred A. Knopf Inc., for extracts from 'Tonio Kroger' and 'Mario and the Magician' from *Stories of Three Decades* by